and National Lecturer for the *Coleg Cymraeg Cenedlaethol*. This is his
fourth book, and his previous works include *On Rawls, Development
and Global Justice: The Freedom of Peoples* (Palgrave Macmillan, 2011),
recently reprinted with a new preface.

Carl Death is a Senior Lecturer in International Politics at the
University ⟨ ... ⟩s and an
Associate E⟨ ... ⟩k is *The
Green State* ⟨ ... ⟩

THE BASICS

Available:

AMERICAN PHILOSOPHY
NANCY STANLICK

ANIMAL ETHICS
TONY MILLIGAN

ARTIFICIAL INTELLIGENCE
KEVIN WARWICK

BIOETHICS
ALASTAIR CAMPBELL

EVOLUTION
SHERRIE LYONS

FOOD ETHICS
RONALD SANDLER

FREE WILL
MEGHAN GRIFFITH

HUMAN GENETICS (SECOND EDITION)
RICKI LEWIS

METAPHYSICS
MICHAEL RAE

PHILOSOPHY (FIFTH EDITION)
NIGEL WARBURTON

Forthcoming:

CONSCIOUSNESS: THE BASICS
KEITH FRANKISH

**EASTERN PHILOSOPHY
(SECOND EDITION)**
VICTORIA HARRISON

ENVIRONMENTAL ETHICS
BEN DIXON AND MAHESH ANANTH

LOGIC (SECOND EDITION)
J.C. BEALL

PHENOMENOLOGY
DAN ZAHAVI

PHILOSOPHY OF MIND
AMY KIND

GLOBAL JUSTICE

THE BASICS

Huw L. Williams and Carl Death

Routledge
Taylor & Francis Group

LONDON AND NEW YORK

First published 2017
by Routledge
2 Park Square, Milton Park, Abingdon, Oxon OX14 4RN

and by Routledge
711 Third Avenue, New York, NY 10017

Routledge is an imprint of the Taylor & Francis Group, an informa business

British Library Cataloguing in Publication Data
A catalogue record for this book is available from the British Library

Library of Congress Cataloging in Publication Data
A catalog record for this book has been requested

ISBN: 978-1-138-81629-9 (hbk)
ISBN: 978-1-138-81630-5 (pbk)
ISBN: 978-1-315-74619-7 (ebk)

Typeset in Bembo and Scala Sans
by Book Now Ltd, London

To my mother, who taught us that justice begins in the home.

To the next generation, to whom we owe a more just world.

CONTENTS

ACKNOWLEDGEMENTS

Feedback on drafts of this book was generously provided by Stephanie Collins, Sherilyn MacGregor, Aoileann Ní Mhurchú, James Pattison and Huw Rees, as well as the anonymous reviewers. Lucy Vallance and Sarah Gore from Routledge offered support throughout while Siobhán Poole was instrumental in ensuring the initial idea came to fruition. Wyn Williams made a valuable contribution in organizing the index and assisting with proofreading. Thank you to all those who have provided help and inspiration since our initial encounter in the Department of International Politics, Aberystwyth – where it all began.

INTRODUCTION

'Global Justice' is a phrase that has become increasingly popular in the study of politics and its practice in recent decades. It is deployed by a variety of individuals and institutions, from governments and international organizations to popular social movements, and from philosophers in their comfy chairs to activists manning the barricades. It is a phrase that is steeped in possibilities – and we might say optimism – about the possibility of changing the world. Yet it elicits as much confusion as it does interest, perhaps inevitably given the variety of uses it is put to, by a variety of different people.

In this book we provide an introduction to some of the various contexts in which it is invoked. Our aim is to give you, the reader, some sense of what it means to those who debate and use the term. In so doing, we hope to provide you with a foothold that can help you orientate yourself in the multitude of discussions and practices where the term is put to use.

Justice is an unwieldy and ubiquitous term, which has more than one meaning. We might think of the criminal justice system in the first instance, and in this context the idea of retributive justice is particularly important: how we deal with and punish wrongdoers. Another idea that is often referred to is reparative justice, which entails the idea of making good for a past wrong. Neither of these two terms is incidental to the study of global justice. Yet it is probably the ideas of social justice and distributive justice that relate most directly to how the term is used in politics. When justice comes up in political debates, it is often in the form of questions such as '*who is owed what?*' and '*what duties to each other do people have?*'

Traditionally these are questions that we have been accustomed to addressing within the context of the nation-state. For example, when we think about the great social movements and campaigns of the past, more often than not they have been about people demanding what they feel is due to them from their governments. In the context of the United Kingdom we might think of the Chartists or the Suffragettes. We think of them as groups that have demanded greater justice and a greater share of political power, such as votes for the working classes and votes for women, in these specific cases. Philosophers, for their part, have attempted to analyse, understand and sometimes help articulate these claims, putting these political actions on more solid foundations.

These are the types of claims that are primarily evoked by the phrase 'global justice' – but rather than claims against nation-states, these are often claims against diverse actors in world politics, from individuals and private businesses to collections of states and global institutions. Despite the recent provenance of the term, global justice is not such a new idea. There have always been causes that have crossed borders and have had global dimensions. We need only to think about those who campaigned against the transatlantic slave trade, or those involved in colonial struggles against imperialist oppression (Keck and Sikkink, 1998). Religious movements have often sought to promote their own vision of justice on an expansive and evangelical scale. The notion that we have a moral relationship with those beyond our own state can be traced as far back as philosophy itself, notably when the Greek Stoics professed that they were *citizens of the world.*

That said, questions about who is owed what, and by whom, have become increasingly complicated in nature because of the increasing interdependence of our world and the sense in which our fate is increasingly tied to the activities of people and agencies all over the world. Indeed, it is this fact of interdependence, and the sense that the world is becoming smaller, which eventually caused philosophers to think about issues of social justice as ones that might pertain across state boundaries. In the aftermath of World War II, our collective fate seemed to be tied ever closer by the spectre of nuclear war. With the establishment of the United Nations and institutions such as the World Bank and International Monetary Fund, it became even clearer that our economies, our resources and our politics were becoming more intricately linked. The Great Depression had exemplified only too well the influence of economic events in one part of the world on others, and that poverty and inequality can be found in all countries. The world wars were cataclysmic, not least because of the manner in which they drew in combatants from the four corners of the globe. The developments that had led to this level of interdependence only deepened and expanded post-World War II, and there was a growing sense that the richest countries had a capability and a duty to aid others around the world. In January 1949, US President Harry Truman declared in his inaugural address that 'More than half the people of the world are living in conditions approaching misery. Their food is inadequate. They are victims of disease. Their economic life is primitive and stagnant. Their poverty is a handicap and a threat both to them and to more prosperous areas. For the first time in history, humanity possesses the knowledge and skill to relieve the suffering of these people' (in Escobar, 1995: 3).

Today we live in a world where the global scope of justice is evident in two main ways. First, cases of injustice – such as poverty, or climate change – exist worldwide and transcend national boundaries. Second, the causes of injustice and efforts to address injustice are global or transnational in scope. The ongoing refugee crisis in Europe demonstrates how the effects of politics and conflict cannot be contained in one part of the world. The financial crash of 2008 and the subsequent fear of further crises demonstrate the extent to which the global economy is now even more integrated. On a more mundane level, the clothes we wear – often produced in far-away sweatshops for low wages under poor working conditions – serve as a constant reminder that the comforts of those in the most affluent parts of the world are deeply bound up with social structures in other parts of the world. The global nature of social, political and economic issues that affect us all is reflected in the proliferation of international charities and in the activism and campaigning which cuts across state boundaries. In this sense, it would be irrational and indefensible for us *not* to be thinking in terms of issues of justice that are global.

Indeed, study, research and thinking about these questions have increasingly extended its purview beyond issues of the just distribution of resources, rights and political power. A succinct account of the study of global justice mentions no less than 10 different subject areas: human rights, just war, humanitarian intervention, terrorism, economic injustice, gender justice, immigration, environmental issues, health issues and natural resources (Brock, 2015). No doubt we could identify others such as international law. These subjects are often disaggregated by authors and treated separately, but there have equally been attempts to provide perspectives on global justice that span a wider range of issues (Rawls, 1999; Caney, 2005; Barry, 2012).

Writing a book on *the basics* of global justice, therefore, presents some challenges in terms of plotting a satisfactory route. Rather than providing you with a systematic survey of *all* the possible subjects, debates and causes that might fall under the rubric of global justice, we have approached the subject from a perspective that tracks the development of the *study* of global justice in political philosophy while also providing a sense of how campaigns for global justice have been taken up *in practice*. In so doing, we will at certain stages broach most of those subject areas listed above, but the main aim is to provide you with an engaging account of how certain ideas and practices have developed.

As will become evident in the opening chapters, the academic debate denoted by the term global justice developed in the first instance among philosophers as a discussion of how we should reinterpret questions of distribution on a global scale. Questions around resources, aid, the global economy and rights were, therefore, at the heart of these discussions, although from the very start it was clear that such debates would encroach on issues of conflict, intervention, war and the environment – fields of study in their own right, of course, and issues that themselves could be discussed discretely in terms of justice. The Just War Doctrine is arguably as old as philosophy itself, while environmental justice – rightly or wrongly – has been studied separately for as long as global justice.

In some senses it would be legitimate to confine this book to the study of this academic debate alone, and it is what other more general texts on the subject have tended to do (Brock, 2009; Mandle, 2006; Armstrong, 2012). The fact that most existing studies do this is one good reason to take a different approach. In this book we seek to widen the conversation and include perspectives more closely connected to the struggles of activists and movements for global justice, as well as considering different philosophical traditions which have not always been part of mainstream academic debates on global justice. As much as the philosophical debate is important, interesting and (hopefully) inspiring, the campaigning and sacrifices of those fighting in the name of global justice are also an essential element of a broader discussion about what global justice means.

The relationship between these imagined social roles – 'the activist' and 'the philosopher' – takes us to the heart of some difficult and perhaps intractable questions about the nature of philosophy. Philosophers have tended to acknowledge the importance of activists in two contrasting ways. Some philosophers modestly claim that their role is to interpret, understand and elucidate the issues of global justice and that they stand aside from the fray; Ludwig Wittgenstein admonished his fellow philosophers to leave everything as it is (2009: #124), and from such a view the philosopher contributes little to the cause directly. Others, following Marx's observation that the point of philosophy is to change the world (2000: 173), might be more ambitious. However, such an attitude would assume that the primary role is to articulate ideas and concepts that buttress the attempts of those – activists, but also other political agents – who seek a more just world. We believe that whichever of these perspectives is adopted, there is intellectual value in engaging more closely with activist campaigns for global justice. Politically, however, the reason why we have written a book on global justice is because we think it is important to try to change the world for the better, and philosophers have their role to play in that struggle.

From a perspective of providing an introductory text on global justice, intending to complement teaching in this area, there is also a value in linking philosophical debates to a closer study of actual campaigns for justice. The campaigns, techniques, issues and ideas that are deployed by many activists and movements may be more interesting and accessible than some of the more abstract debates. There can be an emotional resonance here too: these are the people often experiencing injustices, who are pushing the boundaries, and are key in cajoling, persuading and sometimes forcing other agents into realizing more just policies and actions. This can lead to difficult debates: we may conclude, philosophically, that certain campaigns in the name of global justice are misguided, unhelpful, or just plain wrong. But a closer discussion between fields of study devoted to studying what we *should do* to achieve global justice, and those who study what social movements *have done* to change the world, can enrich both.

This book aims to combine an introduction to the study of academic debates on global justice with closer engagement with actual campaigns for global justice. The philosopher and the activist share a common goal in exposing the inequalities in the world and offering a clearer way forward. Of course we must remember that these labels – 'the philosopher' and 'the activist' – are only artificial labels, or ideal types. They are a shorthand for a particular type of practice or activity. Many philosophers are also activists in all sorts of ways, and activists think hard about the conceptual and moral dilemmas their campaigns involve. Yet it is notable that many texts on global justice remain at the level of abstract debate, and often do not explicitly acknowledge the people who have sought to translate these principles into specific struggles and policies and reforms.

For this reason we think a book more engaged with activist and alternative perspectives on justice will be interesting and useful. Students coming to the subject for the first time will probably want to know about elements of both theory and practice. From the point of view our role as teachers and researchers, we also agree that there is a place for a book that marries the two elements and provides students from philosophical and politics backgrounds with the basics in both respects. Philosophy students can benefit from a better grasp of the realities of fighting for global justice, while politics students can benefit from some philosophical knowledge about the assumptions upon which activists do what they do – and how these ideas can be accounted for in a philosophical manner. Lastly, we also share the conviction that in terms of the study, and cause of global justice, one way forward may be through a more self-conscious engagement between the dual roles of philosophy and activism, where the aim is not to 'win' the debate but to learn from each other.

WHY DOES GLOBAL JUSTICE SEEM SO FAR AWAY?

Looking at the state of world politics today, one might be forgiven for thinking that we are further away than ever from the goal of global justice. Even without a clear definition of the concept, we can be fairly certain that a world with debilitating poverty and deadly conflicts, hurtling towards environmental destruction, is riven with injustices. Given the achievements of human civilization, the wealth of some parts of the world, and our capacity for intelligent thought, it may often strike us as perverse that we live in a world where some die from overconsumption while others die from malnutrition, where statesmen (for they are most often men) pursue violence rather than peace, and we seem willing to endorse a way of life that is destroying the conditions which allow us to thrive in the first place. To expect that we can achieve a utopia may be naïve, but equally, it seems that our problems are so acute that they must arise out of a certain level of stupidity.

Perhaps some form of ignorance is involved, but in working towards a more just world we need to understand our contemporary challenges against the background of a shared history steeped in violence, and practices, traditions and *understandings* in world politics that continue to define the present and militate against addressing our shared problems. To take one example that tells us a lot about how we have understood world politics: if one looks at the history of humankind then one constant has been the practice of organized violence and war. We can look back at what we might consider highly civilized societies, from the Greeks, to the Romans, Renaissance Italy and the modern empires of France and Britain, among others, and see that violence, war and domination of others was integral to their success.

The notion of peaceful coexistence has often been a minority pursuit. In the west it was the Quakers, a sect within the Christian faith, who in the seventeenth century were one of the first groups to adopt pacifist beliefs after the Protestant Reformation, while the ideal of a peaceful worldwide federation was given philosophical expression in the work of later Enlightenment figures such as Immanuel Kant (1983). In mid-nineteenth-century Britain, figures such as John Bright, Richard Cobden and Henry Richard were recognized as moral and principled in their campaigns for peace (although their view of western superiority might seem unpalatable today: see Hobson, 2012: ch. 2), but they were ultimately ineffective in attempting to address the culture of war. A century later, with the end of formal colonialism, the impact of two world wars fresh in the memory, and the spectre of nuclear war on the horizon, it is no surprise that the peace movement gained more traction. Yet international politics continued to be dominated by conflict, with the Cold War between the United States and Soviet Union often being played out through proxy wars in the so-called 'third world'. With the end of the Cold War came a new optimism and the hope that we would see a more peaceful world materialize as the benefits of liberalism and democracy spread. Yet the evil of war persists, and it continues to divide political opinion on how to avoid it. It is instructive that the response to the British Labour Party installing an avowed pacifist, Jeremy Corbyn, as leader in 2015, has been to lampoon him in the press and the political establishment, over issues like his demands for a political solution to the Syrian war and his call not to renew Britain's nuclear missile deterrent.

It seems the idea of international politics characterized by violence and conflict remains the order of the day, and those who suggest otherwise are still liable to be dismissed as dangerous dreamers. The persistence of conflict is explained by many who study international relations as the inevitable result of certain traits of world politics. Those who tend to characterize this realm as one of cyclical conflict are known as realists, and they come in various guises. Classical realists such as Hans Morgenthau (1946, 1948), who became popular after World War II, relate this pattern in good part to the flaws of human nature and the desire to dominate and practice power over others. Neo-realists, the most famous of whom is Kenneth Waltz (1959/2001, 1979), suggest that conflict is inevitable on account of the anarchic international system. Unlike the state, which has a monopoly of power and is an overwhelming force, the international context is characterized by many agents with similar capacities who are ruled by self-interest. Such a system is inherently unstable and states are compelled to act to defend their security, arm themselves, and prepare for war. Such actions simply perpetuate instability and a propensity to use violence. Realists essentially reject any notion that we might overcome the inherent nature of international politics, and regard any notion that we might be able to forge any lasting peace through cooperation and federation as at best wishful thinking, and at worst as legitimizing the domination of the powerful (Carr, 2001). Even those aspects of today's international society that seem to suggest an ability to find mutual interests – such as the UN system – are often seen as agreements that are used by the powerful for their own benefit. If they are seen to restrict their power they will ultimately be ignored, such as the case when the United States and United Kingdom ignored the decision of the UN Security Council with regard to their declaration of war on Iraq in 2003.

What has all this got to do with the more specific questions about global justice that we will focus on in this book? Well, it is important to start by acknowledging that political activists and philosophers of global justice are often quite a long way away from traditional, mainstream thinking about international politics. For the average realist, self-interest is the only norm or value that has a place in international politics, and it is self-evident that this is the only sensible way to interpret events. The crux of Waltz's argument is that 'because any state may at any time use force, all states must constantly be ready either to counter force with force or to pay the cost of weakness' (1959/2001: 160). From this perspective, approaching the other defining issues of world politics – such as climate change negotiations, trade agreements and international assistance – with the assumption that we can appeal to values like fairness, justice and the good, is simply wrong-headed. Interaction in world politics always comes back to the battle for power and domination, and in effect policies pursued in negotiations and pacts are merely the continuation of war by other means (to invert the famous phrase of Carl von Clausewitz; see Foucault, 2000).

This is not to say that other ways of understanding of international politics do not have some standing. In this sense we can regard the majority of the philosophies, theories and ideas articulated in this book as part of an expanding body of thought that challenges the basic assumptions of realist thought. What we might broadly term 'international political theory' has become ever more popular and robust since the early 1980s, and what the contributions within this field have in common is that they assume, contra the *realist*, that we can understand the events of international politics in many different ways and with reference to different theoretical frameworks and assumptions. In particular, as Chris Brown (1992) argued in his influential volume, the study of international politics need not be confined to the rather narrow body of thought that has animated the study of international relations since its formal inception in the early twentieth century. Rather, the entire canon of political and social theory stretching back as long as the western philosophical tradition can provide insights and analysis for our understanding of world politics. Realism, from this perspective, is regarded not as an empirical theory that has revealed the truth of international politics. Rather it is seen as presenting a particular normative view of international politics with its own assumptions, which when applied to world politics serve to perpetuate these ideas.

Brown, in articulating his argument, sets out a framework that has become well-worn in the study of international politics and influences some of the discussion in this book. For Brown identified two emerging positions within international political theory that he identified as 'cosmopolitan' and 'communitarian'. The former he associated with the philosophy of Immanuel Kant, and the notion that individual rights should in some sense take precedence over the rights of the state in international politics. This position does not necessarily entail a suspicion or critique of the state (although it does so in many forms), but ultimately it comes down on the side of the individual where any conflict is entailed. The individual is inviolable, an end in itself, which even the state has no right to treat as a means. The communitarian position is, in contrast, identified with the philosophy of Kant's critic, G.W.F. Hegel, which emphasizes the role of the state in caring for and fostering the individual and allowing her or him to flourish as a full citizen. From this perspective it is ultimately the political community that takes moral precedent over the individual. In very general terms, the suggestion is that the cosmopolitan approach sees a good deal more potential for an integrated international order that shares moral ties and values centred on the individual. The communitarian perspective is generally more sceptical of such 'universal' narratives and the idea that working towards a more uniform, global community misunderstands the true nature of human beings and our need to be embedded within deep, meaningful cultural practices and relations.

We will see that the philosophical debate in the field of global justice can be understood against the contours of Brown's discussion (unsatisfactory though he finds the categories for purposes of classification; Brown, 2002a: 17), and these terms can help to locate other perspectives such as those traditions from outside western Europe which are sceptical of more abstract appeals to general or universal moral values. It is also the case that some of the more recent philosophical interventions in the global justice debate, and some of the philosophies practiced by activists, challenge some of the more mainstream ideas that characterize the cosmopolitan-communitarian framework. In our eyes these all contribute to the enrichment and sophistication of debates in international political theory and buttress the inclusive approach of this tradition of thinking. In this regard it should not be forgotten that these perspectives could *all* be seen as challenging the realist assumption about the inevitability of self-interest, competition, poverty and violence. We would do well to regularly remind ourselves of this shared outlook among the din of competing perspectives on global justice.

TEXT BOXES

At various points in the text we will insert boxes. The intention here is to allow ourselves as authors to pursue an idea, example, or discussion that elaborates upon the main narrative. They will often include more detail or complexity than the rest of the text.

In this instance it is an opportunity to provide some very brief definitional comments. It has already been noted that the cosmopolitan-communitarian distinction will be used as a device for structuring the discussion of certain philosophical positions. It should be noted that for many in the philosophical debate, these terms have now become defunct, and there is a recent tendency to use 'globalist' and 'statist' in their stead. Using the original terms is not meant as any expression of preference – it simply reflects the tendency in this book to relate the

(Continued)

(Continued)

debate in a (largely) chronological format. In very broad terms this approach reflects a pedagogical preference in terms of teaching philosophy, one which maps the development of the debate and sets out ideas with regard to their place in (or outside) a particular canon of thought, rather than, for example, setting out ideas in a more thematic fashion.

Also, we attempt some consistency with regard to the use of the terms 'philosophy' and 'theory'. It is more commonly the case with regard to debates about global justice that 'theory' and its variants are used, rather than 'philosophy': global justice 'theorists' rather than 'philosophers'; or 'global justice theory' and 'global justice theorizing' rather than 'global justice philosophy' and 'global justice philosophizing'. It is debatable whether the terms suggest any great difference, although some may have strong opinions on the matter. The distinction is no doubt related to a more general contrast between the terms 'political theory' and 'political philosophy'.

It has been suggested previously that the distinction relates to levels of analysis, with political theory explaining political ideas and phenomenon arising in everyday life, while political philosophy is more abstracted in analysing and evaluating such theories (Crick, 1967). Other explanations seek to connect political theory with the more continental approach (as in the continent of Europe) and political philosophy with the Anglo-American tradition, or account for it simply in terms of practice dependence: theorists take on the label in politics' departments and political philosophers adopt the role when placed in a department of philosophers. In a book where a wide array of ideas are discussed, which include theories about, and theorists of political economy, development and other related fields, it seems helpful to deploy the term 'philosophy' and its variants, simply in order to distinguish easily discussions and thinkers that are grounded in moral and normative analysis and evaluation of political principles, values and concepts.

STRUCTURE

The chapters in this book are presented in a way that is largely self-contained. You should be able to pick out any chapter and read it without needing to reference another part of the book. That being said, there is also a narrative that develops across the chapters. While we do not propose that we are putting forward a robust argument about global justice and how it should be studied, there are some assumptions we have or claims that we make, which can be regarded as an intervention into the field of debate, as well as a commentary on the subject matter.

In general terms the first half of the book concentrates on the philosophical debate surrounding global justice. Here, in keeping with the commitment mentioned above to a certain method for teaching philosophy, we provide an outline of how this debate has developed over the last half-century or so, giving particular attention to certain well-known figures. Rather than aggregate different positions and provide indicative accounts, we have chosen here to focus on the key ideas of certain thinkers. While there are no doubt disadvantages to such an approach, the hope is that you are provided with a sense of how these academic debates develop, the actors involved, and most importantly you get a taste of the very particular concepts, arguments and ideas that are put to use.

In the first chapter, we begin with what we have termed the communitarian perspective on global justice (some further definitional comments will be in order here). Two key reasons dictate this as a starting point. First, we introduce the key figure of John Rawls, who casts his shadow over much of the subsequent debate, and in many ways began a method of philosophizing about politics that would prepare the field for many subsequent contributors, especially in the Anglo-American academy. Second, it allows us to discuss a perspective that is less radical in its approach and more attached to the reality of world politics. That is to say, thinkers such as Rawls advocate philosophizing about the world as it is, and as such their position tends to advocate the ethical role of the state, cohering with a vision of the world as a Society of States, for which we need normative guidelines on issues such as human rights, war and poverty. We thus examine Rawls' arguments for philosophizing in such a way, we look at some of his key concepts, and we attempt to understand how he applied these insights to world politics. This analysis is accompanied by a section on the work of David Miller, who argues for the moral importance of states but combines this communitarian conviction with arguments of a different kind for articulating our duties of justice to distant strangers. In general terms we can regard these thinkers as trying to 'humanise' world politics, by showing that moral arguments are relevant and there are very strong 'cosmopolitan' reasons why we should help other people and societies, even if for very good practical and moral reasons we live in a world that is organized according to the priorities of nation-states.

In the second chapter, we turn to key figures in the cosmopolitan tradition. These are thinkers who in very general terms dispute the primacy and particular ethical value of the nation-state and tend to view it more as an important tool for ensuring individual needs are met. As such, they are less concerned with how states treat each other or the moral arguments that apply to these relations – they are wholly focused on how we can transform world politics in ways that undermine state power and ensure that it is individual rights that represent the ultimate currency. We are citizens of the world not just citizens of a state, they argue, and our politics should reflect this. In this regard we turn to philosophers who were in many ways inspired by Rawls' egalitarian views on justice, but believe he did not apply them in a radical enough form to the global context. At various stages figures such as Charles Beitz, Thomas Pogge and Martha Nussbaum have set about this task. We begin with Beitz, who played a key role in the debate, and it is emphasized that he was presenting arguments that represented more than an attempt at justifying assistance to the poorer parts of the world. He was arguing for a *different way of understanding* world politics in general. In that respect, although we will find that thinkers such as Pogge and Nussbaum have developed sophisticated and important contributions in the context of global poverty, there has been a tendency to sideline this broader, all-important challenge to traditional realist concepts of world politics, which are still pervasive in practice and theory.

The third chapter presents us with a set of philosophical perspectives that aims to demonstrate just how much variety now characterizes the debate, and how these contributions are attempts to challenge and destabilize some of the ideas and assumptions that have become embedded. In many ways this is a very promising and heartening development, as it shows how the currency of global justice is all the more valuable today and that discussing world politics with reference to this term is becoming a more accepted practice. We look at how a variety of thinkers have applied new perspectives and have attempted to intervene in and change the nature of the debate, both in terms of the issues studied and the methods of enquiry. The chapter begins by considering the argument that a 'third wave' of global justice philosophizing has recently occurred, before analysing recent contributions inspired by prominent 'republican' and 'recognition' perspectives. Iris Marion Young provides an example of a more critical approach that outlines a 'structuralist' account of global injustice. The chapter concludes with contributions from Simon Caney and Alison Jaggar, the former bringing questions of climate justice squarely into the debate, the latter doing likewise with question of gender. A number of these perspectives give voice to the activist and open up avenues for thinking around the debate that foreshadow some of the activist-inspired ideas in the latter half of the book.

In the fourth chapter, we engage with more empirical issues, in the first instance through an analysis of the ideas and theories that have been used to buttress some of the philosophical arguments examined. One of the premises of the philosophical debate is that while setting out ideal principles on the basis of rational argument is important and worthwhile, there is also a role for philosophers in debating how these ideals might be achieved, and what the particular moral arguments are that arise in relation to these problems. In a way this reflects two key questions the philosopher faces: (i) on what basis do we account for duties of global justice? and (ii) what are the most efficacious and morally robust ways for realizing these duties? In this chapter, we see that in addressing the second question – specifically with regard to a fundamental problem of global justice, absolute poverty – key thinkers employ different understandings of underdevelopment. We look at how these interpretations map on to their philosophical arguments, and in so doing raise some questions about the theories and empirical information that are constitutive of global justice philosophizing.

At this point we broaden the analysis to look at how some of these narratives have influenced recent policy debates. In particular we look at the impact of the Millennium Development Goals (MDGs) and the international intervention in Afghanistan as instances where some of these ideas have been at work, with varying levels of success.

The MDGs were intended to achieve greater global justice, but were seen by many as fatally compromised, too weak, or promoting a western ideal at the expense of diverse local values. The invasion of Afghanistan and subsequent attempts to build a stable state shows how the realization of justice can involve very difficult choices and dilemmas, and the (arguable) perversion of aims for a more just and secure world order. We ask whether these recent developments mark a crisis for global justice, and suggest that one way ahead in terms of enriching the philosophical and theoretical debate may be a more thorough engagement with both the actual movements struggling in the name of global justice, and a more fundamental questioning of the assumptions of liberal political theory. Indeed, this echoes the calls of some philosophers in more recent times to 'deparochialize' the debate (Maffettone and Rathore, 2012: 2).

The fifth chapter begins with this debate about whether global justice is parochial and/or Eurocentric. It considers the argument of John Hobson (2012) in some detail, who takes on a range of theorists for implicitly assuming the moral superiority of western culture. It then considers a number of ways to respond to this charge, and the first avenue is to consider more closely some of the more prominent activist campaigns in recent years, including movements for debt forgiveness, environmental justice, anti-racist movements, and divestment and empowerment campaigns. While it is true that these movements as a whole would not regard themselves as part of the liberal political tradition, the situation is somewhat more complex than these groups issuing a flat rejection of its values and ideals. As such, you will be encouraged to reflect on some of the points of connection and tension between the values underpinning these forms of activism and the more mainstream theories of global justice.

The sixth chapter considers an alternative way to broaden and deparochialize the global justice debates, by examining very different approaches to the concept of justice. Again, however, these are approached through the movements and campaigns of global justice campaigners, but particularly focus on those who promote alternative visions to the liberal project. In particular, we look at food sovereignty movements, campaigns for degrowth, and ecocentric movements and theorists, paying particular attention to the conceptions of justice that provide the basis for their action. Rather than seeking to entrench the notion of a binary relationship between traditional liberal views on the one hand and alternative perspectives on the other, we are interested in particular in the potential for expanding the conversation and the possible interactions that might be developed through greater engagement between philosophers and activists.

In the conclusion, we reflect on some of these broader issues and focus in particular on the ways in which the ideas in this book might be used by students to inform their study (for example, in formulating research questions for projects, dissertations, and even theses). We outline how we have brought together the philosophy of global justice and the activism of the global justice movement – providing philosophers an insight into the world of the activist, and encouraging the activist to sharpen their philosophical and ideational tools. We hope that in combining a short study of these two aspects of global justice in today's world, we have suggested one way forward in terms of the study of global justice. Rainer Forst, an influential German philosopher, recently claimed, 'the academic discourse about global justice is not a global discourse. It is dominated by certain views, and it would be good to globalize this discourse' (Flikschuh, 2013: 52). By bringing together the narratives around philosophy and activism, we aim to contribute to this process of expanding the conversation.

1

FROM SOCIAL JUSTICE TO INTERNATIONAL JUSTICE

IN THIS CHAPTER . . .

. . . we trace the beginnings of the modern philosophical debate around questions of distributive justice in the international context. In particular we focus on John Rawls as the seminal figure in much of these debates and look at how he inspired others and presented his own views on these questions. Rawls, it will be explained, has come to represent one strand of thinking – sometimes referred to as communitarianism – that is viewed as a less radical perspective in the debate, as it is tied to the current reality of a world of sovereign nation-states. Before exploring another popular strand, known as cosmopolitanism, in the next chapter, we will discuss another figure often equated with Rawls' view, namely the English philosopher David Miller.

JOHN RAWLS

There are two key reasons that we begin our account with Rawls. The first of these is because he has become such a dominant figure in the world of political philosophy – most especially in the Anglo-American academy where the global justice debate initially began in earnest. The British philosopher A.N. Whitehead (1979: 39) once famously said of Western Philosophy that it may be considered a footnote to Plato. In many respects one might characterize modern political philosophy – in its mainstream Anglo-American form – as a footnote to Rawls' theory of social justice. We will attempt to elucidate this influence here.

The second reason we begin with his work is because of the direct role he has played in the global justice debate. In the first instance, Rawls inspired others, such as Charles Beitz and Thomas Pogge (whom we will discuss in the next chapter), to develop ideas that have proved to be extremely important. Moreover, Rawls himself later made a significant intervention that laid out his 'communitarian' perspective and helped to define the contours of the debate up to the present day.

COMMUNITARIANS AND COSMOPOLITANS

Attributing the label *communitarian* to Rawls is not without its difficulties. The term came to prominence in cognate debates around Rawls' philosophy in political theory, where the term was used to describe his critics – such as Charles Taylor (1992) – who believed Rawls' liberalism failed to acknowledge the communal roots of the self and our moral and political values. Yet Rawls' response revealed that he was sensitive to these considerations and saw them as informing his perspective, allowing for the possibility that his own position was that of a 'communitarian' articulating and defending the particular emergent liberal political values of western democracies. Stephen Mulhall and Adam Swift's book, *Liberals and Communitarians: An Introduction* (1996), is considered the go-to text for understanding the development of this debate.

For some it might seem counterintuitive to label Rawls as a communitarian because of the primacy he accords individual rights, and indeed there are some who view his attempts to blunt his critics' arguments, by emphasizing the embedded nature of the individual within political and social structures, as problematic and inconsistent. Catherine Audard in her work draws out the tension she sees between

(Continued)

(Continued)

what she terms the 'moral individualism' of his early work and the 'social holism' of its later development (2007: 258). However, in the context of international political theory and the global justice debate, the terms take on a slightly different connotation.

As noted in the Introduction, Brown's use of *cosmopolitanism* and *communitarianism* is employed to help negotiate the different perspectives that arise in normative perspectives on world politics, and here *communitarianism* is associated specifically with the Hegelian idea of the *state* as an ethical institution that allows the individual to flourish. It therefore takes on an elevated moral significance that may be interpreted as taking precedence over the individual – and this is certainly evident in more extreme forms of communitarian realism that see little place for valuing the individual's rights in the face of state interests (see Erskine (2002) for discussion of this breed of communitarianism). This is in contrast with the so-called Kantian idea of 'cosmopolitanism' where the status of the state is largely secondary to the inviolability of the individual.

Rawls – and Miller – might therefore be said to be communitarian in the sense that their views on world politics accept the moral position that the state is of fundamental importance and value to the individual, taking precedence over other collectives and levels of government, as a result of which we should be tentative about challenging its authority and remain committed to reforming the state system, rather than undermining it. Rawls' most revealing quote – where the Hegelian theme of the individual being 'at home' in the state is at its most prominent – occurs in the *Law of Peoples*:

Leaving aside the deep question of whether some forms of culture and ways of life are good in themselves (as I believe they are) it is surely a good for individuals and associations to be attached to their particular culture and to take part in its common public and civic life. In this way belonging to a political society, and being at home in its civic and social world, gains expression and fulfillment. This is no small thing. It argues for preserving significant room for the idea of a people's self-determination and for some kind of loose or confederative form of a Society of Peoples, provided the divisive hostilities of different cultures can be tamed, as it seems they can be, by a society of well-ordered regimes. A proper patriotism is an attachment to one's people and country.

(1999: 111–12)

That being said, if we think of Rawls and Miller as 'communitarians', we also need to understand they are of a very different hue to communitarian realists, because they also have a deeply cosmopolitan, Kantian strain to their thinking.

Both see moral values extending beyond the state to the global realm, and both take a far more conditional approach to the authority of the state; Rawls, for example, will often cite instances where individual rights will trump the right of the state. Indeed, it will be argued here that unlike other communitarians such as Thomas Nagel (2005) and Richard Miller (2010), both Rawls and Miller believe duties of justice – and not just weaker humanitarian duties – extend beyond the nation-state. For this reason some might choose to describe them as cosmopolitan. In this sense, we see that the concepts of cosmopolitanism and communitarianism are more helpful in drawing out and identifying elements of thinking in individual theorists, as opposed to playing the more cumbersome role of dividing thinkers in two camps.

Rawls himself does not attribute the term communitarian to his own thinking in the global context, although he does explicitly reject the cosmopolitan position (1999: 119–20); he understands the term in a narrower sense as representing thinkers such as Beitz and Pogge in the global justice debate, who advocate for global redistribution on the basis of the individual's rights. We get a sense, therefore, of why these categories – and categorizing in general – have been problematic in the debate, and why many other terms have been used: Andrew Kuper described Rawls' position as 'thin statist' (2000: 640); Charles Beitz chose 'social liberalism' (2000: 677); more recent discussions have seen the descriptors 'globalist' and 'statist' (Risse, 2012) gaining currency, as well as 'cosmopolitan' and 'non-cosmopolitan' (Brock, 2013). However, as with Brown's original categories they should all be understood in the terms of their particular context, and the limits of their application recognized.

To understand Rawls' status, it is important to appreciate the context within which he published his now legendary work, the 500-page tome *A Theory of Justice* (*TJ*) ([1971] 2005). One might summarize the story with the old saying, 'cometh the hour, cometh the man'. As academic wisdom has it, Rawls began to emerge as a political philosopher in the period when his subject most needed him. In short, the academic climate was such in the Anglo-American world that the notion that political ideas and values could be discussed and studied from a moral perspective had lost its currency.

Philosophers known as the 'logical positivists' had made it fashionable during the 1930s to believe that unless one was making verifiable statements of empirical fact, then one was talking 'nonsense' – whether it be religious, political or moral beliefs. In the same period – and partly as a consequence – it was becoming increasingly fashionable to treat politics as a 'science'; a realm of study that lent itself to analytical, experimental and theoretical approaches inspired by the natural sciences, rather than philosophical debates about values and principles. No doubt the horrors of World War II made it more difficult to think of politics as a 'moral' realm, as many important philosophers became absorbed in the question of asking what had gone wrong with western civilization.

Yet this tendency to extract moral discussions from politics could only last so long, and indeed it was the question of war that partly sparked a revival of interest in this kind of debate. Many Americans in the 1960s became interested in the question of the nature of a just war, in part because many wished to condemn the war in Vietnam, and in part because some wished to defend Israel's right to defend themselves during the Six-Day War. Just and unjust wars therefore had to be distinguished. It was during this period that Rawls began in earnest to piece together the key elements of his philosophical vision and it came to fruition with the publication of his magnum opus in 1971, which would contribute significantly to restoring political philosophy to its former status.

It is difficult to quantify the significance of his work. To give a sense of his accomplishment, an analogy might be made with the Beatles. The fab four have a legendary position in the pantheon of popular music, because in many senses they came to define it through their legacy. Mainstream pop music since their day can invariably be compared with the music they produced and it is doubtful whether it will ever emerge from their shadow. Moreover, the Beatles, despite projecting a very modern and original sound, created music that was deeply embedded in harmonies and melodies that had their roots in the classical music of major western composers such as Bach, Handel and Beethoven (whom they famously instructed to 'roll over').

Rawls of course did not philosophize in a vacuum, and as he notes in the opening pages of *TJ,* his work is a modern take on a form of political philosophy that had its roots in the western enlightenment tradition, taking inspiration and key motifs from figures such as Locke, Rousseau and most especially Kant. However, the way in which he recreated it for the modern day has left a legacy that shows no sign of slackening, to the extent that for some in the Anglo-American academy political philosophy is essentially Rawlsian philosophy. In many ways, Rawls' immediate predecessors who inspired him are overlooked in the same way as the Beatles' forerunners.

The analogy is by no means perfect, of course. In truth, the Beatles' music had another great influence that had combined with the traditional western harmonies to lay the basis for rock 'n' roll, which emerged from African-American musical traditions. They are part of an ongoing tradition of white musicians who have tasted success through appropriating others' music (this theme of non-western traditions is one we will return to in the context of political philosophy). Another element the analogy cannot capture is the sense in which Rawls was actually responding to, or railing against, an orthodoxy that had come to define those debates that did attempt to engage with moral values in politics – namely utilitarianism. The principle that moral philosophy should cleave to the general principle of 'maximizing the general happiness' was something that Rawls wished to challenge fundamentally.

This desire came in part from his belief that the utilitarian standpoint could be misused in such a way as to justify the abuse of the rights and interests of the minority, in the name of the general good. Bearing in mind Rawls' upbringing during 1920s and 1930s' America, in a staunchly liberal and politically aware family living in the ethnically diverse Baltimore City, he himself would have been deeply aware of the discriminatory nature of the society he lived in. If his political philosophy is known for anything, above all else it is the priority it gives to the integrity of the individual, and their fundamental equality and liberty. Indeed, it is these aspects of his work that would be at the heart of later debates relating to ideas about world politics.

THE RAWLSIAN LEGACY

So what are the fundamentals of Rawls' political philosophy that would prove to be so influential, not only on the subject as a whole, but on later debates relating to justice in the global context? The approach that he took was one that sought to emulate the great philosophers of the past, by using a concept known as the social contract. This is an idea that can be traced as far back as Thomas Hobbes (1588–1679) and his famous text, *The Leviathan* (1651). In a very general sense the idea of the social contract is to articulate and justify the grounds on which we live together as part of a political society. It is true that philosophers such Hobbes, John Locke (1980), Rousseau (2011) and Kant provide very different visions of this social contract, but they all hold in common the idea of individuals coming together to will into existence a political society, where they agree on fundamental terms for living together. In essence, they all use this device to set out what they consider to be the first principles for the state.

It is this idea that inspires Rawls' vision, but whereas earlier philosophers would generally provide a story of the original contract – a quasi-anthropological account of how it came to be – Rawls is explicit in his argument that he is using it as a strictly hypothetical device. That is to say, Rawls does not want us to imagine actual people coming together to discuss the terms for living together. Rather he wants to present a sort of timeless thought experiment, which can be used as a tool for working out what the most fair and just principles are for a modern democratic society. In this 'original position' imaginary individuals are denied knowledge of their own preferences in order to guarantee 'neutral' principles as the outcome of their discussion.

THE ORIGINAL POSITION

In Rawls' 'original position' we must imagine individuals behind a 'veil of ignorance'. These individuals, like us, have a capacity for justice and a conception of the good (a set of values and priorities, such as a religious worldview, for example). They will also know about the basic facts of how their society is ordered so they are not ignorant of its basic structures and institutions. However, they do not know their own beliefs, their status, their wealth, their job, their gender, or even which generation in time they belong to. In essence, they are denied all the knowledge that could allow them to create principles of justice that would favour their own position. From this original position, therefore, neutral, fair and just principles for ordering the society should emerge.

This is not necessarily the most intuitive of ideas to grasp in the first instance, and Rawls suggests one way we might understand his thinking. 'Perfect procedural justice' he likens to the familiar scenario where we endeavour to divide a cake fairly. In this situation the obvious answer is to assign the knife to the person who chooses last; they are therefore compelled to ensure a fair division or distribution of the cake, because they do not know which piece they will receive. Given this scenario, as with the choosers in the original position, the rational, self-interested thing to do is to ensure the arrangement you agree to (the division of the cake, or the basic principles of the society) give you the best chance of securing what you want.

The original position is therefore akin to the cake scenario, albeit a more complex version. This is reflected in the different term Rawls uses: 'pure procedural justice'. The former is perfect in the sense that we can know pretty much exactly what a fair result will look like and we can formulate a procedure to ensure it. In the latter case, however, such as with the distribution of social goods within a highly complex society, we cannot know beforehand what such a result will look like. The best we can do is design a pure procedure that we can be assured will produce a fair result, whatever that result might look like.

The principles which Rawls' original position produces are well known but not entirely straightforward. They are principles which are framed to regulate the basic structure of the society, meaning its economic, legal, political and social institutions, as it is these which largely dictate how freedoms and resources are distributed, and therefore whether or not a society is just. Rawls identifies only two key principles. The first relates to the basic freedoms and dictates that the society's basic structure is to be arranged such that we can all be assured of these liberties: freedom of speech, freedom of assembly, freedom from arbitrary arrest, and all those other freedoms we take for granted in a liberal society.

The second is more complex, relating to the distribution of opportunities and resources. The first part secures fair equality of opportunity; fair in the sense that it is more than merely formal equality of opportunity where positions are open to all in theory but in practice only some have a genuine ability to pursue those positions. This 'fairness' is to be secured through the second part of the principle, known as 'the difference principle', which ensures that all inequalities must be to the benefit of the worst off. Thus, inequality in of itself is not deemed to be problematic, but where increases in inequality lead to those with the lowest expectations being worst off, they are to be prevented. For example, we might imagine a huge increase in wealth for some might, through the taxation system, lead to increased wealth for those who are worse off – but the exponential rise in the wealth of a minority might actually render their relative position weaker, because of a loss of political agency, for example.

Now it is often assumed that the most crucial aspect of Rawls' theory is the original position. This is understandable given that it provides the context for revealing his principles of justice. However, the focus on this concept and the subsequent rendering of the two principles often disguises the fact that there is an equally important aspect to Rawls' political philosophy that needs to be grasped to properly appreciate his ideas. This is especially so with respect to his ideas on world politics, as we will see later.

What is often overlooked in brief accounts of Rawls' work such as this is the method he employs in his philosophy, an approach which for him ultimately justifies the ideas and principles he puts forward and sets them on solid ground. This method aims at what he terms a reflective equilibrium, his claim being that for any moral theory to be valid and well founded, it needs to reach this state. This requires that the key elements, especially the key principles of the theory, are aligned with what he terms our 'considered judgements'. These judgements we can understand as being our everyday beliefs that we carry with us; not simply our snap judgements or intuitive reactions but rather those values and ideas that orientate our moral lives and that we articulate when we think about important questions in earnest.

Now, it is not simply that we create our moral theory, such as a theory of justice, so that it lines up accordingly with these considered judgements. The idea, rather, is that our theory represents a set of key ideas and concepts that helps us reflect on these everyday ideas, draw out their rationale, challenge them, and ensure that on rational reflection they are suitably well considered and coherent. We are encouraged to go back and forth between the theory and the judgements testing one then the other, so that we may find that either, or both, need to be adjusted in order to reach a suitable equilibrium.

One helpful analogy, as elucidated by Chandran Kukathas and Philip Pettit (1990: 7–8, 69–71), is to consider the relationship between everyday language and grammatical rules. We may check our use of a certain phrase or construction against the theoretical guidelines, and it may be that we correct our use, or it could be that in moving between the phrase and the rule that we discover it is the latter that might be better adjusted, to create more cogent and suitable guidelines. Importantly, neither the rules nor the everyday language are considered to be entirely stable and permanent. Likewise in the case of our considered judgments and our theory of justice: what is important is that they stand up to critical scrutiny and that we are able to arrive at a theory that is coherent and provides a robust framework against which we can judge our behaviour.

Rawls believes that the construct of the original position provides us with the theory of justice that is in reflective equilibrium with our considered judgments on fairness and social justice in liberal democratic societies. In a sense, we can think of the rational, self-interested choosers behind the veil of ignorance as capturing the individualistic values we hold dear, while the veil itself is a device that helps to represent our concerns with fairness and equality. Moreover, it is in what he calls 'wide' reflective equilibrium; this means that the theory Rawls has put forward is tested against other 'contenders' such as the principle of utility. An important and lengthy part of *TJ* (1971: §12) is the passage where Rawls takes four different theories that might in some sense be regarded as being in reflective equilibrium with our considered judgements on justice, and seeks to show why it is his version of the social contract that is the most apt. In particular, he is able to make the case that the worst off in a society regulated by his conception of 'democratic equality' will be better off than under competing conceptions.

THE DIFFERENCE PRINCIPLE

One way of approaching the difference principle is to think of Rawls' project as bringing together aspects of liberal and social democratic thought. He not only wanted to elucidate how the safeguard of liberal, individual rights is all important in allowing everyone to pursue their own aims; he wanted to show how freedoms and rights must be supported with material resources and a fair basic structure. The socialist will always be ready to point to how some formal rights and freedoms do little to protect people where material inequalities abound; we need only think about the old adage that everyone is equal before the law to appreciate this. Individuals may well be equal in principle, but where an individual has huge wealth and the ability to employ a team of crack lawyers to support their case, they are in a far more powerful position than the average person. In lay terms, therefore, a priority for Rawls is to provide a convincing argument for creating a level playing field that ensures we all can exercise our freedoms and rights in a similar fashion, regardless of our initial starting point in society.

As we have noted, Rawls' second principle is divided into two parts, the first part ensuring fair equality of opportunity with regard to all posts and positions in the society. Maintaining such a fair equality of opportunity is dependent upon the second – 'difference' – principle. It relates to the distribution of basic resources such as wealth, education and healthcare, which must be arranged so that people's basic needs are met in the first place. Furthermore, in order to sustain fair equality of opportunity this second principle must ensure a material position that allows all individuals to take full advantage of society's opportunities and compete on a level playing field.

We must not assume, however, that what Rawls has in mind is a crude material equality where society is organized so as to ensure the same level of wealth between all. Rather, he is seeking a balance whereby people are rewarded for hard work and encouraged to prosper, yet they do not reap such benefits that they are in a far more powerful position than others in society, so undermining their rights and freedoms and the sense of the society as a cooperative venture. To this end, the difference principle demands that inequalities are only permissible when they ensure that those in the lowest tier are relatively better off: 'the social minimum' that represents their position, always 'maximizes the expectations of the lowest income class' (2001b: 145). We might imagine a society where everyone lives in the same material condition as the starting benchmark, and when inequalities are then permitted the social minimum must always create more expectations than this initial starting point.

It is important to note that not all inequalities will have this effect, even if they increase wealth for the worst off; such as when one individual or a minority group gains a disproportionate amount of influence and power. This speaks to the complexity of the difference principle; it is not just a distributive principle that relates to financial resources. It ranges across all those elements that make up what Rawls terms 'the basic structure' of society including the political constitution, and 'the main elements of the economic and social system' that influence the life prospects of those people within it (1971: 7). Therefore the inequalities sanctioned, let us say, to encourage certain individuals to create more wealth, might lead to greater wealth for others through the tax system, but render them worse off in general terms because an elite group of individuals gain more power and influence to skew economic, legal or political arrangements to their benefit (an ability to perpetuate and monopolize certain elitist parts of the education system, for example). It is worth noting that Rawls recognizes the complexity of deploying such a principle and that identifying the exact social minimum that maximizes the expectations of the worst off is as much an empirical question as it is theoretical: 'where this limit lies is a matter of political judgment guided by theory, good sense, and plain hunch, at least within a wide range. On this sort of question the theory of justice has nothing specific to say' (1971: 246) (he would make similar comments with regard to the limits of philosophy in discussing the goals of foreign policy).

With his difference principle, we are able to recognize the deeply egalitarian nature of the liberalism proposed by Rawls and the influence

(Continued)

(Continued)

of socialist thought on his underlying philosophical assumptions. For a defining aspect of this principle is the way in which it is informed by the idea that 'undeserved inequalities call for redress' (2001: 165). It is not simply the case that it is preferable to regulate inequalities to ensure everyone is able to pursue their own preferences; in a deeper sense Rawls wishes to suggest it would be unjust because the advantages that many of us enjoy are not in any moral sense deserved. It would go against our deeply ingrained sense of fairness not to create a level playing field, when so many of us benefit from circumstances beyond our making.

Rawls states explicitly that we may not coherently claim that inequalities deriving from the position we are born into, and the natural talents we are endowed with, are 'deserved' in the usual sense. Moreover, he even makes the case that our 'superior character' is largely a result of 'fortunate family and social circumstances in early life for which we can claim no credit' (1971: 89). Here we have echoes of the early utopian socialists, who stated similar arguments, such as 'the character of man is, without a single exception, always formed for him . . . and is chiefly created by his predecessors that they give him, or may give him, his ideas and habits, which are the powers that govern and direct his conduct' (Owen, [1815] 1991: 75). Rawls does not wish to make the more extreme case that we cannot be morally responsible for any of our actions, yet he is equally forthright in drawing our attention to the complexity of factors at work in the life of any individual. Many factors are out of our control, and while we are sometimes able to make our own luck through good choices, on other occasions brute bad luck intervenes. These considerations are particularly poignant when we consider some formative experiences in his own life: the death of two of his brothers from diseases contracted from Rawls, and his time as a soldier in World War II – in particular the death of his friend on mission that Rawls avoided, simply because he was required elsewhere because of the particular blood type he could donate (Pogge, 2007). Mitigating the worst excesses of misfortune and bad luck is a foundational theme in Rawls' work.

However, Rawls does not wish to make the principle of redress the only basic tenet of his distributive principle, and it is in the way he weaves it in with other considerations, such as the need for economic efficiency and incentives, that the originality of his perspective is evident. Material equality in of itself is not a substantive good for Rawls, although a distributive system that works to ensure a level playing field helps to remind us that we are part of a cooperative system for mutual benefit, and engenders feelings of fraternity that sustain it. We should, however, encourage and reward hard work and innovation with a suitable system of recognition and rewards. This is the balance that Rawls seeks with the difference principle, which speaks to the demands of fairness, both in rewarding effort and ingenuity, while mitigating the worst effects of misfortune and the natural lottery of life.

In essence, there is nothing that stops someone becoming stupendously rich according to this principle, in so far as their wealth does not render others worse off, or compromises the principle of fair equality of opportunity. However, it is not difficult for us to think of individuals with disproportionate wealth and power in this day and age, which suggests that the inequalities Rawls has in mind are of a far more limited nature than those that characterize many states today. He might well describe our contemporary UK and USA as being 'callous [,] meritocratic' (1971: 100) societies, missing the effects of a difference principle that could help to sustain feelings of fraternity, and serve as a constant reminder of our duty 'in enriching the personal and social life of citizens, including . . . the less favored' (1971: 107).

It is with Rawls' two principles that the philosophical debate on global justice might be said to have begun in earnest. It provoked a reaction from a number of philosophers who sought to develop his ideas in the international context. Rawls himself provided a minimal sketch of how he envisaged applying his original position to world politics, but it did not stretch to arguing for redistribution of wealth between states in any form. He imagined representatives of states, denied knowledge of their own territories, coming together to decide on international principles of justice, which largely reflected the conventions of the day. Rawls' main motivation for presenting this sketch seems to have been to discuss issues of just war and conscientious objection, inspired no doubt by recent events in Vietnam.

It should be noted in the context of this discussion that there is another text that was published shortly after Rawls' book, which can also be credited with a lasting role in debates on global justice. This was Peter Singer's famous paper, *Famine, Affluence and Morality* (1972), which attempted to offer a philosophically informed response to the Bengali Famine of 1971. In many respects this was a ground-breaking text because, unlike *TJ*, it directly addressed the question of redistribution of wealth across borders and the duties we have to distant strangers. Singer came at the issue from a broadly utilitarian perspective, arguing that where we have the power to do so we should prevent bad occurrences; in the 'strong version' of this argument it would require doing so to the point of marginal utility, i.e. to the point of causing ourselves as much suffering as the dependents (the Bengali refugee in this case). Even the moderate version – preventing bad occurrences to the point of sacrificing 'something morally significant' – would require a 'great change in our way of life' (1972: 241).

It is interesting that in the academic debate Singer's name in this regard does not carry quite the same cachet as Rawls and those inspired by his work. This reflects Rawls' stature and the fact that his social contract approach has superseded utilitarianism in terms of its popularity in the mainstream. The notion that Rawls' own principles of justice could be extended across national boundaries was taken up almost immediately in Brian Barry's (1973: 129–32) extensive response to Rawls' theory. He suggested two reasons for this, which he believed were implicit in Rawls' own account. In the first instance, if those choosing the principles wished to ensure fairly equal outcomes for individuals by mitigating inequalities and the misfortune of some, then they would in the first instance be concerned with extending the scope of the principles worldwide. They would no doubt be aware, Barry argues, if they were citizens in certain states, their material prospects could well be dire.

The second argument he proposed was that even if we accepted the state-centric Rawlsian perspective, the representatives of these states would, for the same reasons, posit a principle of international redistribution to ensure a certain level of material equality between states. We will look in detail at how these ideas were developed by those following Barry's lead in the next chapter. Firstly, however, we will look at how Rawls subsequently developed the sketch of world politics he first offered in *TJ*.

RAWLS' *LAW OF PEOPLES*

By the time Rawls came to fully articulate his theory of international justice in 1999, figures such as Charles Beitz and Thomas Pogge had been developing their radical, cosmopolitan perspectives that demanded far-reaching measures including global redistribution. In some ways, Rawls' *Law of Peoples* (1999) – which developed further a paper he wrote in 1993 under the same title – has become the representative response from the communitarian perspective. As with all of Rawls' work, a sizeable secondary literature has arisen around *LP*, but the reception has been far more sceptical, even scathing, in comparison to his original work.

Much of this critical response came from cosmopolitan thinkers, and revolved around the fact that Rawls did not appear to reform or develop his views on world politics in a more radical direction. His acolytes had hoped that the initial sketch he drew in *TJ* and the ideas in his 1993 paper would be rescinded, on the basis of a more radical interpretation of his theory, in keeping with Barry's arguments. They went so far as to accuse Rawls of philosophical inconsistency in espousing a libertarian theory of international politics, in comparison to the egalitarian liberalism of his earlier work.

It is certainly true that Rawls' perspective appears more 'libertarian' or cautious in comparison to some of the ideas we will learn about in the next chapter. He does not advocate a global distributive principle or a global taxation regime, and the fact that he puts states rather than individual persons at the centre of his theory is indicative of a communitarian perspective more tied to the here and now, rather than demanding radical change. Certainly the rights and the status of the individual have become more important in world politics, but it remains very much the dominant assumption that states (or their representatives) are the primary actors and referents in terms of day to day politics.

Another aspect that is worth keeping in mind with regard to *LP* is that issues of poverty and redistribution are one small part of what it as an attempt to sketch a general 'theory of international politics'

(1999: 19). Whereas authors such as Pogge dedicate entire volumes to the problem of global poverty, Rawls discusses it in very general terms across a handful of pages in a very short book. Indeed, in one respect Rawls views *LP* as a short guide for liberal foreign policy; a work that sets out moral principles, normative standards and practical views on how to conduct international politics in a manner consistent with liberal values. It is therefore both a more and less complete work than a good deal of the literature focused on global justice. More complete because it embeds these concerns within a wider treatment of interconnected issues of world politics, and is presented as a direct challenge to realist thinking in the field of international relations. Less complete, in the sense that it has far less to say in terms of practical detail than other works on global justice, which are more focussed on the specific issues but less engaged in the bigger picture.

The picture he constructs emulates the earlier vision in *TJ*: representatives from different states come together in an international original position to discuss the appropriate principles for relations between states. However, there are significant ways in which Rawls developed his initial suggestions. In the first place he clarifies an element that is given little attention in TJ, namely that Rawls envisages an initial contract between *just* states. This goes some way to explaining why he did not extend his arguments to distributive justice, as the states in question are assumed to take care of their citizens and do not require assistance. In *LP*, Rawls reconstructs this approach with two original positions, in a way that reflects the sense in which it is a 'liberal' theory.

In the first place we have an original position between what Rawls calls 'liberal peoples'. These all, in theory, comply to a liberal political conception of justice that ensures their citizens are secure, with their basic rights respected. They agree on a basic charter for the law of peoples that includes traditional principles, such as respect for sovereign autonomy, commitment to treaties and reciprocal relations. They also include principles to protect human rights, a right to self-defence against outlaw states, and a duty to assist burdened societies. For Rawls, the real test for these principles is whether they can be adopted by other states who do not themselves abide by a liberal conception of justice. In the same way that Rawls believes non-liberal individuals in his ideal liberal society would endorse his two principles of justice, he reasons that other, non-liberal peoples in the ideal Society of Peoples would also endorse the charter of the *Law of Peoples*.

For Rawls this is a big test: the law should represent first and foremost a moral framework that Rawls believes reflects the values of liberal democratic societies. However, because it is liberal it should be able to incorporate other political perspectives, and this is reflected in the second original position. Here, representatives of non-liberal, decent peoples, which may have various religious or other conceptions of political justice – all of which respect a basic set of individual rights – go through the same process and it is argued that they would agree to the same basic principles. Thus we have a secure set of basic principles that define the relations between liberal and non-liberal peoples. Rawls is careful to note, however, that this is an open-ended list and there may be others in addition, such as ones relating to the global economy.

As well as liberal and non-liberal peoples, Rawls also offers other categories, to help order our moral thinking with regard to entities on the fringes of the Society of Peoples. He conceives of another category called 'benevolent absolutisms' that are characterized by political orders that do not respect political rights and claims to representation, yet succeed in protecting the other basic rights of their citizens. 'Outlaw states' are those that are expansionist and seek to disturb the peace, or are guilty of egregious crimes against their own people. 'Burdened societies' are the category most relevant to our discussion as they fail in their duty to provide worthwhile lives for their citizens, because of their poverty. These are political communities on the fringes of international society that in one way or another are unable to respect, or choose to defy the law.

In working through Rawls' taxonomy it is worth noting two significant points. Firstly you will have noticed that he uses different terms: people, state, society. This is no accident; through employing the term 'people' for the reasonable members of his idealized international society, he is defining them against the traditional understanding of the term 'state', which has typically implied an absolute immunity from external approbation and intervention, and an unencumbered right to go to war. This reflects the general view Rawls has of politics, which is that it is a moral realm to be governed by justice, and this normative concept of a people captures what modern states should be, namely sensitive to such moral standards, peaceable and in reciprocal relations with others. That his outlaws are labelled 'states' reflects the sense in which Rawls views the word in a problematic manner, associated with the type of realist view he hopes to challenge. We might take the term 'burdened *societies*' to reflect the idea that these are potential 'peoples' that aspire to reciprocal, peaceable relations once they have returned to, or achieved a level of capability sufficient to serve the interests of their citizens – rather than seeking to challenge the rule of law.

The second point is that this categorization Rawls puts forward is not meant as a direct representation of how the world is. Rather, the most helpful view of them is as idealized representations that approximate to the types of states that exist in the world. They should help to simplify, clarify and elucidate our views, and think through morally consistent and – hopefully – efficacious actions and policies. Discussing the notion and implications of an outlaw state can help us recognize and respond consistently when certain states are behaving in bellicose and violent ways; the ideal types of non-liberal and liberal peoples can help us hold such states to account and ensure they behave according to their supposed moral standards, or help us recognize when they are in danger of stepping outside the law; the concept of a burdened society identifies those states that are in need of our assistance and encourages us to think about how we can address their issues. Rawls intends these concepts to be of use to policymakers and activists seeking to pursue a just course of action in world politics.

With respect to discussions of global poverty and questions of distributive justice focussed upon in this book, it is the *duty of assistance* to burdened societies that is the crucial principle. The trigger for this duty to be put into practice is where a society, be it for historical or short term reasons, lacks 'the political and cultural traditions, the human capital and know-how, and, often, the material and technological resources needed to be well-ordered' (Rawls, 1999: 106).

'Well-ordered' is Rawls' choice phrase for a society that is able to uphold the basic rights of its citizens.

While it is the fate of *individuals* within these societies that is seen as the benchmark for action, it is important to remember that this duty is conceived as one that holds *between peoples*. That is to say, members of the Society of Peoples are duty bound to act as part of a legal agreement between each other, not because of a direct duty to the individuals suffering, but because the burdened society has essentially fallen outside the law and must be assisted in (re)gaining its place within the Society of Peoples. This is a very different moral argument for assistance than we will come across elsewhere, with its priority of peoples over persons emphasizing what we have termed the communitarian (or thin statist/social liberal) character of Rawls' approach.

What does the duty entail? In many ways the substantive actions to be taken are less than clear, and this has been part of the controversy around the principle. Rawls warns against throwing funds at the problem and rejects the idea of ongoing redistribution as part of the solution. He also advises that it is not an easy problem and there is no quick fix. In fact, one of the most important resources he seems to think is that of 'advice' – not only in the technical sense, but also with regard to addressing the political culture that informs the institutional arrangements of the society in question. In this respect he takes his lead from Amartya Sen (1999), who has used powerful empirical arguments to demonstrate that famines, poverty and suffering have often been caused by the lack of proper open and democratic institutions.

Rawls recognizes that financial resources play a part and some contributions will be necessary, but it is this focus on securing responsive and effective institutions that has led many of his critics to regard him as advocating far too little in terms of assistance. On the other hand, it should not be surprising that a political philosopher, whose own 'domestic' theory places so much emphasis on the arrangements of the society's basic structure, should regard the same elements as being key to improvement in the context of burdened societies. Nor can one extract Rawls' ideas from the debates in which he was involved. In many ways he can be seen as offering a counterpoint to the cosmopolitan focus on the redistribution of wealth and their emphasis on trade and the global economy. While he does not rule out measures relating to these issues in attempting to address such situations, he clearly thinks that such a duty needs to be conceived with a focus on creating stable, decent institutions that will ensure a level of autonomy in the long term.

THE CRITICAL DEBATE ON THE *LAW OF PEOPLES*

It is fair to say that Rawls' *Law of Peoples* was not greeted with the same fanfare as his first major publication. To a large degree this is to do with the intellectual context. As alluded to, many philosophers inspired by Rawls believed he had taken a false step in his original views on world politics, and they hoped his 1993 paper was an aberration that would be put right in his book length study. However, he maintained his basic views, which led cosmopolitans such as Allen Buchanan (2000), Simon Caney (2002), Charles Beitz (2000), Martha Nussbaum (2002) and Thomas Pogge to accuse him of 'libertarian rule-making' (Pogge, 2001: 251) and of failing to transpose the radically egalitarian nature of his domestic theory to the global context. It is worth noting that the text has been equally criticized from the more conservative perspective, with some arguing that his theory amounts to an overly ambitious cosmopolitanism that does not take account of the fundamental differences and conflicts between states (Jackson, 2005; Geuss, 2005). In a sense, one can interpret this two-pronged attack on the text as a reflection of Rawls' attempt to steer a course between cosmopolitanism on the one hand and realism on the other. Perhaps it was inevitable that his 'realistic utopianism' would cut no ice with either of these rival perspectives.

There were two general strands to the cosmopolitan critique. Firstly, many were of the view that the principles Rawls envisaged allowed too much leeway for the abuse of individuals by governments. In short, the baseline of human rights he advocated for members of his Society of Peoples was set too low. Indeed, it is true to say that many of the more ambitious elements of the Universal Declaration of Human Rights are absent from the list that Rawls believes those in the international original positions would settle upon. The second strand relates to the specific question of redistribution, and incredulity on the part of his critics that Rawls should not choose to transpose his difference principle, or a version of it, to his international theory. As Barry had argued originally in response, why would representatives not choose such a principle to ensure more substantive equality?

While these criticisms became somewhat embedded in the narrative of the global justice debate, there were dissenting voices that saw some virtues in Rawls' approach and disputed the image being painted by his critics. Chris Brown (2002b) welcomed his more realistic utopianism, while authors such as David Reidy (2007) sought to cash out the potential extent of measures such as the Duty of Assistance, and the policies advocated with regard to ensuing a fair global economy. In the hands of these more sympathetic interpreters, his views seemed more attuned to the egalitarian aspects of his earlier work. In fact, it has been argued that the duty of assistance can lay the basis for a whole raft of measures relating to financial redistribution, assistance with state building and taxation infrastructure, technical assistance and development, as well as policies relating to the global economic structure (Williams, 2011: 140–53). In the final analysis, the differences with cosmopolitan measures seem not so fundamental – it is the acceptance of non-democratic political orders, and the justification in terms of a duty to peoples rather than individuals, which provide the most significant contrasts and suggest his contrasting, communitarian perspective.

One particular aspect of the debate may go some way to explaining why Rawls' theory appeared so unsatisfactory to his critics. There was a lack of acknowledgement of the consistency in method he deployed (James, 2005). While they focused on the transposition of one principle in particular, Rawls grounded his theory in the method of reflective equilibrium. This explains why he could not endorse a cosmopolitan position because his theory would require principles that articulated the 'considered judgements' prevalent in the international public political culture. This of course would endorse more recent ideas about human rights and assistance, but it would equally recognize the primacy of states and their perceived moral worth as the vessel for communal political life. Tied to the present political reality in the global context is also a recognition that it does not constitute a cooperative venture for mutual advantage in the same

(Continued)

(Continued)

systematic way as states, while states are autonomous to an extent that could never be true of individuals. Thus although Rawls recognizes the need for far-reaching 'special' measures in relation to burdened societies, as a whole the relationship between well-ordered societies is not one that demands or justifies a permanent distributive arrangement, reminiscent of his difference principle. Rawls' views, are of course, not without their problems, but it is fair to suggest that his approach to global poverty and other issues in world politics is now recognized as being far more cogent and prescient than his initial critics suggested.

DAVID MILLER – COMMUNITARIAN OR COSMOPOLITAN?

Rawls is one of two key philosophers who are regarded as communitarian challengers to the cosmopolitan perspective. The other is David Miller, a highly regarded English philosopher who is most associated with his defence of nationalism. In the context of the global justice debate, his contribution has been a notable one for this very reason. As a thinker known for his strong moral case for liberal nationalism, it is significant that he should extend this political theory to the global realm, in such a way that articulates moral responsibilities beyond the nation–state. This is particularly so because historically, and in the discipline of international politics, such a strong nationalist position is associated with the view that moral political principles are limited to within state boundaries. Beyond the state is anarchy: a system where self-interest is the first and only rule (Waltz, 1979).

Before we look at how Miller articulates our duties to those beyond our national borders, it is worth noting the argument he offers in favour nationalism. This is helpful in one respect in appreciating the ideas that cosmopolitan thinkers are railing against, especially those who wish to deny there is any particular moral status pertaining to the state (some might assign some moral value to the state, but regard it is as very much secondary to the individual). Miller holds the belief that the nation–state is an entity that is constitutive of individual identity, and in a positive sense. It is unique in offering five elements that are vital in fostering solidarity: 'a community constituted by mutual belief, extended in history, active in character, connected to a particular territory, and thought to be marked off from other communities' (Miller, 2000: 31–2). Such large scale solidarity is vital to the functioning of the nation-state, which requires a broad sense of community in order to fulfil the role of guaranteeing collective goods, protecting the vulnerable and ensuring just relations.

Miller's account, of course, does not take the cosmopolitan course of questioning the nation-state as the basis of our social organization, and in this sense he is aligned with Rawls in his theorizing and believes our moral and political philosophy 'bends to accommodate pre-existing sentiments' (Miller, 2000: 32). This 'Humean approach' as he refers to it, leaves in place everyday sentiments 'until strong arguments are produced for rejecting them'. While Miller might point to the benefits of the state with reference to the dramatic rise in living standards in some societies, post-World War II especially, cosmopolitans would no doubt claim there are very strong reasons for rejecting the priority of the state, some of which we will pursue in the next chapter.

We are left in little doubt from Miller's perspective that the nation-state is integral to the lives of human beings, imbuing them with core meaning and values. Yet what we discover is that Miller is not a hard-line nationalist. He believes: (a) it is possible to conceive of political values beyond the state, and (b) these political values can circumscribe the principles of the state. Some might argue that a well-developed and tightly integrated enough global community does not exist to the extent to create and sustain such foundational principles, and that only the nation-state is suitably placed for this role. Not so, argues David Miller, but it is interesting that the way in which he arrives at principles of justice for the global realm emulates cosmopolitan thinking.

Ultimately, Miller argues that our primary moral responsibilities may be to our compatriots – and indeed our ethical relationship with them entails substantial duties – but we also have secondary duties of global justice to others because of their basic status as human beings. As such, even though we might not have a political relationship with them as members of the same state, when there are humans whose basic needs are not met and are threatened with danger and death, there is a general responsibility for international society to protect them.

Miller might be criticized for similar reasons to Rawls, in that he provides comparatively little detail with regard to how his general principles might be put into practice, and the detail he does provide suggests scepticism about the importance and effectiveness of measures with respect to the global economy. In fairness, Miller is interested in the first place in how we might describe and distribute responsibilities and much of his work is dedicated to setting out these subtle philosophical differences. One key argument, for example, is the idea that a collective such as a state can be held 'responsible' for certain outcomes. Much of this takes on importance when Miller discusses who should do what, and it is these questions rather than *how* the responsibilities are carried out that are the priority for him.

What Miller terms 'outcome' responsibility is particularly important because this implies that an actor (individual or collective) understands the possible outcome of their actions, and this is a morally more significant type of responsibility than mere 'causal' responsibility, which can occur when an action leads to an outcome because of unanticipated consequences. An important strand in Miller's thinking is his view that states bear outcome responsibility for the difficulties they face, and that obstacles or difficulties caused by the global structure do not mitigate these responsibilities. This accounts for why he gives comparatively less attention to such factors; in essence Miller thinks that despite the fact that the global economy is sometimes unfair and unequal this should not lead us to believe the international society should bear more responsibility than the state itself. In keeping with these views is a tendency to assign problems of poverty and underdevelopment primarily to national state structures and local political culture.

His arguments for responsibility are particularly important with regard to foreign assistance. In the first instance he is happy to assign remedial duties of justice to the international society where the basic needs of individuals are not met. Miller describes duties of justice as being strong, inasmuch as they compel others – in theory – to act. There is no moral choice and so there is an element of enforcement (although it is an open question to what extent this makes sense on a global level, where there is no enforcing institution akin to the state)

However, Miller (2007: 257) argues that Zimbabwe is an example of a state that has received assistance in the past on this basis, but has failed to reform itself and act in ways that respond to their citizens' basic needs. In this instance, according to Miller, the international society has done its duty and the fact that outcome responsibility rests with the state means a strong duty of justice no longer holds. Any remaining duty to those suffering is a weaker, humanitarian duty that can be fulfilled on a voluntary basis, but there is no longer an element of compliance. This is of course controversial, and there are many analysts who point out that Zimbabwean politics is far more complex than Miller's analysis would suggest (e.g., Scoones *et al.*, 2012), but the point is largely an illustrative one for Miller's emphasis on national, domestic responsibility.

Rawls and Miller are similar in their view that more complex and onerous responsibilities apply to our fellow citizens within the state than distant strangers in foreign lands. Nevertheless, they recognize that such duties do exist and that we are compelled to act when others suffer. However, they might be said to differ in two subtle but important ways. Miller is more forthright in his views that the moral imperative lies with state actors rather than the international society, and this is reflected in the fact that he is willing to lower the status of global duties to humanitarian duties, where this imperative is not responded to adequately. Rawls regards the duty of assistance as holding in all instances and is less interested in assigning such 'outcome responsibility' – he acknowledges that the state has a role to play and there may be ways in which they need to reform, but the implication is that actions by the international society may be equally if not more important.

The other difference is that Rawls' approach is more strictly communitarian than Miller's. One could characterize the latter's approach as hybrid, in that he emphasizes the nation-state as the primary moral entity in the global realm, but overlays this perspective with a cosmopolitanism that dictates where basic needs are compromised, then duties of justice pertain to the suffering individuals, as individuals. Rawls, on the other hand, presents a set of interstate principles one of which is the duty of assistance. This duty pertains to burdened societies in the first place – not their individual members – and it is enacted in order to bring them into the Society of Peoples.

This is not to say that the suffering of the individual is not central to the duty, as this is taken as the marker of a burdened society, but unlike in Miller's theory, it remains an interstate duty of justice, where it is the condition of the state that necessitates action. Miller's approach might thus be termed cosmopolitan, which may not in practical terms lead to tremendous differences. However, a theory of international justice that remains tied to the reality of interstate agreements could speak more directly to the reality of international politics, and their shared philosophical aim of theorizing on the basis of embedded sentiments and judgements.

CONCLUSION

In this chapter we have explained how John Rawls became such a central figure in the philosophical debate around global justice, because of his role in reviving political theory and his subsequent influence on other thinkers. We have elucidated some of the key ideas from his original work that have been central in this debate, while also outlining his own theory of international politics and his views on global poverty in particular. These have provided a significant contribution as they articulate a communitarian response to the issues of global justice. We have also attended to elements of the critical debate that are worth pursuing in the literature, and suggested how Rawls may have been harshly dealt with in the first place (especially because the importance of his philosophical method was overlooked).

We completed the chapter by introducing another significant figure who is associated with the communitarian approach, namely David Miller. This included a brief outline of his defence of nationalism, and an account of how he deals with the concept of responsibility in order to articulate certain duties he believes hold on a global level. It was suggested, however, that given the significance of the individual in providing the grounds for these duties, it seems Rawls presents us with the more purely communitarian approach, where duties relating to global poverty are articulated in the first place as interstate duties.

In general, it might seem that these analytical, technical debates are far removed from the grim realities of global inequality and poverty.

To invoke a stereotype, is it of any consequence whether (largely white, male, middle class) philosophers sit around on their comfy chairs, smoking pipes, and debating the finer aspects of questions about the foundations for global duties? Some might well be tempted to say the answer is a resounding no – and it is perhaps true that those who dedicate their lives to agitating for change as activists and political individuals might have bigger and more immediate impact.

Putting aside the hope that some of us may have as academics – that our teaching may inform and possibly even inspire students so that they can contribute in positive ways – there are other reasons as to why these academic debates are not inconsequential. These relate to some of the issues we raised in the introduction, which have to do with the way international politics is traditionally conceived in practice and in theory. We must remember that many still subscribe to the idea that politics in this realm has no role for moral arguments, that claims of justice in the cut and thrust of international politics are spurious, and that we should understand world politics and act in such a way that reflects this 'reality'.

In their own ways, both Rawls and Miller contribute normative arguments that reject this 'reality' and both try to articulate ideas that challenge the traditional view that assisting distant strangers is at best a voluntary, humanitarian practice, or a strategic concern with ulterior motives. It is particularly significant that a traditional 'nationalist' such as Miller should argue that despite our moral priorities to our fellow citizens we have strong duties to others. He provides a challenge to realist thinkers, who might regard him as a natural ally for their view that mutual cooperation is circumscribed by the state. Rawls is equally significant in his own efforts to 'domesticate' and 'humanize' world politics. By adapting the social contract to the international level he demonstrates how the laws and practices that have emerged can be justified by a familiar and robust philosophical concept, which has informed our understanding of domestic politics for centuries. However one views social contract theory, one basic statement being made by Rawls – that the realist must respond to – is that we can treat international politics as a realm of moral philosophy: that a more just world is possible.

Taken together, these are two forceful challenges to the realist status quo. They argue that even if we are happy to accept the moral standing of states and the practicalities of world politics as they are *there is nevertheless a strong duty of justice, which cannot be refused on moral grounds, for taking substantial steps towards alleviating the suffering of others.* By claiming otherwise, these philosophers are arguing we have a wrong-headed, immoral and callous view of the world. If our politicians and their various advisors and experts accepted these arguments and acted upon them, the world we live in might look very different.

The philosopher's hope is that others can use their ideas to undermine the dominant realist ideology. In the next chapter we discuss another group of philosophers who argue that the communitarian challenge is simply too weak and tied too fundamentally to the status quo. If we are going to change the world, we must dispense with the illusion of the primacy of the state.

2

FROM SOCIAL JUSTICE TO GLOBAL JUSTICE

IN THIS CHAPTER . . .

. . . we outline some of the key arguments and introduce some of the most prominent thinkers in the cosmopolitan tradition. We look in detail at how some of the earlier, most influential ideas developed through an engagement with Rawls' political philosophy and laid the foundation for what has become a challenging and powerful set of ideals, which rails against the traditional view of international politics. In this respect we pay particular attention to the seminal arguments of Charles Beitz, who used Rawlsian concepts in his critique of these traditional ideas, before moving on to engage with perhaps the most influential of all cosmopolitan thinkers, Rawls' student, Thomas Pogge. This will entail a discussion of human rights and the kinds of practical policies that are characteristic of his perspective. We then move on to introduce other theories that have emerged from the cosmopolitan outlook. The thinkers discussed begin with the same fundamental emphasis on the overriding value of the individual, but as the selection demonstrates, this can produce very different projects. We look first to another, 'dialogical' tradition of cosmopolitan thought that has its roots in the work of the famous German philosopher Jürgen Habermas and tends to discuss the terms on which we justify global principles and policies – rather than arguing for and specifying particular principles in the Rawlsian mode. The chapter concludes with the capability approach, a perspective conceived by Amartya Sen in seeking a meaningful measure of individual poverty, which was later developed by Martha Nussbaum – a philosopher who has strong links with the liberal tradition but is influenced by competing perspectives, providing a link to the further exploration of alternative approaches in the following chapter.

GLOBAL AND INTERNATIONAL JUSTICE

Thus far we have used the terms *international justice* and *global justice* in a way that may seem interchangeable. However, to assume this would be a mistake, because the terms themselves carry very different connotations. Moreover, an understanding of the difference is informative with regard to grasping important philosophical differences. When the term international justice is used, it tends to be with reference to ideas put forward by a thinker such as Rawls, who regards world politics as being primarily about relations between states. As we have seen, this is reflected in his international theory and his 'Law of Peoples', which is largely about identifying the moral duties that hold between states (or peoples, to use his normatively charged term). The focus is reflected in the term international justice because according to this perspective, the concept of justice holds between states; its scope is literally international, or between nation-states.

Global justice has a subtly different meaning. The implication here is that relations of justice, marked by strong duties, hold between entities that can in some sense be 'beyond' the state. As we articulated with regard to David Miller's view on these issues, such duties do not need to be mediated by state relations, rather we can consider ourselves as having direct duties to individuals in other states (or, according to some philosophers, other non-human entities) regardless of where we find ourselves. This implies the more radical notion that state boundaries do not have a privileged status in world politics and that relations of justice stretch beyond them. When we deploy the term 'global' as opposed to 'international', we are therefore implying a view of justice that has no particular respect for state boundaries. In this context, cosmopolitan thinkers characteristically present theories of global justice where duties in world politics relate first and foremost to the individual, rather than the state. A communitarian thinker such as Rawls, however, would be regarded as a theorist of international justice in his emphasis on inter-state duties.

Of course, these divisions are somewhat arbitrary, because one might identify both Rawls and Miller in some senses as cosmopolitan, global justice philosophers. Although Rawls emphasizes the priority of states, it is sometimes suggested that he posits natural duties of justice to individuals as the basis for his duty of assistance and an allegiance to human rights, while Miller attributes the notion of duties beyond those to our fellow citizens to the basic needs of other individuals. Cosmopolitans, on the other hand, may also give some weight to the fact that states are key agents in the fight to ensure justice, or provide an important context for individual development.

However, what might be taken to divide the two approaches is that communitarians maintain that the state has a privileged moral standing, which defines it as the primary agent in the context of world politics, because of its centrality for the human personality and the extent of the value it embodies (think here of Rawls' emphasis on the intrinsic good of culture, the importance of a shared public life and the significance of a proper patriotism that he sees embodied in a 'people'). This is not an insignificant difference with cosmopolitans, because ultimately they are more inclined to say 'take it or leave it' when it comes to the entity of the state; theirs is a more radical approach in the sense that it does not entail protecting or privileging the state on the basis of exceptional moral values. If moving beyond a Society of States is what is required in order to ensure a more just world for individuals, then we should see no issue with dispensing with the privilege of the nation-state as the primary site of justice. The demands of the individual take precedence every time over the type of collective values that for many are overexaggerated, or even imagined.

In this chapter we will look at how this moral outlook is set out in more detail by particular philosophers. They all share in common this idea that ultimately it is the individual that is the relevant unit of moral concern from the perspective of world politics, and that world politics should be organized and structured to this end.

Moreover, in this particular discussion it is worth noting that we are dealing with one specific, if ubiquitous, approach, namely liberal cosmopolitanism. That is to say, one can hold a cosmopolitan world view that privileges the individual, questions the authority of the state, but articulates a different moral approach from liberalism. We have encountered one alternative already, namely the utilitarian Peter Singer (1972) who, in his argument for extending our moral duties to other individuals beyond national borders, articulated a formative global theory of justice which he has since developed in more sophisticated ways. While we focus on the more dominant liberal voices in this chapter, in the next we will move onto some other cosmopolitanisms that are tied to very different normative outlooks, some of which question how radical liberalism can really be.

CHARLES BEITZ ON POLITICAL THEORY AND INTERNATIONAL RELATIONS

For some critics, liberal theorists are presented as rather staid, perhaps a little old-fashioned and lacking a radical edge. Yet it is too easily forgotten how challenging these original arguments were, and how they remain radical in fundamental ways when viewed against the reality of world politics today. In particular, when we refer to Charles Beitz's book on *Political Theory and International Relations*, we need to remind ourselves of the overarching argument it represents, which is a rejection of the traditional ways of regarding international politics, either as an everlasting power struggle or as a realm of loosely connected and nominally cooperative states. Beitz's influence should not be forgotten in this regard; he helped to legitimate the discussion of world politics in terms of principles, values and progress, and in so doing is recognized as one of those who first brought ideas of political theory back into the study of international relations.

One measure of his success is his impact upon debates surrounding Rawls' discussion of international politics. Rawls, as we have seen, limited his discussion in *TJ* to principles of just war, articulating a vision of a loosely configured international society characterized by the value of autonomy. This vision was associated with 'the morality of states' perspective that Beitz critiqued, because of the limited way in which it interprets the scope of justice in the international realm. Thus although we began with Rawls in terms of gaining a background for the global justice debate, it is with Beitz that one sees these discussions beginning in earnest among philosophers.

The history of the debate is important to emphasize, in one sense because those who are involved in contemporary global justice debates, and those who seek to challenge their apparently regressive nature, may sometimes be guilty of turning in on themselves and forgetting the primary target. That is say, contemporary thinkers may now see some problems with some of the oversimplistic assumptions in earlier arguments, or have identified how some elements of liberal ideology undermine their claims to progressiveness, but they nevertheless occupy similar territory, inasmuch as they offer a powerful rejection of the status quo. When set against these more traditional outlooks, they have much more in common than is frequently recognized.

Appreciating the overarching structure of Beitz' book draws our attention to this fundamental issue of undermining these traditional realist outlooks. Moreover, it highlights the scale of the challenge that he and other philosophers faced in attempting to challenge assumptions about the nature of international relations. He begins with a critique of the realist outlook that he labels '*International Relations as the State of Nature*' – a reference to the way in which it characterizes world politics through reference to Thomas Hobbes' infamous image of a stateless society, one where life is 'solitary, poor, nasty, brutish, and short' (Hobbes, [1651] 1982). As states lack a Leviathan to which they have ceded their power, so the reasoning goes, they are trapped in constant competition, necessitating a perpetual readiness for conflict. This starting assumption buttresses the conviction that analysing world politics in moral terms is inappropriate; as with Hobbes' state of nature, arguments about justice and right are irrelevant where the only rule is that of competition and no covenant exists. Where any moral sentiment is allowed, it is framed in terms of justifying the interests of the state. For Waltz (1959/2001: 209), it is foolhardy to ignore the primary importance of survival in the balance of power of international politics: 'the balance of power is not so much imposed by statesmen on events as it is imposed by events on statesmen'.

Beitz was therefore not simply putting forward his own cosmopolitan theory; more fundamentally he was arguing for the legitimacy of thinking about world politics in moral terms rather than simply self-interest. That Beitz felt obliged to make these arguments – through reference to increasing levels of cooperation in international relations and the claim that not all such action is self-interested – shows the scale of the task. It is as well that we remind ourselves of this because as we noted in the introduction, the same view continues to hold sway in the practice of international politics and its study in the academy.

However, Beitz was not only satisfied with clearing the way for a political theory of international relations – he had to advance it further in order to pave the way for his more radical arguments. To achieve this he critiques what he describes as the most prevalent alternative to the 'state of nature' account, an approach he entitles 'the morality of states'. This is a historical tradition that harks back to legal theorists such as Samuel Pufendorf (1994) who himself rejected the Hobbesian understanding of international relations. He disagreed that justice pertains only within the conditions of a covenant, and turned to the idea of natural law to argue that such duties are prior to political institutions (and in fact represent commands from God).

In order to conceive of justice pertaining to states, Pufendorf has to interpret them as moral persons, analogous to individuals; however, the duties he outlines as fundamental to international law are much weaker than those we are familiar with in the domestic realm. A basic reason for this is the argument that states are far less vulnerable than individuals, and therefore a similar level of cooperation and commitment are not required in order to maintain their security (a theme echoed in Rawls' rejection of a global distributive principle). However, the analogy pertains sufficiently for Beitz to characterize the 'morality of states' as 'the international analogue of nineteenth century liberalism' (1999 [1979]: 66). States, as with individual citizens in this period, are to be treated as autonomous and immune from intervention, while there are no moral rules regarding the structure of economic relations, thus combining 'the liberty of individual agents with an indifference to the distribution outcomes of their economic interaction' (1999 [1979]: 66).

In broad terms the rest of Beitz's work is dedicated to challenging these libertarian moral values as the cornerstone of international relations. In the second part he takes on the assumption of autonomy, while the third part tackles the issue that would become central to philosophical discussions of global justice, namely the distribution of economic advantage. In arguing against the idea that states have an overriding right to autonomy, he seeks to employ competing moral arguments that weaken this claim and demonstrate that maintaining autonomy in many cases can lead to more serious injustices, such as when an imperial power exerts its hold over a colonized people demanding self-determination. These types of questions are by no means irrelevant to issues of global justice, but here we focus on what became the most prominent arguments, which pertain more directly to the redistribution of wealth.

In this case we see that Beitz has taken a more complex route to a similar conclusion reached by Brian Barry in his initial critique of Rawls' Original Position: that in actual fact there is every reason to extend it to the global realm and posit global distributive principles. Beitz is effectively arguing that not only is states' autonomy conditional; neither do they have an absolute right to their economic product. The redistribution of wealth and resources that occurs within states should be replicated on a global level.

Beitz sets out this claim with two different arguments. The first develops a point made by Barry: that given the way in which Rawls sets up his international original position, representatives of states behind the veil of ignorance would surely choose to set out a distributive principle along similar lines to the difference principle, in an attempt to ensure that no state is significantly poorer than any other. That is to say, the state representatives would want to ensure a redistribution of resources that would guard against severe inequalities between states, to prevent some individuals ending up in societies that are appreciably less well off than others. Theoretically this seems consistent with the desire of individuals in the domestic original position to ensure a fair equality of opportunity that is not undermined by excessive inequalities. It should be noted, however, that there is an empirical assumption as well that is not so easily accepted, namely that an abundance of natural resources, or a redistribution of their product, will necessarily translate into greater material abundance within a state (literature on the 'resource curse', for example, argues that abundant natural resources can lead to a poverty trap, see Ross, 1999, and Collier, 2007: 39).

The second argument is the more sophisticated and significant, for it takes Beitz unequivocally beyond the framework of the 'morality of states' in his thinking. That is to say the first argument pertains to a world order governed by the relationship between states, but the more radical approach throws this framework into question. In this case Beitz argues that rather than positing representatives of states in an international original position, it is preferable to conceive of a global original position where we have individuals as representatives of individuals, in the same manner as the first original position. This scenario immediately dissolves the priority of states in world politics because those choosing principles for the international order are doing so, not on behalf of the interest of states, but rather the interests of individuals. In effect, the globe is being treated as one extended cooperative entity, for which it is apt to choose principles of social justice governing the lives of all people in the same way, regardless of their position or country. So rather than largely autonomous states (with their potentially different conceptions of justice) being the primary subjects of justice, and accruing the benefits of redistribution to be used according to their own principles, we are talking in terms of a global society where rights and resources are to be distributed according to the uniform, Rawlsian two principles.

Such an argument depends upon Beitz's extension and development of his claim that the world is no longer characterized by nation-states that are culturally, economically and politically autonomous. To the contrary, he argues, we now live in a world so interdependent and interconnected we are justified in claiming that it represents a global cooperative venture for mutual advantage, reminiscent of the nation-state. 'If social cooperation is the foundation of distributive justice', he states, 'then one might think that international economic interdependence lends support to a principle of global distributive justice' (1999 [1979]: 144). He cites the development of international investment and trade, and the proliferation of multinational corporations as key evidence (1999 [1979]: 145).

Following Rawls' lead, Beitz assumes that the circumstances of justice – where duties of justice hold – apply to those goods, and the products of those goods, that are the result of our mutual endeavour. Essentially, Beitz argues that much of what is produced in the modern world is a direct result of cooperation across borders: 'interdependence in trade and investment produces substantial aggregate economic benefits in the form of a higher global rate of economic growth as well as greater productive efficiency' (1999 [1979]: 145). Beitz characterizes these emerging global activities and organizations as 'the constitutional structure of the world economy' (1999 [1979]: 148) with far-reaching distributive implications in terms of the relative benefits and losses made by actors within that structure. The extent to which this emerging global economic structure resembles the configuration and effects of a nation-state's economy is significant enough to claim that principles regarding equality of opportunity and distribution should apply uniformly across the different territories. Such principles will seek to maximize the position of the worst-off individuals, while disregarding whether such policies are co-extensive with national borders (Beitz, 1999 [1979]: 153).

Significantly, Beitz later revised his position by claiming that it is not the fact of interdependence that should be seen as laying the basis for such a cosmopolitan argument (1983: 596). Rather there is a more fundamental value at work that is more important than interdependence, which may or may not be taken to be well developed enough to necessitate 'global' duties of distribution. Rather, these duties rest in the first instance on the morally more secure ground of a conception of the individual as free and equal. This moral fact enjoins us to consider what principles of justice should apply to the institutions that have an effect on their lives. Thus principles of justice are to apply to global institutions and economic interactions not because they constitute a cooperative venture for mutual advantage, but rather because in a more basic sense they impact upon individuals' well-being and their capacity to pursue their ends.

Beitz thus moves from a justification of cosmopolitan principles on the basis of the social contract model pursued by Rawls. We do not need to be 'fellow citizens' in a global society to ground duties of justice to each other – our very humanity is a substantial enough basis for these duties. Arguments about global institutions become secondary in the sense that they pertain not to justification, but ensuring the circumstances where these duties are enacted properly.

The basic moral status of individuals, and the question of ensuring their entitlements are met through effective policies, are the two key themes in the work of the most significant figure in the cosmopolitan tradition: Thomas Pogge.

THOMAS POGGE

Pogge is a philosopher who is now recognized as much for his practical contributions to campaigns and debates about global justice as he is for his academic work. In a sense this is particularly fitting, because more than any other he developed the philosophical study of global justice through a more thorough engagement with empirical questions about the causes of poverty. He has come to develop a series of sophisticated policy recommendations that are grounded first and foremost in his cosmopolitan philosophy.

This was not always the case, however, and if we look at his earlier book, *Realizing Rawls*, we see that Pogge in some respects followed in the footsteps of Barry and Beitz. In the latter sections of this book he put forward a similar case that in its most 'elegant and unified interpretation' Rawls' theory can be applicable on a global scale (Pogge, 1989: 242). However, Pogge did not pursue the application of these exact theoretical arguments to the problem of global injustice in later works. It might be said that the theoretical ideal of establishing a global order aligned with the difference principle was put to one side, and that instead of this intellectual exercise, Pogge began to develop arguments that aimed at having purchase and leverage in the real world of politics.

Therefore, although Pogge, like Beitz, was inspired by Rawls, he would take the application of the latter's principles on the global scale as the springboard for developing his own arguments. This is not to say that the Rawlsian motifs or moral ideals were foregone, simply that he began to develop his own moral and practical vocabulary that aimed at articulating an appealing and practical cosmopolitan vision. He expresses the rationale behind his proposals in relation to one particular policy for redistribution, in which he says 'Modesty is important if the proposed institutional alternative is to gain the support necessary to implement it and is to be able to sustain itself in the world as we know it' (Pogge, 2008: 211).

This vision was advanced in its mature form in *World Poverty and Human Rights* ([2002] 2008), which is an impressive combination of moral argumentation and policy recommendation. In this work Pogge provides what is perhaps the most oft-quoted characterization of the cosmopolitan position:

> Three elements are shared by all cosmopolitan positions. First, *individualism*: the ultimate units of concern are *human beings*, or *persons* – rather than, say, family lines, tribes, ethnic, cultural, or religious communities, nations, or states. The latter may be units of concern only indirectly, in virtue of their individual members or citizens. Second, *universality*: the status of ultimate unit of concern attaches to *every* living human being *equally* – not merely to some subset, such as men, aristocrats, Aryans, whites, or Muslims. Third, *generality*: this special status has global force. Persons are ultimate units of concern *for everyone* – not only for their compatriots, fellow religionists, or suchlike.
>
> (2008: 175)

This expresses very effectively the sense in which it is the individual, above all else, that is the chief moral concern for the cosmopolitan, and this is true of each individual regardless of where they are in the world. In more concrete terms Pogge sees this commitment being expressed in terms of the concept of human rights, and the claims that such rights make on behalf of each individual. These claims are nowhere near as ambitious as Rawls' domestic principles of justice and the comparative level of wealth they demand, yet they do entail for Pogge a 'social context and means that persons normally need, according to some broad range of plausible conception of what human flourishing consists in, to lead a minimally worthwhile life' (2008: 54).

Pogge is clearly sensitive to the fact that given the variety of different cultures and values that exist across the world, the body of human rights proposed as credible and likely to meet with an *overlapping consensus* (a phrase he borrows from Rawls) will have its limits. However, unlike Rawls, he has not been accused of pandering to indefensible attitudes and customs, and probably the biggest contrast between the two is the extent to which Pogge asserts the central importance of democratic and electoral freedoms. Whereas Rawls suggests that individuals can still be part of the deliberative process of politics through group representation, Pogge is adamant that the individual be respected further, with opportunities for all to vote and take office. In this regard he is the more 'aggressive' cosmopolitan in as much as he believes democratic orders need to be promoted in order to secure the necessary rights and opportunities for people to live worthwhile lives.

It is interesting that Pogge's views have been subject to far less criticism than Rawls' greater tolerance of non-liberal orders. As the discussion of Beitz' work suggests, it was not so long ago that the key principles of the international order were autonomy and non-intervention – yet in the mainstream debates on global justice today it is accepted as the default position that principles and policies aimed at addressing poverty will entail democratization. It is not so much that this attitude is surprising, given that historical and empirical evidence suggest the benefit of democracy for addressing poverty; rather it is the sometimes uncritical manner in which these ideas are asserted that is potentially problematic. For even if we are convinced that democracy works (and presumably Rawls recognizes this – in invoking much of Sen's work on democracy as a justification for his own call to address the political culture) it is entirely another matter whether we are justified or wise in promoting it or 'forcing it' upon other states. There may be cause for questioning in this instance whether Rawls, with his more tolerant perspective, is more attuned to the practice and reality of international politics than cosmopolitans such as Pogge.

Part of the reason that the difficulties with the practicalities and morality of promoting democracy are put to one side is Pogge's conviction that no such promotion would be required were we to establish a more just global order. It is at this point that we begin to engage with the more empirical elements that are central to his arguments. He is well known for arguing that the global rich – largely from Western democracies – sustain a global structure that systematically works to undermine the lives of the global poor.

Pogge (2008: 297, n251) has some sympathy for the kinds of arguments put forward by Marxist thinkers such as Immanuel Wallerstein, who argue that the lack of democracy in many parts of the world is a direct result of the foreign policy and global order maintained by rich western democracies. Capitalism curtails global justice, to put it bluntly. Pogge in particular points to the practice of international bribery by rich states and corporations alike (Pogge, 1998: 500), and the fact that this is accompanied by huge debts that have often been incurred by dictators and military regimes. In such circumstances it is incumbent upon rich countries to cancel such debts as populations suffer. These issues will be returned to in later chapters, but for now they are prime examples of the sorts of policies and attitudes that lie at the heart of Pogge's interpretation of the problem of injustice.

His general view of why the world is so divided today can be summed up in one quotation: 'The affluent have been using their power to shape the rules of the world economy according to their own interests and thereby have deprived the poorest populations of a fair share of global economic growth' (Pogge, 2008: 207). He recognizes that there may be other competing interpretations accounting for present inequalities, namely the exclusion from the use of natural resources, and the effects of a common and violent history (i.e., imperialism). Yet what is most important for Pogge is not which interpretation is the most persuasive, rather the fact that all three perspectives lead us to the same conclusions: that current inequalities are unjust and their 'coercive maintenance [i]s a violation of negative duty', and they can all agree 'on the same feasible reform of the status quo as a major step toward justice' (Pogge, 2008: 205).

Here it is worth pausing a moment to grasp the import of Pogge's reference to 'negative' duties. These kinds of duty are regarded as ones where, in contrast to 'positive' duties, they enjoin us to refrain from committing particular acts, as opposed to actively taking up particular, additional tasks. Specifically, Pogge makes the claim that the 'global rich' are actively harming the global poor through imposing and perpetuating a global order that results in them being denied the basic needs required to fulfil their entitlements. As such, what is required from the global rich is not a positive duty to make a substantive contribution to raising the living standards of the poor, rather they must refrain from supporting and perpetuating this deleterious global order. In Pogge's eyes, the most affluent 7 per cent of the population's planet foreseeably reproduce the order that has been shaped over the last 35 years, and more – and most importantly the resulting poverty could be mitigated by refraining from this collusion and designing a new system. Significant in this respect for Pogge's general approach to the problem of global poverty is the fact that he is making the argument for reform and change on the basis of negative duties, which are regarded as less arduous than positive duties. This is representative of his attitude that proposals must be modest in order to gain and sustain support.

In addition to addressing the structural inequalities in the global economy built up through various trade agreements, reforming our foreign policy, our arms trade and the behaviour of our economic representatives, Pogge also recommends other measures in order to level the playing field and address the biases towards the global rich. One of his arguments relates to the copyrights imposed by Western countries on pharmaceutical products – drugs and medicines – while another is a *Global Resources Dividend (GRD)* that would redistribute wealth accumulated by those extracting and benefiting most from the world's natural resources.

This latter policy provides a more focused and realistic version of the kind of distributive principles advocated by Barry, Beitz and Pogge in earlier works. Pogge acknowledges the potential problems associated with development aid (2008: 213–14), yet he is adamant that such a redistribution of wealth could have hugely positive results were it embraced by the most affluent. He cites two reasons to hope that such a policy might be regarded as a realistic proposition. In one of the few passages where he gives some attention to the realist tendencies of international relations, he suggests that ultimately it will be prudential for the more developed states to begin to share more wealth and ensure greater prosperity in order to promote more democratic, stable and affluent states. Such a suggestion is also implied in Rawls' presentation of the duty of assistance, where he notes that in the first place it might be more readily accepted for more self-regarding reasons, rather than through any feelings of affinity.

However, Pogge also sees grounds for optimism in the fact that he presents what he takes to be a compelling moral argument. He says that moral convictions *can* shape international politics, citing the abolitionist movement, and he suggests a 'similar moral mobilization may be possible also for the sake of eradicating world poverty – provided the citizens of the more powerful states can be convinced of a moral conclusion that really can be soundly supported and a path can be shown that makes only modest demands on each of us' (2008: 217).

KOK-CHOR TAN

It would in some sense be remiss to provide an introduction to the global justice debate, and cosmopolitan thought in particular, without reference to one of those who has contributed significantly throughout the various stages. Kok-Chor Tan has been a prominent figure, ever since some of his initial responses to Rawls' LP, which we can identify as one of at least three significant contributions.

Tan, in a similar vein to other cosmopolitan thinkers, was critical of Rawls' international theory, as sketched out in the original 1993 paper and the later book, because of the limited set of rights and resources it recommends for individuals. However, it can be suggested that Tan's critique in Toleration, Diversity and Global Justice (2000) was a more sympathetic attempt to trace the consistencies in Rawls' position and to demonstrate how the 'political' liberalism Rawls developed in the 1980s and 1990s inevitably led to the ideas he presented. Rather than claiming Rawls had turned his back on his radical egalitarianism, Tan made sense of his international theory as part of the development of his oeuvre – reflecting the increasing emphasis in Rawls' work on toleration as the touchstone for liberalism, and the attendant requirement to limit the reach of freedom and autonomy in the global context. The book remains a must read for anyone seeking to get to grips with global justice philosophy. In setting out his arguments Tan elucidated his own 'comprehensive liberalism' that emphasizes individual autonomy over the competing liberal value of toleration, grounding his argument in the claim that individuality and cultural diversity are mutually affirming. This ultimately constituted a 'strong' cosmopolitan position arguing for extensive rights and resources to buttress individual autonomy, regardless of place or context.

In his second major contribution, Justice without Borders (2004), Tan set out to demonstrate how such a strong cosmopolitanism and its supposed impartial, universal character can be rendered consistent with communitarian demands. This can be regarded as a more difficult challenge because such a cosmopolitanism sets out the ideal of

(Continued)

(Continued)

global society where substantive equality exists between individuals – reminiscent of the types of Rawlsian argument originally put forward by Beitz and Pogge. Tan thus rejects a 'sufficientist' approach that many subsequent theories have proposed, seeking only a minimum set of rights and resources, which might equally be more easily squared with the entrenched societal structures of certain nation-states. He argues that nationalist and patriotic commitments can be consistent with obligations of global justice, insofar as they are limited by core cosmopolitan principles. One might understand Tan as attempting a similar project to Miller in attempting to bridge the gap between cosmopolitan and communitarian approaches, but from the opposite direction – and where Miller might argue that certain cosmopolitan arguments may have to be yielded where tensions emerge, so Tan is more likely to circumscribe communitarian commitments.

His most recent foray into the debate (Tan 2012) represents somewhat of a new departure and could quite easily be considered in the next chapter, where alternative philosophical approaches are considered. This is because Tan elucidates and strengthens the particular impulse driving his vision for global justice, namely luck egalitarianism. This is a philosophical position informed by some of the arguments Rawls' deploys for his difference principle and which have been discussed by philosophers such as Jerry Cohen (2001), namely that societal institutions should mitigate against the worst effects of brute bad luck (the flipside being that we can also hold individuals responsible for bad 'option' luck, brought about by bad choices). Tan argues that such an intuition can be expanded so that global institutions operate to mitigate those elements of bad luck that do not occur because of bad choices. An obvious example of this is the fact that an individual can do nothing about being born into a poor society. It should be noted that Tan's perspective remains hugely aspirational, even utopian, in seeking to equalize the vagaries of bad luck on a global scale. This is illustrated by the fact that such 'egalitarian justice' is limited to those above a threshold of basic needs; in the case of those beneath this line we are enjoined to offer them humanitarian assistance regardless of their choices. Only once the needs of all these individuals are met will the demands of luck egalitarianism be truly global in scope.

DIALOGICAL COSMOPOLITANISM

Up to this point we have explicitly positioned our discussion within the mainstream Anglo-American tradition of philosophizing, associated primarily with the Rawlsian tradition. We hope we have explained why this is a legitimate approach. It may be worth noting that these cultural divisions can be somewhat misleading; Pogge is a German philosopher after all, and as we turn towards another tradition that began in his homeland, we begin with the Scottish thinker, Andrew Linklater. Linklater is a notable figure in the tradition of another approach to cosmopolitanism, although it has not figured so directly in discussions of 'global justice'. This approach, known as dialogical cosmopolitanism, begins with some very different assumptions. It puts to one side the types of questions that are key to the Anglo-American tradition, involving the just distribution of resources and rights. Rather than focusing on the application of ideas about 'social justice' to the global realm, 'dialogical' cosmopolitans seek instead to emphasize the importance of equality with regard to political dialogue. Rather than the distribution of goods taking centre stage, it is broadly speaking the creation of equitable structures for dialogical exchange that receives their attention, setting out the grounds on which principles and policies can be justified convincingly.

This type of approach is broadly associated with the one contemporary philosopher who stands shoulder to shoulder with Rawls in terms of the breadth of his achievement and influence, namely the German philosopher Jürgen Habermas (1989, 1992, 1997). He himself is associated with the famous 'Frankfurt School' which came to prominence in the 1920s through figures such as Theodor Adorno, Max Horkheimer and Herbert Marcuse. In very broad terms, these thinkers had in common the fact that they advanced new and challenging interpretations of Marxist traditions of thought. A key element here is the assumption that our material environment conditions our categories of thought. A central theme of the Frankfurt School was thus the possibility of extracting ourselves from the deleterious effects of capitalist modes of thinking, and providing the grounds for a *critical* social science that can allow us to evaluate and influence our way of being. Providing an account of how we are thoroughly conditioned by our material reality, yet are able to emancipate ourselves to reason and think in an unencumbered way is no mean challenge. Much of the most famous work in this tradition focuses on what went wrong for the pursuit of justice and emancipation in the mid-twentieth century, particularly the experiences of fascism, the Holocaust and the horrors of World War II. *Dialectic of Enlightenment*, for example, begins by observing that 'Enlightenment, understood in the widest sense as the advance of thought, has always aimed at liberating human beings from fear and installing them as masters. Yet the wholly enlightened earth is radiant with triumphant calamity' (Adorno and Horkheimer, 1944: 1). In very general terms it can be suggested that whereas traditional Marxist thought held to a deep conviction about the possibilities of emancipation, the first generation of the Frankfurt school became far less hopeful about our capacity to extract ourselves from the destructive influences of modernity – even coming to believe that human reason itself is destructive or oppressive.

Habermas is often presented as the antidote to his more pessimistic predecessors; the philosopher who wished to rescue the project of the enlightenment and demonstrate that emancipation may be, in some form, possible. Although his work has ranged across a variety of subjects it is the 'dialogical' or 'discursive' approach to issues of political and social theory which is most strongly associated with him. Habermas is associated with the view that we are able to bring about progress in society that does not necessitate harms to certain groups, and that this is achieved through ensuring, in broad terms, dialogical exchange between individuals on the basis of equality. To this end, one hypothetical construct developed by the early Habermas was the 'ideal speech situation'; it provides an ideal for a situation where an exchange of ideas can happen that does not foreclose the contribution of some, and ensures that power relations do not influence the course of the debate. Through this intersubjective process we can arrive at ideas and ideals that incorporate the appropriate needs and desire of the body politic. We can hold out the hope that we may be able to exercise our reason in a critical manner, which can to some degree transcend the conditioning influence of our social reality.

It is this tradition of thought that Linklater believes can be transposed to international society in order to articulate the idea of cosmopolitanism. It should be emphasized, of course, that while he sets out his ideas beginning from this very different theoretical perspective, the core of his ideas is identical to that of the so-called 'distributive' cosmopolitans such as Beitz and Pogge. From the perspective of both traditions we have moral duties to each other because of our common humanity, and these take precedent over the demands of the nation-state.

Andrew Dobson (2003, 2006) identifies this very useful distinction between dialogical and distributive approaches in his critique of cosmopolitanism. For Dobson (2006: 168), one of the elements of dialogical cosmopolitanism that gives it its special character, and an advantage over distributive cosmopolitanism, is the sense in which it emphasizes the need to ensure the inclusion of marginalized voices. In particular, this offers a more promising response to critics inspired by communitarian or postmodern perspectives that place such a great emphasis on the way in which cosmopolitanism falls short of its universalist aspirations. We will examine such criticisms later, but these thinkers share a tendency to view the cosmopolitan project as an attempt to expand particular western values globally, rather than a genuine attempt to articulate a truly 'universal' moral and political vision.

Linklater is sensitive to the way in which marginalized voices can be excluded, and the Habermasian foundation to his thinking allows him to articulate a moral ideal that pays particular attention to this problem. We are encouraged to engage with the 'other', to respect their status through reflecting on our shared humanity, and to encounter them in a moral way that puts to one side relations of power and focuses instead on coming to an intersubjective understanding of our common needs. A key difference that emerges here between a Habermasian approach and a more Rawlsian attitude is the sense in which the former is far more open-ended in nature. That is to say, the Rawlsian approach tends towards identifying hard and fast principles in light of our common humanity and our nature as human beings, and on that basis advocates quite specific outcomes, measures and policies. Linklater, however, is keen to advocate for a cosmopolitanism 'with no fixed and final vision of the future' (1998: 48–9). No doubt he would agree with many of the types of measures Pogge proposes, but given that the focus lies on the *process* of conceiving principles, rather than the principles themselves, such an approach will be more preoccupied with focusing on the nature of global institutions and the opportunities they provide for open dialogical exchange, unencumbered by inequalities of power and status.

These tendencies in Linklater's work are emulated and developed by thinkers who have engaged more directly with debates in the 'distributive' tradition, and who approach the subject from a position more embedded within Habermas's philosophy. Linklater himself begins from a more international, sociological perspective. He is in part interested in the way in which international society is increasingly developing along cosmopolitan lines that can be elucidated by a Habermasian perspective, which seems to both capture how there are greater levels of intersubjective agreement and also provides a normative framework for justifying its further development.

A figure such as Rainer Forst – a student of Habermas – is a political philosopher (referred to by some as belonging to the 'third generation' of Frankfurt school scholars, or even the fourth) who in his earlier work followed in his supervisor's footsteps, and engaged increasingly with Anglo-American thinkers with respect to issues of justice. He criticises its predominantly distributive paradigm for placing an excessive emphasis upon the question of the distribution of *goods*. It is not this, in his view, that represents 'the first question of justice' (2005: 33), rather it is the distribution of *power*. This is the most basic and important of all resources or goods that we can have, and in this sense it is not what we have, but rather the 'way we are treated' (2007: 260) that is the ultimate measure of justice.

This implies a rather different way of interpreting our role in the political order: instead of being recipients of goods we are agents who demand a justification of that order. This is a particularly Habermasian theme that connects us to the emancipatory thrust of the original Frankfurt school. We must possess power: to deploy it in order to question the system that we are part of, insist upon legitimate justificatory reasons for that system, and challenge those that dominate and distort communication in our society. Before we articulate and try to realize our ideal principles, we need to ensure a public sphere where political debate can disclose current injustices.

Forst's discursive theory of justice is interesting not only in its Habermasian roots, but also because of the different scope that it posits in terms of the subjects of justice. That is to say, his theory tends towards a position that is neither communitarian nor cosmopolitan in its outlook. It is neither statist nor globalist. That is to say, where the former would tend to see questions of justice defined largely by the state, and the latter places far more emphasis on the global structure, Forst's perspective hones in on 'sites of justice' (2012: 196) where the justification of social and political structures actually occurs. According to the emphasis on power, in order to secure just arrangements we must ensure that wherever there are 'sites' where the order is justified, people must have the opportunity and leverage to criticize and even veto those justifications, and partake in the process of recreating them in more acceptable ways.

In some ways this approach is reflected in the critical aspects of Pogge's theory: he, for example, attempts to provide an account of the status quo and a causal explanation of how global institutions came to be, which reveal to us unsatisfactory justifications which we are empowered to challenge. However, Forst emphasizes the manner in which justice in the contemporary world has a distinctly *transnational* aspect that cannot be captured by statist or globalist accounts. Relations of power cut across state boundaries but are not often truly global: one can think about multinationals that operate across a discrete number of territories and dominate particular local elites. In fact, for many individuals, they are stuck within a web of multiple forms of domination exercised through the structures produced by local, national, regional and global actors.

One proponent of a discourse theory of global justice is Julian Culp, who provides a helpful definition of the central tenet of such an approach: 'that the formulation of principles of distributive justice must primarily concentrate on the socio-political conditions that would secure a fundamentally just structure of justification, within which further distributive principles of justice would then be determined by way of collective deliberation' (2014: 15). This neatly summarizes how the emphasis is placed on ensuring structures that eliminate dominant powers, while the principles that follow are indeterminate.

Culp, in contrast to Forst, regards the transnational approach as problematic in one sense, in that it does not commit to the idea that the global level constitutes an appropriate site of justice. In other words, although it is more promising and flexible in capturing the way in which there are multiple structures that impact on our lives – which do not cohere with national boundaries or are not truly global in scope – it is problematic in failing to acknowledge the existence of a basic global structure within which these other sites of justice exist. A proper recognition of this global structure, as itself a site of justice, will entail a number of policies in order to ensure that it can be deemed just and free from power asymmetries.

This produces an interesting effect if we compare such a theory to the other cosmopolitan approaches we have discussed above. In practical terms we are talking in terms of instigating the kind of distributive policies advocated by Pogge and his GDR – *but not because this is a principle of justice necessitated by a prior account of individual rights and entitlements*. Rather, these policies are seen as *instrumental* in creating the socio-political conditions at the global level that ensures the representatives of all states are able to contribute to the deliberation and creation of international laws and regulations.

Culp also develops his 'discourse-theoretic Internationalism' in a more practical direction, by engaging in the possibilities it represents with regard to the more specific questions around development policy. In particular, he quite rightly draws attention to some of the key issues in the field, in particular problematic assumptions about development equating to economic growth, its tendency to encourage paternalism, and the danger that it represents Eurocentrism in the values it propounds. These issues will be considered in more depth in later chapters. Culp's general argument is that while other approaches to development, such as the capabilities approach of

Amartya Sen and Martha Nussbaum, challenge the central importance of growth, they are more likely to fall foul of the other accusations because they posit specific outcomes.

A discourse focused approach is, as we have emphasized, more open ended, and as such maps on neatly to one of the ideals of development: the emancipation and recognition of individuals as agents able to fulfil their own potential. Culp puts forward a persuasive claim: that working to ensure in the first instance that they are in an adequate position to partake in the discursive process of defining development goals and normative aims is a more promising approach than the outcome orientated tendencies of the distributive tradition. These claims certainly demand a response on behalf of the distributive tradition, and whether it is destined to cleave to an approach that can be accused of ethnocentrism and paternalism in specifying particular outcomes – rather than coming to a consensus on the basis of reciprocal dialogue.

SEN, NUSSBAUM AND CAPABILITIES

The final cosmopolitan 'project' to consider in this chapter is the capabilities approach, associated most prominently with Amartya Sen and Martha Nussbaum. Rather than seeking to identify particular principles and policies aimed at addressing global poverty, or arguing for the most convincing arrangements for debating appropriate principles, they are specifically concerned with analysing the nature of poverty, and what aspects of the individual's condition must be addressed to alleviate such poverty. Initially, in the work of Sen, this took the form of an extension of the Rawlsian approach, and in this sense we return to the Anglo-American tradition at the beginning of this final section.

Sen was concerned with the question of 'Equality of What?' and the 'measure' of justice being used by Rawls in his theory. This is the concept of *primary goods* that is constituted by the rights, opportunities and resources guaranteed by the two principles of justice. Sen's basic argument is that while these goods are imperative, in the final analysis they do not represent the correct measure of equality (or poverty, for that matter). This is because the goods in themselves do not guarantee that persons can pursue their chosen way of life. Sen makes the crucial point that we all have different abilities and we live in very different contexts, and what matters in the end is whether we can convert our goods into actual capabilities. For a very basic example, we can think about how within a nation-state such as the UK the same level of financial resources for someone living in London as compared to elsewhere leaves them with a comparative capability deficit.

Sen therefore put forward his capability approach as an alternative 'measure of justice' that claims it is actual freedoms – the ability to do or become something – which represents the appropriate measure. There followed some debate with Rawls (1999: 13; 2001: 169–73), who claimed that implicit in his theory is the concept of capabilities, because the two principles of justice guarantee, as a baseline, a substantive level of freedom that ensures the worst off is guaranteed fair equality of opportunity. In his view this 'social minimum' clearly designates a minimum capability set otherwise the worst off would not be able to compete on broadly equal terms.

This debate aside, Sen's critique has led to a substantial interest in capabilities as a concept and he himself developed it with regard to his work on development (Sen, 1999). Key to Sen's perspective is the claim that we should measure development not in terms of economic growth or other indicators, rather the capabilities – actual freedoms – individuals accrue through these processes. Famously, development for Sen (1999: 3) is 'a process of expanding the real freedoms that people enjoy'.

It might be said that this approach comes into its own in the context of situations of poverty, as they provide a more focused analysis of the exact freedoms that people are denied, and a more accurate measure of the capabilities we should be aiming to enable. Rawls' perspective, in contrast, is aimed at outlining the general principles of justice for a liberal democratic society where it is assumed the level of relative scarcity of goods is such that no one should be in a position of such poverty. The 'social minimum' provides a helpful indication of where the baseline should sit, but the focus on distributing goods for 'fully cooperating members of society over a complete life' (Rawls, [1993] 2005: 21) means he does not develop the conceptual tools for looking in detail at how those below the minimum might be assisted.

This tendency of Rawls to bracket his theory of justice and delineate it in such a way as to put other claims to one side represents a starting point for Nussbaum in *Frontiers of Justice* (2006). She views Rawls' theoretical approach as the social contract approach 'in its best form', but her general project is to argue that it cannot address the 'unsolved problems of justice' in an adequate form (2006: 3). These unsolved problems of justice include global poverty, disability and the status of the non-human; all issues that Rawls believes are beyond the scope of his concept of justice as fairness (or at least, that would require a thorough reworking of the idea). While Rawls made no attempt to rework his ideas with regard to disability and the status of the non-human, his attempts to extend justice as fairness to 'international law and relations between political societies', or issues of global poverty, are regarded by Nussbaum as unsatisfactory (2006: 21).

In particular, she argues that the Rawlsian approach is restricted by the fact it rests on the assumption that the parties in the social contract have similar capabilities and co-operate for mutual advantage. This in effect excludes many from the initial contract, and we are given no account of how they might then be regarded as equal partners who are 'owed justice rather than charity' (Nussbaum, 2006: 118). Her critique of Rawls' approach to burdened societies reflects this general point, because in her view they are treated in an analogous fashion to individuals with disabilities. They cannot be conceived as contributing to mutual advantage and they are excluded from the original position.

Nussbaum, as you may have anticipated, prefers the cosmopolitan route that disregards national boundaries. She agrees with Barry, Beitz and Pogge's argument that 'national origin is rather like class background, parental, wealth, race and sex: namely a contingent fact about a person that should not be permitted to deform a person's life' (2006: 264). However, she interprets Beitz and Pogge as being committed to the contractarian approach, which yields the same problem with regard to individuals who are not net 'contributors'. This is a questionable interpretation, based on the account given here, which has suggested that both appeal to the more fundamental ideal that our fellow humans entail duties on our behalf because of their basic humanity. Pogge sets out this basic intuition on the grounds of what this basic humanity demands, namely the notion of 'human flourishing' which is constituted for him in terms of our experience, success, character and achievement (2008: 36). Human rights represent the currency through which we can demand the institutional conditions to facilitate the ability to flourish.

In this regard, the originality of Nussbaum's approach lies not so much in her rejection of the contractarian approach, nor in her notion that it is 'human dignity' (2006: 274) that provides the moral foundation and motivation for organizing global institutions in a just fashion. It is rather the influences that inform her approach and make it arguably philosophically richer than other cosmopolitans, and the deployment of 'capabilities' as a helpful and suitable measure of this idea of human dignity. One notable element about capabilities as a concept is that it constitutes a subtle shift in emphasis with regard to rights and justice, because of the focus on actual freedoms. As Nussbaum notes this goes against the grain of the American tradition in particular, which traditionally cleaves to a concept of 'negative liberty'. This perspective tends to foreground the importance of ensuring a sphere of liberty for the individual, unfettered by state intervention in particular. A capability perspective regards this preference as misleading, because ultimately such a sphere of action is premised on the notion that individuals will have basic capabilities to practice in the first place. The freedom to starve or freeze, without the capabilities or social support to flourish, is no freedom at all for Nussbaum. In this respect we see the influence of Karl Marx on Nussbaum's thinking, especially the focus he places on 'opportunities for activity, not simply quantities of resources', (Nussbaum, 2006: 75), the emphasis on 'truly human functioning' in achieving a dignified life, and our need for 'a totality of human life-activities'.

The other significant influence on Nussbaum is the Greek philosopher Aristotle, in particular with regard to the themes of animality and the social nature of human beings that come to the fore in her conception of capabilities. Aristotle is famous for his contention that we are by nature 'political animals' and that we find 'deep fulfilment in political relations, including, centrally, relations characterized by the virtue of justice' (Nussbaum, 2006: 86). While the liberal contract tradition thus posits an apolitical conception of the good life, an Aristotelian outlook places social and political relations at its heart. Nussbaum also emphasizes the manner in which this conception of the human makes room for appreciating our physical constitution, our 'animal body . . . whose human dignity, rather than being opposed to this animal nature, inheres in it and in its temporal trajectory'. This emphasis has the effect of undermining the norm posited by the contract theory of fully functioning individuals as it recognizes that over a lifetime we will spend considerable periods being needy and requiring care. Entitlements to assistance, resting on our need for a dignified life, are thus applicable to everyone and exclude no one. Such a conception that 'stresses the animal and material underpinnings of human freedom . . . also recognizes a wider range of types of beings who can be free' (2006: 88). There are thus implications in terms of the scope of justice that Nussbaum elaborates in her work on nonhuman animals, and variations on this theme will be returned to in Chapter 6.

This conception of the person is reflected in the basic list of human capabilities that Nussbaum sets out as constitutive of a minimally dignified life:

1 Life, in the sense of not dying prematurely or not being worth living;
2 Bodily health, including nourishment and shelter;
3 Bodily integrity, including security from sexual assault and also opportunities for sexual satisfaction;
4 Senses, imagination and thought, entailing extensive education and freedom of expression;
5 Emotions, including to love, grieve and avoiding fear and anxiety blighting our development;
6 Practical reason, entailing the ability to form a conception of the good and reflecting on one's life plan;
7 Affiliation, including the ability to live with others and show concern for them and to have the 'social bases for self-respect and nonhumiliation';

8   Other species, living with concern for the world of nature;
9   Play, enjoying recreation;
10 Control over one's environment, including an ability to partici-
    pate politically and hold property.

These capabilities are not deemed to be in competition with the
notion of human rights, rather for Nussbaum they provide a moral
basis for those rights, articulating in particular the needs we have
that can make demands for rights fulfilment legitimate and politically
powerful. In this sense Nussbaum's approach is similar to Pogge's in as
much as they both articulate conceptions of the human good, which
lay the basis for our entitlements that can be articulated as rights –
which in turn are used as claims against the institutions that influence
our lives. In fact, with another ten basic principles that Nussbaum
outlines, in this instance for regulating the world order, she emulates
many of the ideas put forward by Pogge, thereby reflecting a similarly
'systemic' view of the causes of global poverty. For example, she cites
redistribution of wealth, regulations for multinationals, a fair global
economic order, an institutional focus on the disadvantaged, and
promoting education (2006: 315–24).

One notable addition is the injunction that the family, while pre-
cious, is not to be considered 'private'. It is here we see the other
significant influence impacting on Nussbaum's perspective, namely
feminism. She emphasizes how millions of girls die of neglect because
families do not want another female to feed and because the state
does not do enough to protect them. The fact that such gendered
differences in care exist reflects in part the tradition of 'the home as an
inviolable domain of personal prerogative' (2006: 322). Nussbaum is
recognized for her earlier work on development and women (2001),
and her feminism finds expression elsewhere in her later work with
references to the need to emphasize the importance of care work
(2006: 214) and the effectiveness of the capability approach in drawing attention to actual inequalities faced by women, especially in
the family (2006: 290). Yet despite her commitment to Marxist,
Aristotelian and feminist modes of thinking, and her focus on the
individual experience of poverty, Nussbaum also remains a staunchly
liberal cosmopolitan whose work sits comfortably next to the distributive and dialogical traditions outlined above.

CONCLUSION

Recognizing the various influences from beyond the liberal main-stream in Nussbaum's work – and her standing as a liminal figure on the threshold of alternative thought – seems to be an appropriate juncture at which we can draw this discussion of liberal cosmopolitan to a close. In the next chapter, we will engage directly with other cosmopolitan perspectives that have recently made explicit contributions to the debate around global justice, and have sought to do so using concepts and approaches that challenge the liberal perspective. In Nussbaum's view, such challenges are to be welcomed in order to refine the liberal project. We may assume that the perspectives we have discussed here, including Beitz and Pogge's moral, distributive cosmopolitanism, and the dialogical approaches of Linklater, Forst and Culp, might all be subject to critique and improvement, but that they share a basic moral force in placing the individual at the centre of our vision for world politics. Nussbaum states:

> If . . . we hold that the most important insights of liberalism concern the equal worth of persons and their liberty, we should conclude that these criticisms do not disable liberalism; instead, they ask us to reject some common liberal strategies in the name of the deepest and most central liberal goals. They challenge us to produce a new form of liberalism, which rejects feudalism and hierarchy in an even more thoroughgoing way than classical liberalism did, rejecting the hierarchy between men and women in the family and the hierarchy, in all of society, between 'normal' and atypically disabled citizens. Such an account sees the bases of social cooperation as complex and multiple, including love, respect for humanity, and the passion for justice, as well as the search for advantage. Its political conception of the person holds that human beings are vulnerable temporal creatures, capable and needy, disabled in many different ways and 'in need of a rich plurality of life-activities'. This sort of revised liberalism offers a great deal.
>
> (2006: 221)

No doubt some of the contributors to the debate would agree with Nussbaum's sentiments. Others do not. As we advance through the more recent and variegated philosophical literature, and then engage more with the actual campaigns run by global justice activists, we will discuss a growing scepticism about the validity of the liberal worldview. However, it remains true to say that mainstream debates within the global justice literature have been profoundly shaped by liberal thought on the meaning of terms like justice, freedom and equality. Indeed, it has often been liberal theorists who have most consistently sought to refute the realist assertion that global politics is necessarily a realm of power and domination where social progress is illusory.

3

BEYOND COSMOPOLITAN
AND COMMUNITARIAN?

IN THIS CHAPTER . . .

. . . we demonstrate the breadth of the philosophical debate on global justice. Inevitably, this chapter can only give an indicative sketch of the different philosophical perspectives that have sought to criticize or build on some of the approaches discussed so far. In this respect we aim to give a clear account of what such perspectives add to the debate, rather than attempt an overview for each. They have one thread in common, namely that they represent either a conscious attempt to expand, push beyond or question the framework of the debate whose emergence we have detailed in the previous chapters. These developments have occurred along the lines of engaging with new topics, but also engaging with new philosophical methods or concepts. The general direction of travel in the chapter is to move from those approaches that are regarded as the heirs to the main-stream debate to those perspectives that raise the more fundamental questions about the contours of the debate thus far and link more explicitly with the perspectives engaged with in the latter half of the book – many of which are far more critical of the liberal assumptions of global justice philosophizing.

The chapter begins with the claim that there has recently been a 'third wave' in mainstream global justice theorizing, and we consider the claim put forward by Gabriel Wollner with respect to the thinkers he uses to exemplify his argument. We then turn to two popular philosophical traditions – republicanism and recognition theory – that have challenged the liberal orthodoxy for some time in the field of political theory and have more recently been deployed with the same intent in the global justice debate. The next section then outlines a contribution to the debate from a philosophical figure, Iris Marion Young, who before her untimely death was always at the critical margins of the mainstream political theory and, in the context of the global justice debate, raises some difficult questions about the predominant individualistic outlook – while also making a significant link with the activist perspective.

The final two sections will then move on to engage with those developments that signal the more fundamental challenge to the global justice debate as it has been conducted thus far. In the first instance, we consider the arguments around climate justice that Simon Caney presents. Caney himself hails from the mainstream Anglo-American tradition and has little desire to disrupt conventions, but in shining a light on the centrality of environmental issues to the global justice debate, he implicitly suggests the need and potential for shifting the terrain of the debate in a significant manner. Similarly, Alison Jaggar's move to discuss global poverty from an explicitly feminist perspective throws up many questions about how the global justice debate has been conducted up to this point. These considerations set the scene for later chapters where we engage with more critical, activist-orientated perspectives that have not intervened in the debate in the same conciliatory manner, but may have a great deal to contribute in this ever-growing conversation. Indeed, there are many parallels between some of the perspectives presented here and the alternative ideas that inform some of the activism analysed in later chapters. In this chapter, however, we remain focussed on philosophers who have sought to engage with and influence the academic debate on global justice as described thus far – rather than seeking to undermine or reject it.

A THIRD WAVE?

There remains genuine scope within traditions of mainstream political theory to augment the global justice debate in interesting ways, which may shine a light on previously disregarded problems and possibilities. In this section we turn to an interesting claim that has recently been advanced by Gabriel Wollner: that we have borne witness to a 'third wave' in the global justice debate, which sets the standard for subsequent debates. He gives an account of three recent, substantial contributions to the literature from Aaron James (2012), Laura Valentini (2011) and Matthias Risse (2012) in order to substantiate this claim and argues that they represent a combined challenge to the previous cosmopolitan and non-cosmopolitan narratives in significant ways. It is an interesting claim in one particular respect: although he characterizes them as moving beyond the previous dichotomies, they are theorists embedded in the liberal mainstream; as such the next phase in global justice philosophy, by implication, will be constituted by a more thoroughgoing examination of prevailing traditions, rather than cleaving to other radical alternatives.

In the case of Valentini, it is her 'coercion framework' that entails particular attention (a concept that invokes the republican perspective attended to later in the chapter). She begins from the liberal premise that the role of justice is to assess coercion while advancing the case that we need to think about this concept in a broader manner. Interactional coercion relates to cases brought about by group or individual action, and systemic coercion relates to cases precipitated by systems of rule. A consequence of this perspective is that questions of justice become disaggregated over different levels, because coercion occurs in numerous ways, so that different duties will pertain between different actors. For example, states will have duties to each other to uphold effective sovereignty, while global economic institutions will have duties to individuals. This perspective is also burdensome for individuals, who bear duties of justice as actors within coercive systems such as the global economy, or members of states who practice interactional coercion.

It should be noted that Valentini is not unique in taking such a 'coercion' approach; Nicole Hassoun (2014) has recently combined such a perspective with a version of Beitz' original interdependence argument. Hassoun makes the general case that globalization has led to such intensive interdependence that individuals across the globe are subject to coercive institutions that they are incapable of legitimating because of their dire poverty. Intriguingly, the case for assisting these individuals is made, not on the basis of protecting their rights but on the basis that the legitimacy of global coercive institutions requires a basic level of capability among their subjects.

With regard to James, his chief aim is characterized by Wollner as an attempt to address scepticism relating to applying fairness to global trade. He aims to provide a sketch of 'structural equity'; however, the prior step is making the case that fairness should apply to the institution of trade in the first place. In this instance he argues that such trade constitutes a set of social practices that could be otherwise structured, and such practices raise questions about how they should be organized to everyone's satisfaction – thus fairness is held to apply. Secondly, because global trade entails that some lose at the domestic level – for example, those in the British steel industry affected by Chinese production – a justification is entailed that is sensitive to questions of fairness.

James' response to this challenge utilizes the 'complaint' model from the contractualist tradition. He seeks the principles that will provoke the least amount of complaints from participants. He argues (1) that appropriate principles would entail gains from international trade being distributed equitably, (2) that trade does not augment national income at the expense of individuals within the state (probably entailing some form of social insurance), and (3) that gains from international trade should be distributed equitably within the state.

In Risse's case it is the concepts of *pluralist internationalism* and *common ownership of the earth* that demand particular attention. His form of internationalism represents an important departure, it is claimed, from the 'globalist' and 'statist' scopes of justice (associated with those we have heretofore described as cosmopolitan and communitarian). This is because Risse argues in accordance with the latter that special duties pertain within the state, but *also* holds that strong duties of justice exist beyond the state in the same manner as cosmopolitans. It should be noted that the supposed originality of

Risse's perspective would appear to depend on an interpretation of a figure such as Miller as having rejected such a possibility. However, we have previously suggested that Miller himself is happy to endorse strong rather than humanitarian duties on a global level as well as at state level.

The *grounds of justice*, which are a set of conditions that necessarily generate norms of justice, are perceived by Risse to rest on a number of different grounds, such as state membership and common humanity, but it is the notion of *common ownership of the earth* that Wollner regards as particularly significant. According to this secularized version of a seventeenth-century principle, going back to figures such as Hugo Grotius, a question of justice arises out of the fact that everyone relies on the earth, its space and resources. This entails a basic distribution of these original features that should provide the opportunity for everyone to fulfil their basic needs. This return to a previously overlooked historical principle opens up new conceptual space in the discussion of migration and climate change, for example (Wollner, 2013: 26).

Wollner elaborates on how these three theorists enrich the global justice debate, and indeed he claims that in drawing out and elucidating issues such as 'scope' we are led to a more sophisticated understanding of theories of justice in general. As it is the business of philosophy to clarify and elucidate, these developments are of course to be welcomed. However, it is somewhat more difficult to endorse Wollner's other claims with respect to how they have moved the debate on in a decisive fashion.

It is not clear, for example, that previous theories have been insensitive to the differing levels of justice and that they have been unequivocally state-focused or global in their approach. Miller for one unequivocally identifies duties of justice at state and global levels. Neither is it clear that they have not taken the 'requirements of action guidingness seriously' – critical guidance for actors is implicit or explicit in many of the ideas we have examined. The promise of the third wave laying the basis for more general and extensive theories of global justice might seem to overlook such efforts by Beitz, Caney and Rawls. Pogge in particular might also baulk at the final suggestion: that these latest theories are innovative in taking empirically informed normative theory and closing the gap between philosophy and policy.

None of this is to question these authors' achievements, of course, and it goes without saying that they contribute to the enrichment of the academic debate. Wollner is also more convincing in his claim that developing accounts that adequately articulate the complexities and variety of questions of justice – be they global, transnational, national or even local – is a challenge that will not be easily overcome. Not only is this a question of identifying these different 'sites' of justice; there is also the issue of how the different duties that arise may conflict or be in tension for particular actors. How, for example, should a state balance duties to their own population with the claims of those outside? He is surely correct in claiming that these types of questions will preoccupy philosophers in the immediate future.

REPUBLICANISM, RECOGNITION AND GLOBAL JUSTICE

Having looked briefly at the suggestion that there are is an identifiable 'third wave' in mainstream global justice philosophy, we now pick up on contributions from other mainstream currents in contemporary political philosophy, which have recently been extended to the global justice debate. They are essentially liberal, in so far as they accord with the basic assumptions of the equality and inviolability of the individual, but they differ in terms of their historical roots and the way in which they set out these basic intuitions. The first example is that of Republican political thought, which focuses on the concept of freedom as non-domination.

Quentin Skinner, a historian of thought, is recognized as being most influential in reinvigorating republican thought. He has focused in particular on the way the central concept of freedom differs from the liberal notion of negative freedom – which has traditionally concentrated on the idea 'non-interference'. The Republican concept, however, suggests that it is the ability to avoid the *domination* of others that is fundamental.

Republicans argue that the liberal idea fails to capture the political ideal of freedom in its entirety; the classic example is the case of a slave with a good master who leaves him largely to his own devices. So the argument goes, we are committed by the liberal view to acknowledge that the slave enjoys a decent measure of freedom. This seems counterintuitive, because in our everyday understanding of freedom, we would not regard a slave as free, regardless of the life they enjoy. The republican view concentrates on the idea that political liberty should not be contingent, and that it is properly constituted through structural (legal, social, economic) relations that ensure domination is not possible. The slave is never really free when his master might at any time curtail his activities, or even treat him brutally.

This concept connects with another aspect of the republican tradition – going back to the Roman philosopher Cicero – that posits a more active notion of the citizen than the liberal tradition. Such a republican view regards every individual as a participant in the society's political life, and opting out is neither morally desirable or realistically conceivable. Phillip Pettit is the author most often associated with this contemporary strain of thought and he has recently suggested how a 'Republican Law of Peoples' might be imagined. He follows Rawls in some key respects, beginning with 'states as they are' as the basis of his philosophizing. This, he acknowledges, marks him off from other republican thinkers such as Lawrence Quill (2005), Steven Slaughter (2005) and James Bohman (2007), who have taken a more radical approach, looking at what transformative action in the international context will better serve individuals.

Domination in Pettit's terms is the presence of alien control, which can occur through an actor interfering, invigilating or intimidating another in such a way that reduces the others substantive options. Non-alien control, on the other hand, might occur through reasoned argument or permission on behalf of the actor. The particular evil of domination, in his view, is the way in which it undermines mutual respect. This evil relates not only to our actions as individuals, but also to those organizations such as representative states, where we seek to act together. Thus Pettit reformulates the republican doctrine: 'the free individual is protected against the domination of others by an undominating state *and undominated state*' (2010: 77).

In setting out his international vision Pettit notes certain standards to distinguish between effective and representative states on the one hand, and ineffective and non-representative states on the other (the burdened societies, outlaw states and benevolent absolutisms of Rawls' Society of Peoples). The former we can understand as undominating states, and they seek relations to ensure they are undominated in the international realm. He then sets out to sketch the ideal reciprocal relations between representative states – what he calls a 'regime of respect' (2010: 72).

Sources of domination in the international sphere include other states, powerful private bodies such as corporations, and public bodies such as the United Nations and International Monetary Fund. Pettit argues against any form of global state or empire as a means to address such sources, on account of their propensity to domination. While a network of international bodies underwritten by public law may be ineffective, he regards them as vital in providing the context in which states can relate to each other in a reasoned manner, providing the possibility of reasoned deliberation and forms of non-alien control.

The other path towards mitigating domination suggested by Pettit is an intriguing notion that weak states can band together in order to address inequalities of power, and challenge dominating states. This could even be seen as one rationale behind the European project of greater integration, for example. This analysis is extended in some respect to dealing with the domination of private non-state bodies, as he argues that where states unite as a collective, powerful private bodies will be less likely to isolate and dictate harmful, dominating policies against particular, weaker states (this speaks to contemporary attempts to crack down on tax havens, for example). This is also a crucial point at which Pettit argues the republican model is distinguished clearly from the Rawlsian approach, arguing that for mutual respect to exist states 'must be powerful enough to command respect from each other: to force one another to display respect' (2014: 86). This recognition of the nature of power politics and Pettit's claims that his approach is 'incentive compatible' (2010: 87) provides a genuine challenge to the claim that Rawls' approach represents an attractive via media between cosmopolitan and realist perspectives.

This strain in Pettit's philosophy comes to the fore in his brief treatment of ineffective, non-representative states. International action with regard to these regimes is likely to be motivated because of self-interest and the fact that the potential environmental, health and security problems they may constitute will be regarded as generating possible existential threats. Pettit's argument that such states 'may generate waves of illegal immigration into richer countries, threatening the political cultures of those regimes' (2014: 90) has particular resonance in Europe as we write this book in 2015–16. More optimistically, he points out that self-interest may emanate from another source, namely electoral pressure exerted by publics in representative regimes, who can create pressure for aid and humanitarian intervention. Pettit is ultimately silent, however, on the most difficult of all issues, which is the only credible long-term solution: establishing effective and representative states in their place. In one respect, this is where the real work of global justice theorizing might have to begin.

Developments in the political theory of *recognition* with respect to global justice are also at a formative stage. Nevertheless, there is much to suggest that this could be a fruitful marriage of interest, in particular with relation to what might be considered, if not the 'blind spots' in the current literature, certainly those areas that have been given less attention. Specifically, the suggestion is put forward that there has been a tendency to ignore aspects of global justice that do not focus on the issues of distribution and redistribution – and that similar attention needs to be given to issues of inequalities of status and political participation. In this regard there are close connections with the dialogical cosmopolitanism encountered in the previous chapter, as well as to many of the frustrations expressed by activists with the limits of global justice philosophy which we will consider in latter chapters.

Recognition theory has its roots in the German philosophical tradition, in particular those schooled in Hegel's thought. Their claims are most readily articulated through the work of Nancy Fraser, who along with Alex Honneth is one of the two key figures who has laid down the terms of the debate around recognition theory (Fraser and Honneth, 2003). In contrast to Honneth – who is also associated with the Frankfurt School – Fraser has begun to set out the relevance of recognition theory to the problems of world politics. For her, it is the notion of status, and more specifically the parity of participation, which is the most adequate measure of justice.

Within this conception of justice, recognition is seen to be in interplay with the issues of redistribution and representation, and all three must be addressed to ensure parity of participation for the individual. Representation is the political dimension that requires rules and boundaries to be drawn in such a way as to facilitate this parity. Redistribution, as with Rawlsian theories, relates to the need for a distribution of resources that secures a substantive equality. Recognition, finally, relates to ensuring that there is no inequality of status that provides an obstacle to the ideal.

There is much to be done to set out how such an approach can provide insights with regard to global justice, and arguably other theories are not framed quite as narrowly as is suggested by some of the advocates for recognition theory (e.g., Burns and Thompson, 2013: 10–11). Political issues feature heavily in Pogge's work, for example, while Caney (on the cosmopolitan side) and Rawls (on the communitarian side) are just two examples of fairly integrated accounts of the issues of global justice (however schematic). However, where Fraser's account might provide real traction is with regards to the principle of recognition and the equality of status it demands.

In this sense, recognition theory speaks both to the concerns of dialogical cosmopolitans and their focus on equitable political institutions that mitigate power relations and also to the concern from feminists and postcolonial theorists that certain groups have been structurally marginalized, overlooked and denied true recognition and equal status. A number of the more mainstream theories have, it seems fair to say, made less nuanced and sophisticated contributions with regard to the problem of status between states, peoples and various other groupings. In particular, giving sufficient attention to historical relations and developments can help us understand current problems – racism and sexism being some of the most immediately obvious. Doing so in a persuasive manner might seem to be facilitated by the theoretical scope that Fraser's status model of recognition implies.

For Fraser, the most important question in contemporary political thought is who has the right to be included in social and political life, and in this respect, basic recognition of an individual or a group's status is the fundamental issue. The widening and deepening of globalization has led to a more complex situation in terms of recognizing whose parity of participation has to be protected within these ever-changing political structures. Whereas traditionally it has been relatively uncontroversial to acknowledge that questions of political membership have to do with who is and who is not recognized by the state, the transnational and global nature of economic, political and social interaction has destabilized these assumptions.

Fraser (2008) resists an uncomplicated conversion to cosmopolitanism, however, as she sees deep problems with the idea that we can conceive of ourselves as fellow subjects of justice, on account of abstracted common characteristics that sideline our social relations. There are concerns also about the way ideal or utopian theorizing overlooks the realities of influential power relations. That said, she leaves open the desirable possibility of creating a global 'we' (despite the Hegelian tradition suggesting that such a 'we' requires the 'other'). Although Fraser has resisted the temptation to engage more directly with cosmopolitan and global justice theorizing, her rich work has many points of connection to the debates already covered in this book, as well as others to come in the subsequent chapters. Her focus on 'parity of participation' seen through the prism of recognition, resources and representation would seem to provide a potentially robust and thorough account of global justice.

Finally, in giving an account of why recognition theory has been slow to embrace issues of global justice, Burns and Thompson reflect on its Hegelian roots (2013: 14). As noted in our introduction, Hegel is often characterized as the forerunner of modern communitarianism, and the assumption that shared values hold across states but not beyond. This scepticism is exemplified by Fraser's resistance to the abstractions of cosmopolitanism. States constitute a 'lifeworld', and it is within this context that recognition of groups and their contribution to the whole makes sense. In this sense, part of the project for recognition theorists is to resist this characterization of Hegel and to draw out the ways in which he, and some subsequent Hegelians, attempt to negotiate a middle ground between the two extremes. This is a useful reminder that when we debate contemporary issues and ideas, we cannot dismiss or deny the influence of the history of philosophy – even if one is seeking an outright rejection of that past.

IRIS MARION YOUNG AND STRUCTURAL INJUSTICE

The notion of a third wave suggests a particular direction in which the tide will turn over the coming period. Republicanism and recognition theory are two perspectives well placed to influence future debate because of their recent importance in political philosophy more generally. Our engagement with activism in the next chapters will entail an encounter with more radical approaches, but here we turn to one figure who offers a particularly notable set of ideas that combines different influences in a unique manner – and links her ideas explicitly to the activist approach.

Iris Marion Young may therefore be described as a different kind of philosopher who represents another possible inspiration for future debate. There is no doubt that she was an original and multi-faceted thinker who was influenced by many different currents of thought. She died an untimely death at the age of 57 in 2006, but her biography attests to the variety of subjects and ideas that animated her work, including gender, identity and justice.

She is often identified with the rise in prominence of 'identity politics' as a critique of liberalism in the late capitalist era. Such a perspective eschews the liberal focus on the individual and explicitly extends the subject of justice to groups – and in particular oppressed groups. It seeks to elucidate the nature of that oppression, often focusing on the types of prejudices and values that lie behind it – with a view to challenging these norms and emancipating these groups. It is a key tenet of such approaches that conventional liberal philosophy cannot effectively address these issues of group identity that are so central to the inequalities that persist in our societies, and that in order to secure a more just world we need to move beyond its traditional categories of thought.

This broad perspective has many points of connection with feminist political philosophy, while one can recognize a clear link between these types of arguments and the importance that a philosopher like Fraser attributes to bringing in the politics of recognition to the global justice debate. However, with specific regard to this debate, we will focus on one particular intervention from Young, which is neither explicitly feminist or identitarian in approach, but elucidates another original contribution that provides an alternative account of the causes of global injustice – with some interesting implications. Indeed, feminist theorist Alison Jaggar refers to Young's social connection model (2014b: 36) in explaining the virtues of her own gendered approach to global justice, which avoids misattributing responsibility because of its more sophisticated recognition of the structural forces at work.

Young's account begins with the first of the two key questions outlined in the introduction, namely how we account for duties of global justice. Rather than being grounded in political relations that hold between states, or our status as human beings, she regards the connections that exist between people, as a result of social processes, as the basis for duties and obligations. These social processes are characterized as *structural* by Young, and social injustices, causing harm to individuals, arise as a direct result of these processes being at work. Her account of the social structure is rich and complex and exemplifies the way she brings different intellectual influences to bear on her ideas; we will characterize it here in basic terms as the outcome of past collective actions that creates rules, resources and positions within which actors currently act – and which can have collective results that are unintended. Her definition of structural injustice is as follows:

Structural injustice exists when social processes put large categories of persons under a systematic threat of domination or deprivation of the means to develop and exercise their capacities, at the same time as these processes enable others to dominate or have a wide range of opportunities for developing and exercising their capacities. Structural injustice is a kind of moral wrong distinct from the wrongful action of an individual agent or the wilfully repressive policies of a state. Structural injustice occurs as a consequence of many individuals and institutions acting in pursuit of their particular goals and interests, within given institutional rules and accepted norms. All the persons who participate by their actions in the ongoing schemes of cooperation that constitute these structures are responsible for them, in the sense that they are part of the process that causes them. They are not responsible, however, in the sense of having directed the process or intended its outcomes.

(Young, 2006: 114)

Such structural injustices almost inevitably occur through highly complex connections in their transnational or global instantiations; Young uses the example of sweatshops and the various individuals bound up in their continued existence to give a sense of this complexity. It is here that the interesting implications of Young's *social connection model* emerges, as she tries to give an account of how we can attribute duties, despite what appears to be an impossibly difficult situation whereby responsibility can be disaggregated to different individuals or groups. In fact, Young develops her model because she argues that current accounts of responsibility demand that we trace the connection between an injustice and a perpetrator, and operate according to a *liability* model. In her view such structural injustices preclude this possibility.

It might be appropriate in cases where, for example, a factory manager breaks laws that in turn cause harms. We might allow that Pogge's attribution of responsibility to the global rich stretches this liability model to its limits, by identifying a direct and clear causal connection. In the example of the sweatshop, however, we have a situation where the most powerful agents within the structure are removed from such direct relationships making blame, in the traditional sense of liability, harder, if not impossible to attribute. Yet surely it is inappropriate to suggest that they are *not* implicated in any meaningful way. Young articulates this intuition of how responsibility pertains in such a context:

> The social connection model of responsibility says that individuals bear responsibility for structural injustice because they contribute by their actions to the processes that produce unjust outcomes. Our responsibility derives from belonging together with others in a system of interdependent processes of cooperation and competition through which we seek benefits and aim to realize projects.
>
> (2006: 119)

This is a very different concept of responsibility to that of the liability model, as it has the effect of dispersing responsibility across an indefinite amount of actors, while it also acknowledges that the injustice comes about, not through direct volition, but because those actors are part of a complex historical structure.

RECTIFICATORY JUSTICE

Young's recognition of the complexities of oppressive structures turns our attention in one way towards the historical processes that led to them being established and perpetuated. It is not surprising, therefore, that her 'structural injustice' approach has been regarded as applicable to colonial history, notably by philosopher Catherine Lu. This is significant inasmuch as it signals a more recent willingness to address the issue of rectificatory justice more explicitly within mainstream debates (see Kumar and Tan (2006) for an earlier example). In this sense these efforts to expand the scope of the debate should not necessarily be seen as attempts to 'move on' or 'destabilize' some of its liberal assumptions in the same vein as other perspectives in this chapter. Rather we have witnessed a potentially disruptive set of issues being brought more clearly into view; issues that we will return to in later chapters as they have also been raised by many activists.

Lu is particularly interested in how Young's approach can inform our negotiation of historical cases of colonialism, and how we ascribe responsibilities in a situation that involved direct and indirect perpetrators both within and outside colonial territories. She focuses in particular on the very real issues of redress being sought by South Korea for survivors of Japan's 'military comfort system, which used women . . . to provide sexual services to Japanese soldiers during the Asia-Pacific War' (2011: 264). The advantage of Young's structural injustice approach is that its scope moves beyond Japanese political and military leaders, who can uncomplicatedly be assigned moral responsibility. It focuses also on the social structural process of international society that provided a permissive context, in addition to the structures within Korean society that led to 'specific patterns of harms and victims' (2010: 264). It also facilitates a more forward looking approach that buttresses attempts to address the practical issues of ensuring the victims are able to regain sufficient individual agency within their societies. The net result is an approach that assigns political, or remedial responsibility to a raft of actors in Japan, Korea and the international community – across generations if need be – in order to secure the just outcome.

Other thinkers who have attempted to think through the implications of rectificatory justice at an international or global level include Daniel Butt (2009) and Göran Collste (2015). In Butt's systematic

(Continued)

(Continued)

treatment entitled *Rectifying International Justice* he marshals historical, backward-looking arguments in order to question the resistance
to global redistribution more generally. Once we fully appreciate how
our present possessions and resources are premised on immoral acts
in the past, it becomes far harder to resist calls for such redistribution.
While thinkers such as Beitz, Miller and Pogge do discuss imperialism
and the legacy of colonialism it is striking in some respects that they do
not play a more central role in their discussions. Butt provides at least
three ways in which we might easily make the connection between
past wrongdoing and current injustice: namely where we live in states
that continue to benefit from the effects of historic injustice; where
individuals or groups possess property that is not rightfully theirs; and
where there is a collective responsibility in the political community
with respect to a failure to address some historic injustice or other.

Similarly, Collste makes the case for global rectificatory justice in
a wide ranging volume that seeks both to intervene directly in the
global justice debate, and bring considerations from post-colonial
studies to bear on our philosophical discussions of the issue.
Specifically, Collste argues that there should be a global rectificatory
principle that functions alongside any global distributive principle,
and proposes, for example, that the charter of Rawls' Law of Peoples
should include such a rectificatory principle. In terms of speaking
to the agenda of 'deparochializing' the debate, Collste's contribution
is perhaps most interesting in its attempt to bring ideas about the
colonization of minds and cultures into view. This is suggestive of the
possible points of connection between the liberal mainstream and
other critical perspectives.

There are many implications in Young's approach to responsibility that merit comment, but there are perhaps three key points to
draw out. The first of those is the subtle difference in attitude that it
elicits, which Young alludes to by describing it as forward-looking.
The liability model, which tends to underpin other approaches to
global justice, elicits a response that at worst becomes an exercise in
finger pointing and takes away from the most urgent matter, which
is to address the injustice. These structural injustices are ongoing,

and the social connection model exhorts a collective response from those involved in sustaining it. This is a second key aspect that tends to differentiate it from the liability model, namely a collective approach that entails what Young describes as a 'public communicative engagement' (2006: 123), which cuts across various different actors and encourages different individual and collective agents to coordinate their actions.

This ties in with a third notable aspect of the model because it provides a theoretical framework within which we can understand and appreciate the work of activists. In this particular context, she demonstrates how the social connection model fits with the aims and action of anti-sweatshop protesters, who can be characterized as forward-looking in their aims, and engaged with activities that seek to motivate and precipitate coordinated action between a number of actors. Such a claim by Young is of course significant, and suggests one way forward, in terms of the overarching narrative of this book, and the notion that philosophy and activism could and should attempt a more explicit engagement.

THE ENVIRONMENT IN THE GLOBAL JUSTICE DEBATE

Jaggar describes gendered disparities as 'the elephant in the room of global justice theory' (2014b: 23). Some might argue that the same can be said for another major issue, namely the environment and the protection of nature. In these final two sections we move from an engagement with alternative methods of philosophizing about global justice to thinkers who engage with topics that are potentially hugely disruptive in terms of the development of the debate.

Increasingly it has become apparent that we cannot decouple the fate of our natural world from wider issues of global justice, especially economic and social questions (Death, 2014). In the first instance, environmental harms are inequitably distributed: those suffering most from the effects of climate change and environmental degradation are most likely to be in the poorer regions of the world. Secondly, taking ecological concerns seriously leads us to question the assumption that economic growth is the appropriate answer to the problem of injustice. From a common sense perspective the two normative projects of global distributive justice and global environmental justice can be regarded as potentially contradictory.

Of course, neither philosophers nor politicians have been entirely unaware of the implications of environmental issues for debates on justice. From one perspective, the regular global environmental conferences that have been held in recent years could be interpreted as representing an attempt to realize greater global justice in practice (Death, 2010). Here we have representatives of all states convening in order to set out agreements that aspire to be viewed as fair and just, and that seek to protect future generations from the worst side effects of environmental harm. However, they are also in this respect an exemplar of the problems associated with the ideal, because all too often these processes are riven with division and undermined by the self-interest of states, where the less affluent invariably have more to lose, and the richer states abuse their power.

In terms of philosophical discussions, the trio of Rawls, Beitz and Pogge all make provisions for environmental issues within their theories. Built in to Rawls' original position is the possibility of accounting for future generations, as those choosing the appropriate principles are understood as being denied knowledge of the period in which they live. In this regard, it is rational for them to identify some measures in order to ensure the sustainable use of resources. If they do not, they run the risk of being part of society that has been devastated by the over consumption of resources and an attendant environmental disaster. The *duty of just savings* reflects this concern, which is a caveat of the difference principle, ensuring that no redistribution of resources can occur that jeopardizes the chances of the next generation enjoying the same or similar standard of living. This same principle is invoked by Rawls in his discussion of international justice, where he argues that this, or a similar principle, will be part of the political conception of justice for any well-ordered society within the Society of Peoples. The implication is that overconsumers undermine their right to be considered a full member of this Society.

In elucidating his application of Rawls' two principles to the global realm, Beitz too acknowledges environmental concerns, and his resource redistribution principle would have to 'set some standard of conservation' against the possibility of parties to the original position finding themselves in a world with depleted resources (Beitz,

1999: 142). Pogge, when elucidating the conditions for his Global Resources Dividend, is also at pains to argue that it can be directed in such a way as to discourage the use of resources that are 'especially important for conservation and environmental protection' (2008: 212). Indeed, in his view it is the type of policy that can address head on the problem of ensuring collective action, which is so often associated with attempts to address environmental issues. It can enforce the sort of restrictions on consumption that nation states would never voluntarily pursue because the environmental costs are relatively small for them, in the short term at least. This is an argument he has continued to develop, identifying more directly the connection between environmental degradation and global poverty (Pogge, 2011), in particular the sense in which the former contributes to the undermining of human rights in less affluent parts of the globe.

However, even the most ardent advocates will find it difficult to claim that the attention given by these philosophers to environmental issues reflects the scale and immediacy of the problem we face today. We might characterize them as taking the view that environmental concerns are a limiting factor, or one among a number of concerns for the more important business of working out a fair distribution of resources and the most appropriate ways of bringing about a more equitable world. In contrast, Simon Caney is one of the most well-known cosmopolitan thinkers who has set out the challenges of climate justice as a sub-field of global justice. That is to say, rather than regarding it as a corollary of other questions, the approach adopted by Caney is that we can in some respect bracket the problem of climate change, in particular, and think through how this problem is dealt with in a just fashion on a global scale. This seems fairly uncontroversial, because for one thing, it reflects the way in which it is dealt with as a political issue.

He is not, of course, the only philosopher to have addressed these issues (see for example Dale Jamieson (2010, 2014) and Stephen Gardiner's influential work (2012)), and some generic views of how the issue might be dealt with have emerged in recent years (see also Dobson, 2003, 2007). Three key principles have been suggested in terms of the responsibility to tackle climate change: it should be either the polluter, the beneficiary, or those with the ability to address the problem that should shoulder the burden (see Caney, 2005). Some rail against the notion of the polluter paying, as it is argued that in historical terms it is only comparatively recently that we have properly discovered how the damage has been done, and so they should not in that sense be *liable*. This issue with liability relates also to the other two principles, as beneficiaries are rarely responsible for the benefits they accrue, while the most capable bearing the brunt of the obligation might also lead to a disconnect in terms of liability.

In a recent article, Caney (2014) challenges this conception of burden-sharing justice with another approach that he believes must compliment the mainstream perspective – because assigning burdens to actors will not always coincide with the desired outcome of addressing the problem. Harm-avoidance justice is focused not on the distribution of burdens, rather the upholding of people's entitlements and avoiding the situation where they are harmed. Caney's general point is that while focusing on a just distribution of burdens often coincides with the priorities of harm-avoidance justice – i.e., the distribution means the undesirable situation is averted – it is quite often the case that the contrary is true. So identifying who should bear the burden of climate change and distributing it accordingly does not necessarily mean it will be successfully addressed and further harm avoided. In blunt terms, those assigned with the burden because they should address it, may simply choose not to do so.

Focusing on harm-avoidance justice, in Caney's view, entails a recognition that realizing the desired outcome involves sacrifices that some would rather not make. As a result we require an account of what he calls *second-order responsibilities*. Rather than those of the first order, which relate to upholding our part of the bargain, these responsibilities entail we ensure others comply.

Caney gives an account of these responsibilities by beginning with the *tasks* that need to be taken on to avoid the harms caused by climate change. These can range from enforcement and enablement to changing demographic policy and civil disobedience. Implicit here is the number of *agents* to whom we might assign these tasks, such as governance institutions and corporate and public researchers, urban planners and council officials or even 'charismatic individuals'. We are still faced with the crucial question, however, as to why these agents who have the power, in some sense, *should* carry out second-order responsibilities. Caney appeals to what he considers to be 'highly plausible assumptions'

(2014: 142): that we face a state of emergency with regard to climate change, that the agents identified will be effective and able to make crucial differences, and because of their elevated status and their important causal role they bear these duties more heavily than others.

Caney's arguments are put forward in a lucid and traditional analytical style. In this sense he can hardly be described as a philosopher that comes from a radical perspective. In some senses it is vitally important that such a 'mainstream' figure should choose to make climate justice his core concern, as environmental issues have not really gained the traction in political philosophy that one might expect, given the significance of the issues. What is interesting, however, is that Caney makes explicit reference to the role of the activist and the importance of civil disobedience. In fact, he is actively arguing that there can be a *duty* to break the law where this is entailed by second-order responsibilities relating to climate change.

A more general point to pick up on in concluding this section is the place of issues like the environment, or indeed gender, in global justice philosophizing. The environment, for example, has been treated to some extent as a condition on other distributive principles, while in the case of Caney and others we see the issue of climate change being dealt with as a discrete aspect of global justice. Their reason for doing so is because of the ramifications for our rights and entitlements as humans. Climate justice is thus bracketed from the broader concerns of environmental justice that relate to wider issues including animal life, biodiversity, resource degradation and numerous others. The prioritizing of climate justice can be taken as a reflection of our anthropocentric world view; that is the tendency to view nature through the lens of our own human concerns and priorities. This entails an instrumental view of nature, which does not attempt to persuade us that we should consider its inherent value or appreciate it in of itself – at least not in terms of our considerations of justice.

Other philosophers have reflected more upon these more fundamental ecological issues, and we will return to some of these questions in subsequent chapters. To stay within the broadly liberal philosophical tradition for the moment, however, one of Andrew Dobson's key criticisms of cosmopolitanism is what he terms its unexamined 'motivational heart' (2006: 165). In his view the perspective lacks an account of sufficient motivation that leaves us with principles that represent an 'intellectual commitment' but fail to express 'a determination to act' (2006: 165). The key problem for him is that approaches such as Pogge's allegedly depend on an unrealistic good Samaritanism. It appeals to our moral ability to identify with the distant other, and come to their aid, on account of the rather abstract notion of them being human. We are so impressed by the Samaritan, Dobson explains, because he is not liable for the state of the victim. We cannot expect people to be so exceptional in their everyday lives, and so we must rely on motivation brought about by a sense of liability instead.

This is where climate change can play a key motivational role for Dobson, because recognizing the effects of our ecological footprint makes our obligations clear and compelling. Wider environmental issues may again be sidelined, but the manner in which he attempts to make climate change a central and substantive part of the cosmopolitan project speaks to the desire to bring it more squarely into the global justice project. The relationship between environmentalism and global justice will be returned to in subsequent chapters. In the eyes of many 'green' activists, simply challenging the scope of the liberal project, or 'greening' it to a greater degree, will not suffice if we are to properly address the issue of environmental injustice. This is where the radical implications for the global justice debate lie, in a more explicit engagement with these issues – for once we recognize the centrality of environmental questions to justice, it behoves us to consider whether liberal assumptions such as individual rights, economic growth, distinct notions of public and private responsibilities, and an anthropocentric moral universe, are part of the problem rather than the solution.

JAGGAR AND GENDER

Lastly we turn to Alison M. Jaggar's intervention in the global justice debate, which is possibly the most explicitly challenging one to date. She treads a middle path between recognizing the virtues of the liberal philosophical tradition that underpins the debates we have discussed thus far, while also making clear that in her view many of these assumptions need to be reconsidered. Her general point is that to date, the global justice debate – in accordance with the tradition it represents – fails to acknowledge sufficiently the central role that gender plays in accounting for injustice. Traditional liberal thinking on justice falls short of the mark because it ignores – or at the very least fails to emphasize – the way in which women are particularly discriminated against. Because it is in effect blind to this gender imbalance, it cannot offer us the responses required to get to grips with the problem of global injustice adequately.

Jaggar sets out the general challenges to liberal theory in reference to Rawls' *TJ* which she describes as a 'rich and complex work' (2014a: 4) that is 'remarkably egalitarian' (2014a: 5). She also describes it as 'bringing three centuries of Western political philosophy to culmination' and in this sense it represents an apt and explicit target with regards to identifying problems with this tradition (2014a: 5). She describes how anti-colonial struggles and the Civil Rights Movement in the United States challenged its assumptions by highlighting the cultural and symbolic nature of injustice and the way equality requires recognition of the prejudice directed at some groups, and not just economic and political measures aimed at the individual. Feminist philosophy followed a similar path in questioning these same assumptions.

A key development has been the concept of 'gender', which goes beyond the traditional distinction between men and women on account of their biological differences. Masculinity and femininity are instead viewed as identities defined by *social practices and values*, which have a fundamental impact on the way we can live our lives. This basic conceptual idea opens up a perspective that allows us to see how injustices occur in a mundane and everyday manner, within the private as well as the public sphere, and indeed how these injustices are central to the 'normal' functioning of world politics. Women face basic disadvantages because (to quote a famous song), this is a man's world. Institutions are structured to accommodate men and masculine assumptions about politics, development, conflict and the good life. This is expressed in the concept of patriarchy: a social system which functions to ensure the reproduction of masculine power relations, and which tends to favour men and discriminate against women. Think about how it is often automatically expected in many societies that women will be care givers, and will do the majority of household tasks relating to food and cleaning. These roles are often unpaid, and regarded as low status and apolitical, despite being fundamental to the reproduction of society.

The challenges to liberal theory from feminist philosophy are defined by Jaggar through two key concepts. In the first instance there is a challenge to the *domain* of justice: to which realms does justice apply? Here we return to the public/private distinction referred to in the last chapter by Nussbaum, and the fact that the private should not be exempt because of the obvious injustices relating to the distribution of care work, as well as violent crime and sexual offences. The famous feminist slogan of the 1960s and 1970s was that 'the personal is political'; family life, the distribution of resources and work in the household, and the sorts of personal flourishing available to men and women are all shaped by broader, political, social norms.

Secondly, a feminist perspective – in keeping with the identity politics of the postcolonial and civil rights movement – bears a challenge to the traditional *objects* of justice. As well as recognizing the importance of political and economic factors – captured in Rawls' two principles – feminists call for attention to be given to the distribution of respect and valuation of women, as well as their responsibilities in the home. These challenges constitute a critique of the 'gendered' aspects of our philosophical canon, in that they elucidate how the categories traditionally employed bias the focus of justice towards men; in restricting the domain of justice and in failing to recognize the importance of societal prejudices against women and their roles, women are in effect treated as secondary considerations.

These insights on the gendered aspects of our philosophical ideas are exploited by Jaggar with regard to the global justice debate. That is to say, it is not just the obvious cases of discrimination such as female genital mutilation and sex trafficking that fall within global gender justice – those *subjects* of justice that go beyond the traditional scope – but *all* the issues it addresses. Jaggar refers to a number of apparently gender-neutral institutions and policies that are the focus of global justice, and outlines how they have been shown to exhibit disproportionate effects upon women. For example, trade reforms that allow rich countries to dump subsidized agricultural products on poor countries have hit women particularly hard, as they represent the majority of the world's farmers. Developments in global trade, structural adjustment programmes, the expansion of the arms trade, global integration and environmental harm all have similarly gendered effects. The challenge faced by global justice theorizing is not just to identify these inequities, but more fundamentally question whether the categories used in the debate are 'infected' by gender bias (Jaggar, 2014a: 12). Should not female infanticide, for example, be included within an expanded definition of genocide?

Taken together, therefore, reflecting on the gender dimensions of global justice challenges traditional liberal conceptions of justice with regard to domain (e.g., the home), subjects (e.g., sex workers), and objects of justice (e.g., transnational structures such as the organization of care-related responsibilities). Jaggar's perspective is directed towards this latter theme of the objects of justice, by offering what she regards as a *prologue to a theory of global gender justice* (2014b), or an explanatory model to help us understand how gender disparities come about. Helping us understand these processes should in part provide the means for addressing how the relevant objects of justice can be reformed. In a sense, she may be viewed as conducting empirically focused work, similar to Pogge, but doing so through the lens of gender in order to identify processes that have gone previously unacknowledged.

Her model builds on the work of Susan Moller Okin (1989) and Iris Marion Young (2006), in particular the focus on how institutions make women more vulnerable, such as through the ways in which gender roles are assigned. In the case of marriage, for example, among middle-class privileged women in western countries their vulnerability is often increased by the types of work they are expected to take on and the roles they are to fulfil within the household, confining their freedom and agency in comparison to the roles assigned to men. In other contexts the vulnerability can be more extreme, leading to dependence despite situations of violence and abuse. Where married women do seek work, the requirement to combine it with domestic responsibilities can increase the likelihood of economic exploitation by employers because of their comparatively reduced bargaining power. Jaggar applies this model to the transnational or global context to demonstrate how the assignment of gender roles has a distinct role in creating cycles of vulnerability for women. She specifies two particular examples of such cycles, namely domestic work and sex work.

With regard to the first example Jaggar identifies a direct link between a general retreat from citizen welfare to added demands that fall unfairly on women, because they are expected to take up these care roles that are less widely supported. These reductions are related to policies implemented by global institutions such as the World Trade Organization, or neoliberal structural adjustment programmes enforced by the International Monetary Fund which required developing countries to cut social spending on health, education and food subsidies. Therefore, even though the policies are superficially gender-neutral, it is women who bear the brunt of their effects.

Moreover, these cuts create demand for domestic servants in affluent countries, while structural inequalities in the global economy and subsequent poverty in developing countries lead to many women migrating abroad to seek such work. These workers are often exposed to exploitation by their employers in what can be an unregulated work environment, while back home their responsibilities become an additional burden for female members of their family. Jaggar concludes 'women's cheap or unpaid domestic labour underwrites the entire global economy by subsidizing the indispensable tasks of cleaning and care' (2014b: 28).

The global sex industry is also characterized by its dependence on, and exploitation of, women. Although there are male suppliers, the vast majority are female, while the consumers are predominantly male. Conditions vary but a high percentage of workers are extremely vulnerable, trapped in a cycle of violence and exploitation, where the hope of exit is often minimal. Again, structural inequalities in the global economy are at work here, with families in the developing world depending upon remittances from sex workers in the developed world, while increasing numbers of states depend on the tourist industry and the attendant sex work. It is the men who organize the work who benefit most, rather than the women who endure it. The ubiquitous nature of the industry, and the number of women who enter it, is explained by Jaggar in terms of global norms of sexuality that help define such roles (the man as consumer and woman as pleasure giver), 'the gendered inequalities of access to economic resources, and transnational . . . institutions that encourage the emergence of a gender-structured global sex industry' (2014b: 31). Focusing on these two examples through the lens of Jaggar's model provides a revealing picture of how global inequalities are gender specific. It helps to provide a narrative about the particular injustice and exploitation faced by women, which is often hidden by more generic accounts of underdevelopment that focus on other industries or structures.

Jaggar makes a convincing case that gender should be at the heart of our concerns with global injustice and the explanations behind it. It ultimately provides us with a more sophisticated understanding of how we should deal with the objects of justice in the transnational and global realm and their intersection with local institutions, be they cultural norms, practices, or the political and economic institutions that exacerbate problematic and debilitating poverty. It is a question for philosophers of all stripes as to whether these insights can (or should, from the feminist perspective) be absorbed by and accommodated by the liberal mainstream. It is clearly the case that it is not simply one among many problems; global injustice is shot through with gendered inequality.

CONCLUSION

This chapter has attempted to give a sense of how the global justice debate has been inflected by increasingly varied voices, and that there are many perspectives, traditions and concepts that can be employed to elucidate and develop the debate further. The suggestion of a third wave in a sense deepens the debate as it stands, with the promise of yet more philosophical sophistication through developing liberal approaches based on coercion, and a focus on discrete issues such as trade. Republicanism and recognition theory demonstrate that other traditions in mainstream political philosophy may have worthwhile contributions to make in being transposed to the global level and challenging the predominant liberal perspective in certain respects. Turning to Iris Marion Young, we see another approach that exemplifies how disparate traditions and different theoretical approaches – structuralist rather individualist in this case – can serve to widen the debate. The environment and gender are two themes that have also been applied to the philosophy of global justice, and while authors such as Caney and Jaggar take a largely conciliatory approach that seeks to influence rather than undermine the ongoing debate, they are also suggestive of the possibility of a more radical reconsideration of its liberal foundations and a need to include more disparate voices.

Indeed, one of the more strident interventions in the philosophical debate in recent years came in Maffettone and Rathore's volume,

Global Justice: Critical Perspectives, which claimed 'it remains necessary to include more (global) voices into this (global) debate of global reach and significance' (2012: 2). It is their specific aim to 'deparochialize' the debate. Rathore's characterization of those debating the subject is particularly damning, suggesting that '[w]e might even put it crudely that' the primarily western academics involved 'profit off the chronic global poor for the injustices they suffer' (2012: 173). Maffettone for his part is more sanguine about the hopes of embedding helpful insights from other traditions in the debate, and indeed one of the aims of our book, in combining a study of philosophy and activism, is to map out the possibilities in terms of widening the debate – especially in surveying the world of ideas that inspires activists in their struggles.

In this regard, Young is a particularly pertinent thinker, because her work more generally displays an original and productive philosophical pluralism, and also because she seeks to articulate the connections between philosophy and activism (for example, in a famous article from 2001 entitled 'Activist Challenges to Deliberative Democracy', which we will discuss in more detail in Chapter 6). It is notable, however, that this link is also alluded to in the work of others such as Caney and Pettit; as discussed in this chapter they provide a privileged place for the activist and in a very rudimentary sense recognize and provide normative support for their role in fighting global injustice. Turning to activism need not, therefore, be seen as a radical attempt to displace current debates and philosophical paradigms.

It does, arguably, provide a context for addressing some of those areas that Wollner regards as the next steps in global justice philosophizing: complicating the state/global focus through looking at national, transnational and global movements; taking the requirements of 'action guidingness' seriously through understanding the obstacles activists face; laying the basis for more extensive theories that recognize the entire gamut of global justice campaigning, from Stop the War to Anti-fracking campaigns; and closing the gap, not between philosophy and policy, but philosophy and those at the forefront of seeking policy change. In the next chapter it is this last theme of the connection between philosophy and policy that we interrogate, by looking first at the ways in which global justice philosophers have deployed empirical theories and concepts in their normative work, and then examining how these perspectives have inspired have attempts at realizing global justice.

THE PATH TO GLOBAL JUSTICE

THIS CHAPTER . . .

. . . explores the various ways in which creating a more just world is envisaged and proposed in practice. We look at how some of the philosophers we have been introduced to in the previous chapters use ideas and theories about development in setting out their own moral and practical views. We will also look at how some of these ideas have influenced policies pursued by global institutions, states and activists, in their struggle to create a fairer global society.

THE PRINCIPLES OF GLOBAL JUSTICE AND NARRATIVES OF DEVELOPMENT

In the previous chapters, we have touched on the kind of policy ideas that some philosophers have put forward in their key principles, such as Rawls' *duty of assistance*, Beitz's *global distributive principle* and Pogge's *global resources dividend*. These concepts are presented in the first instance as normative principles that arise out of, and can be justified by, those initial philosophical arguments that articulate our duties to distant others. In addition to arising from their philosophical foundations, they also represent ideas about the best way to go about addressing the injustice and poverty that exists across the world.

There is a claim here (implicit or not) on behalf of the philosophers that they have identified the kind of policies that will be morally defensible *and* effective. Indeed, it is fair to suggest that the supposed effectiveness of policies are employed by philosophers to support their moral principles: they aim to present answers that are not simply the result of detached moral reasoning, but that also take into account what works. This is not just a matter of credibility and of wanting to appear in touch with the real world. If they advocate policies with negative or negligible gains with regard to greater equality and less poverty, then these dire consequences will of course undermine their moral arguments. To put it bluntly, moral principles are no good if they do no good.

In making claims about effective remedies for the problems of global justice, philosophers will tend to endorse a certain understanding of what has caused this relative poverty in the first place and what actions will be best placed to improve the situation. It is in this context that we see there are certain consistencies or patterns with respect to how underdevelopment and poverty is understood by different philosophers. Here it is helpful to be able to use theoretical schema to simplify this task. One categorization that has been employed in earlier discussions (see Miller, 2007: 242) is that of different 'development narratives' by Dani Rodrik (2003). In his view there are, in very broad terms, different stories told about how it is that a state may or may not overcome poverty. These can be divided roughly into three narratives.

In the first instance we have an 'integrationist' account (or simply the 'external' narrative in Miller's version). This emphasizes the interplay between the state and the global economy as the key driver in achieving development. Generally it is suggested that the greater extent to which the state is integrated within these structures, the better its chance of overcoming poverty. A particularly popular version of this narrative was the Washington Consensus (Williamson, 1989, 2004), which gained favour in the 1990s after the fall of Communism, and which held (among other things) that states needed to break down barriers to international markets and 'roll back' the state. Rather than the state organizing the economy it should allow the capitalist system to go about its work unhindered.

A second perhaps more traditional story is the 'geographical' narrative ('physical' in Miller's terms). From this perspective, it appears that natural factors (insofar as we regard any state as 'natural') such as accessibility of terrain, length of coastline and, in particular, the natural resources it harbours will have the largest say in whether a state will be able to escape from poverty. In this regard, we might take for granted that oil-rich countries have a massive advantage over other territories because of the wealth they can generate. Influential economist Jeffrey Sachs quotes Adam Smith approvingly in explaining why Great Britain was the first country to industrialize: 'England, on account of the natural fertility of the soil, of the great extent of the sea-coast in proportion to that of the whole country, and of the many navigable rivers which run through it and afford the convenience of water carriage to some of the most inland parts of it, is perhaps as well fitted by nature as any large country in Europe to be the seat of foreign commerce, of manufactures for distant sale and of all the improvements which these can occasion' (in Sachs, 2005: 34).

A third, 'institutional' (or 'domestic') narrative is one which emphasizes the importance of state institutions and political cultures as the most influential factors in overcoming poverty. From this point of view it is how the state manages the business of politics – the economy being central to this – that ultimately leads to further poverty or economic progress. This view has gained greater currency of late with the state gradually being 'brought back' into view as a key determinant of development. Indeed, the term 'statebuilding' has been one of particular popularity, reflecting the idea that it is the institutions of politics that need to be effective to provide the grounds for overcoming poverty (Chesterman, Ignatieff and Thakur, 2005). One choice phrase is the idea that all states are aiming at 'getting to Denmark', with this Scandinavian country representing an ideal, because of the presumed efficiency and justness of its institutions and the standard of living enjoyed by its citizens. This suggests how a democratic system is assumed to be characteristic of the ideal state that 'statebuilding' policies work towards.

It is a recognizable tendency within the study of development (and economic and social science as a whole, it might be said) for those discussing and debating these ideas to hark after a 'silver bullet' – namely a theory or interpretation of underdevelopment that can be reduced to one key explanatory factor. In practice, no one would admit to this type of blinkered thinking; however, they might make the case that despite the plethora of factors that account for certain developmental trends, one can coherently argue that one set of factors (e.g. integration, geography, institutions) is overwhelmingly important. This tendency can become starker in philosophical debates where clarity and simplicity is a virtue. That is to say, in suggesting a 'duty of assistance' or a 'global distributive principle' advocating certain policies, we may see the philosopher cleaving to a particular developmental narrative in the type of principles they argue for.

We can take Beitz's original elucidation of his global distributive principles as a starting point. You will recall that Beitz wants to extend Rawls' distributive principle across borders so that it is applicable to all individuals regardless of their place in the world. This is the path his moral argumentation leads him along, together with an empirical argument claiming that contemporary global relations entail a cooperative venture for mutual advantage. In fairness to Beitz, this work was a ground-breaking philosophical sketch of the possibilities of thinking about justice on a global plane; however, what is interesting in practical terms is that he endorses a developmental narrative that emphasizes the significance of resources over and above other factors. This reflects the geographical narrative mentioned above (although arguably some of his discussion elsewhere relates to the institutional and integrationist narratives), as the reasoning implied is that resources are key: where some states are blessed with copious natural resources and are financially better off, others are entitled to dispensation through what is effectively a global taxation regime. As he states, 'Some areas are rich in resources, and societies established in such areas can be expected to exploit their natural riches and to prosper' (Beitz, 1999: 137).

At this point, the philosopher has inevitably entered the fray with regard to empirical debates surrounding the causes and solutions of global poverty. In the case of Beitz's philosophizing, we can see that the equivalent reasoning has existed in the reality of politics, as he essentially makes the case for the type of redistribution of (financial) resources that has occurred through aid, for decades. More specifically, as he posits the argument in terms of an ongoing duty of redistribution, we have what is a theoretical equivalent to an idea such as the Tobin Tax, which suggests resources must be redistributed not as humanitarian aid but as a duty of justice – this is what resource-poor states are owed. Now what Beitz the philosopher has to accept is that there has been more than one powerful critique of the efficacy of financial redistribution of this sort, which can undermine the strength of his argument. He may have provided an argument for how we account for our global duties in a persuasive manner, but this does not necessarily entail a persuasive response to the challenge of fulfilling these duties in an effective and ethically sound manner.

Literature on the 'resource curse' (Ross, 1999; see also Collier, 2007) has long suggested that resource-rich states are often unable to ensure the sorts of level of equality and security that might be assumed, and that many of the world's poor and suffering live within their borders. Because of the ease with which governments are able to ensure vast incomes through taking wealth directly from these extractive industries, often the institutions that are required to protect and promote the lives of ordinary citizens are never established effectively. Intuitively one would suppose oil-rich countries would have the best living standards and least poverty, but experience can prove otherwise. Leif Wenar has made powerful arguments claiming that the political leaders of such states are committing nothing less than theft from their subjects in denying them the benefits of their collective natural resources (2008), while western states, in particular the G8, are complicit in fuelling this crime through their importing practices (2013). The vast natural wealth of certain states, and the attendant financial wealth, can be particularly damaging where governments are not robust and representative. A similar critique of aid has emerged and which has most famously been elucidated by Dambisa Moyo (2009; see also Easterly, 2006). The argument here is that redistribution of wealth via development aid breeds a dependency in developing states, which stultifies the kind of development in terms of economy, industry, government and finance that is required for improved standards of living.

DEAD AID

Dambisa Moyo is a Zambian-born economist who worked at the World Bank and for Goldman Sachs. Her bestselling book, *Dead Aid: Why Aid is not Working and How There is Another Way for Africa*, is

(Continued)

(Continued)

a strident critique of development aid from rich countries to poorer countries. She claims that in the past 50 years over US$ 1 trillion has been given to African countries in development-related aid, but questions whether this aid has made people any better off. In fact, she claims, 'Aid has been, and continues to be, an unmitigated political, economic and humanitarian disaster for most parts of the developing world' (Moyo, 2009: xix).

Why is this? Moyo comes from a firmly 'integrationist' perspective: what is needed is to liberalize trade and integrate into world markets. Aid, in her view, stifles business and trade, encourages corruption, strengthens unaccountable governments, and encourages a child-like or dependent mindset. Her famous example is the donation of thousands of mosquito nets to a poor region. These help people avoid malaria for a few years, but they also put the local mosquito net manufacturer out of business. When the donated nets break or are lost, there is no one to make new nets (Moyo, 2009: 44). Her alternatives to aid are free trade, Chinese investment, microfinance and direct cash transfers to the poor, and international bond markets (see also Easterly, 2006).

Development aid is a highly contentious topic, and opinions tend to polarize along ideological lines. Collier (2007: 100) suggests that the aid debates bring out the worst on the left and right wings of the political spectrum. For the left, aid 'is some reparation for colonialism. In other words, it's a statement about the guilt of western societies, not about development'. The poor are framed as helpless victims. On the other hand, 'The right seems to want to equate aid with welfare scrounging'. It seems overly simplistic to present aid as either the magic solution, or the root of all injustice. Some sorts of aid, in some times and places, can alleviate suffering, whereas in other forms new problems can be created. As Collier (2007: 123) concludes, aid is probably 'part of the solution rather than part of the problem', but it needs to be supplemented with other reforms and political interventions too.

These kinds of criticisms draw our attention to the types of argument that place more emphasis on the 'institutional narrative' and the importance of government structures. In particular, one of the criticisms of the 'resource curse' is that it fails to acknowledge the way in which countries such as Australia, Norway and the United States are relatively resource-rich yet face fewer issues in ensuring their population – on the whole – enjoy a better standard of living. The general point would be that what these states share in common is an institutional capacity that has been built up over time, which makes them adept at using their resources to their advantage and in a way that meets the demands of their citizens to an adequate degree. The state has been built up in a way that allows for using these resources to their economic and the social advantage of the majority. Furthermore, some of the problems associated with an economy dependent on natural resource exploitation – corruption, environmental degradation, stagnation of alternative economic sectors – have gradually been 'outsourced' to neighbours, colonies, or trade partners. Europe, North America and Japan have all achieved high levels of prosperity, resource consumption, and relatively high standards of environmental protection, but this relies upon high levels of natural resource extraction (with the accompanying costs) in the peripheries of the global economy: in Latin America, Africa and Asia.

Much of the statebuilding literature from the likes of Francis Fukuyama (2004) and Paul Collier (2007) looks at the issue of how states can reform themselves in order to 'get to Denmark'. The need for *democratic* institutions is implicit or rather assumed, but the more normatively explicit work of Sen on development sets out persuasive empirical evidence about the role of democratic practices – the equality of women and a free press in particular – and the manner in which it buttresses economic and social progress (1999). In fact, examples of groups such as the Australian Aborigines and the Native Americans exemplify the point that the organization of state structures are key to the treatment of citizens, and it is often when these are inadequate or discriminatory that people's rights are abused.

Tied in with these arguments about the need for developing states to therefore concentrate on emulating the (just) institutional structures of democratic states are some rather thorny issues about the role of culture in buttressing these institutions and securing progress.

There is a line of argument, most stridently advocated by David Landes (1998), which sees culture as the single most important factor; in his view some cultures are more inclined towards the sort of behaviour, values and ideas that can be anticipated to respond better to the supposed needs of development such as the free market, industry and institutional groundwork.

Such arguments can be worryingly essentialist and prescribe certain 'inherent' qualities in people. There is a good deal of discussion about the extent to which certain values and practices can be so easily and reductively associated with certain groups. As much as a thinker such as Sen emphasizes the priority of democratic values, he is very much at pains to demonstrate that at their core lie ideas and practices that have existed historically across the globe (Sen, 2009: 338–55). These are the types of moral issues that face philosophers, who by dint of their arguments, provide ideas and principles that seem to support this particular 'institutional' narrative.

David Miller could be regarded as pursuing a similar argument to Landes, in his emphasis on cultural factors within the institutional narrative (2007: 238–47). Miller does not ignore other contributing factors to poverty, in particular the influence of the global economy, yet he is very much of the view that the key solutions lie within rather than outside the state. In one sense there is an undoubtedly important message in his wish to emphasize that the fate of states lie within their own hands and the policies they pursue, yet in underlining their agency there is what might be regarded as a tendency to convey incapability as a congenital failing. The poor are poor because they (or their leaders) have made bad decisions, to put this perspective in its crudest form.

Rawls is regarded as a philosopher who in a similar vein emphasizes institutions and culture, borrowing heavily off Sen and questioning the efficacy of 'throwing funds' at the problem (1999: 110). Yet his discussion of such policies comes within a broader framework that provides a moral defence of non-democratic states, raising interesting questions and tensions, but ultimately suggestive of different routes of development. His tolerance of the non-liberal and his appreciation of Sen's research forestalls the kind of criticism that can be directed more squarely towards Miller, with regard to the issue of cultural essentialism. There is some debate about the policies

Rawls advocates as part of his duty of assistance, and some claim that it recommends financial, institutional and integrational aspects – attempting to negotiate and account for the different influences on poverty (Williams, 2011, 2014). However, one of his keenest cosmopolitan critics accuses him of what is described as 'explanatory nationalism' – namely the idea that poverty is explained by Rawls largely or purely in terms of factors deriving from within the nation-state (Pogge, 2008: 145–50).

Pogge, on the other hand, is very much of the view that in addressing the issue of global poverty we need to take a systemic view, paying attention to the 'integrationist' narrative. The policies that flow from his moral defence of human rights, and the negative duty to realize individuals' entitlements, revolve around addressing these systemic issues that he sees as being most relevant and basic to the causal chain of poverty. For example, that corruption undermines egalitarian economic goals within a state can be seen, from Pogge's perspective, as the outcome of factors that in many instances lie outside it, such as the behaviour of multinational companies, politicians and other agents within the global context. As much as we may be able to identify unhelpful actions and policies within the state, in Pogge's view we must prioritize rectifying the injustices of the global structure because these condition the behaviour of those within it. Should we do so, we would see very different results. A rule-governed global economic structure grounded in justice and fairness is the foundation upon which just, fair and equitable policies can be expected to flourish within states. We cannot expect democratic states to develop (without great difficulty), which are able to best use their resources in a way that responds to the demands of all their citizens, unless they are integrated into the global system in a fair and equitable manner.

Pogge's arguments are persuasive. In many senses they shine a light on the manner in which those states that have been at the forefront of economic development have played a key role in designing and sustaining a system that – although less directly exploitative than the age of Empire – is certainly designed to maintain their position of relative power. We may want to question the extent to which our own comforts are maintained through what is described as the Western world 'kicking the ladder away' (Chang, 2002). Moreover, in reflecting on these questions with regard to states, we may also want to question why it is certain groups within our nominally democratic societies – such as the Australian Aboriginal or the Native American – are so much more worse off.

One of the most coherent counter-cultural explanations of why our world is characterized by massive wealth alongside staggering poverty is provided by analyses of development drawing upon the political economy of Karl Marx. In a similar vein to Pogge, theorists like Ben Selwyn explicitly reject the integrationist account of development that closer insertion within the global economy will bring development and justice to the world's poor. Rather, he suggests, closer inclusion in capitalist social relations is a deeply violent process which breeds further inequality. The possibility of meaningful equality and human flourishing are precluded by 'capitalism's social relations, in particular the non-democratic ownership of wealth and means of creating wealth by a tiny percentage of the world's population' (Selwyn, 2014: 4–5). As Oxfam pointed out in a report in January 2016, 62 people now own the same amount of wealth as the poorest half of the world's population. On this measure the world is getting more and more unequal. Marxist theorists like Selwyn agree with the vision of development articulated by Pogge and Sen – expanding the real freedoms that people enjoy (Sen, 1999: 3) – but differ in their understanding of how such a process of development can come about. For Selwyn (2014: 5), 'capitalism precludes Sen's vision, as it is founded upon the systemic exploitation and repression of the majority (the world's labouring classes) by the minority (the world's capitalist classes and states)', and produces systematic exploitation within the sphere of production (workplace), within the sphere of exchange (the labour market), within the household (gender and patriarchy), through race and racism, and through the commodification of nature (2014: 14–15).

What, then, explains the existence of chronic poverty, given the frankly copious amounts of wealth in the world? Is it the lack of natural resources, domestic cultural and institutional failures, or global systemic issues? Some combination, no doubt, but philosophers have differed in where they have placed the emphasis, and in the next section we question more directly the application and derivation of these empirical theories, which have been central to the philosophical debate of global justice.

EMPIRICAL ISSUES IN PHILOSOPHIZING ABOUT GLOBAL JUSTICE

Here we interrogate a little further the relationship between the philosophy and practice of global justice – that is to say we look more closely at the way in which philosophers use ideas derived from the empirical study of development in order to buttress their normative arguments. Two specific issues will be identified; firstly that the philosopher has to guard against selecting and utilizing information simply on the basis that it represents the best fit with their moral arguments, as this can lead to the accusation that their understanding of the problem of global poverty is skewed by their normative commitments. The second issue is related, in that we will identify historical precedents for the empirical ideas and theories utilized by global justice philosophers, which illustrate how they were borne out of particular political, ideological thinking that had particular outcomes in mind.

This is not meant as a blanket condemnation of philosophers per se. In one way it reminds us of the limits of their craft and the limits of scholars' scope. Very few have been able enough or brave enough to step over the divide between the empirical and philosophical in a far-reaching manner, as Pogge and Sen have managed. It is meant as a reminder, however, to remain critical as readers and to always question the extent to which a philosopher or theorist can claim they are presenting objective, neutral arguments that are impervious to bias or prejudice – especially in 'applied' contexts such as these. As well as sounding a note of scepticism, questioning the relationship between the moral argumentation and the empirical information it relies upon, we hope, opens out the prospect of further debate and exchange of ideas, and leads us into an explicit attempt to understand more meaningfully what is going on in the 'real world'.

Much of the remainder of this book will look in particular at what we might term the coalface – namely at what is happening among those explicitly aiming at changing the world and realizing the kinds of ideals that philosophers have articulated. Thinkers such as Sen and Pogge in particular have been successful at recognizing the conditions under which things can improve, and what actions we require from politicians in particular. However, we are also interested in assessing how these conditions might be realized, or these actions carried out, through the influence and work of people working in their communities, ordinary individuals and inspiring activists, fighting injustices in their own ways.

Questioning the ways in which philosophers have understood the phenomenon of global poverty and its causes is not an original step – it is something they have done with respect to each other. Indeed, we need look no further than Pogge's accusation that Rawls is an explanatory nationalist. In making this claim we see that Pogge is in essence arguing that Rawls has taken an unreasonably narrow view of the factors that cause global poverty – and that he requires a more sophisticated and expansive understanding that correctly identifies systemic problems as the foundational problem. What is more interesting, however, is the implication that this is not simply a misinformed or partial view of the facts, but that Rawls inevitably presumes this interpretation of the facts because this is what his moral perspective demands.

Rawls, if you recall, is tied to the status quo in his moral perspective of international politics, in the sense that he believes that this is the system for which we should work out our principles – and this system is, of course, characterized by a society of peoples. Because Rawls, so the suggestion goes, understands the world in terms of discrete nation-states that are bound loosely together by political and economic interactions, then he will understand the drivers of global poverty in the same terms – namely decisions and behaviours at state level that are influenced in some small way by the loose global structure they inhabit. Moreover, being wedded to a more communitarian perspective that eschews substantive equality between individuals necessarily steers him away from more radical policies to be pursued at the level of global governance. What this amounts to is an argument that Rawls' moral view conditions his interpretation of the facts, so that he will inevitably choose the theory or ideas that cohere with his prior perspective.

Interestingly, Miller later took Pogge to task in a similar manner, essentially implying that Pogge was denuding developing states of any meaningful agency in his enthusiasm for placing the blame on systemic failures. Miller used the analogy of a roundabout where careful drivers are able to avoid accidents while the careless do not (2007: 240). He is happy to recognize that sometimes the 'engineers' could make a better job of putting together a route that is easy for all, but wishes to stress the point that there will be many who can negotiate the course regardless. Again, the implication here is that Pogge's normative commitments are leading him to interpret the facts about global poverty in a one-eyed manner that places sole causal influence on the systemic issues.

This, it is implied, is hardly surprising given his cosmopolitan moral outlook that plays down the importance of the state, demands far-reaching egalitarian policies at a global level and amounts to a moral perspective that is thus skewed towards the systemic and global plane. These arguments lead us to a slightly problematic and somewhat disappointing notion – that communitarians interpret global poverty as the result of actions by states because this buttresses their moral outlook, while cosmopolitans interpret it as a result of actions at a global level as it buttresses their own moral vision.

Of course, these arguments have been put in somewhat stark terms here, and the truth is that there is more subtlety to the approaches of the philosophers in question. Indeed, as noted earlier there are reasons to argue that Rawls' duty of assistance acknowledges both domestic and global factors in terms of addressing poverty, while Miller in his own work acknowledges that improvements can be made to the global economic structure. Pogge, on the other hand, does not deny the influence of domestic factors, but wishes to argue that they would be seen to be less influential in another world where a more just global regime existed. It would be harsh in the extreme to label them as ideologues on account of their promotion of one version of reality over another.

That said, if we delve a little deeper into the history of some of these accounts of poverty, we discover that there are reasons to be sensitive to the possibility of such ideologically conditioned thinking. Ideological, in the sense that some ideas are conceived not so much with moral principles in mind, but rather more through narrow, politically focused and goal orientated thinking. In a broad sense, the arguments regarding policy priorities in the philosophical literature can be seen to reflect historical debates in the field of development.

The tendency of more communitarian-focused thinkers, such as Miller and Rawls, to focus on the internal aspects of the nation-state – and the 'statebuilding' narrative they emulate – can be linked directly to the early work of influential figures such as Gabriel Almond (1960, 1963). These thinkers, who were largely based in the United States in the post-World War II era, came to be associated with modernization theory. At the core of this theory was the assumption that what was required of developing states was to 'catch up' with their western counterparts in terms of their state structures and capabilities (recent exponents of modernization theory include Collier, 2007, and Sachs, 2005). While contemporary statebuilding is sometimes couched in terms of humanitarian and developmental concerns (and not simply global security – although this is what accounts for its more recent prominence, post Afghanistan and Iraq) the modernization project was more explicitly self-serving. Efforts to increase the stability and security of developing states, while securing allies was a major strategic concern for the United States during the height of the Cold War (Fukuyama, 2004).

As authors such as William Bain have argued (2003), there is also reason to draw comparisons with earlier imperial projects which sought to 'improve' the quality of governance in colonial dependencies. In these earlier narratives we find more explicitly chauvinist attitudes and language, with terms such as 'the standard of civilization' being the order of the day. According to this idea different peoples can be ordered according to their capabilities and potential, and it was the role of the imperial powers to 'civilize' those lagging behind.

Bringing these ideas to the fore does not imply, of course, that thinkers such as Miller and Rawls advocate them, but it is nevertheless important to recognize the historical precedents of the ideas that form part of their thinking. It raises our awareness of further moral dimensions that require consideration, and what the implications might be of policies that seek to fundamentally change the nature of other societies. It can also lead us to ask whether philosophers pay due care and attention to these issues in articulating their arguments.

Similar comparisons can be made with respect to a thinker such a Pogge. Interestingly, he explicitly recognizes the influence of another group of thinkers on his own work – namely the dependency on world system theorists (2008: 297, n251). The most well-known is Immanuel Wallerstein, but perhaps more significant names in historical terms are Raul Prebisch and Andre Gunder Frank. They are significant because in many ways dependency theory was a direct response to modernization theory, and it sought to argue that it was ultimately the dependent position of former colonies within the world system that primarily accounted for their lack of development. From this perspective, states and their relationships are defined by virtue of their place within the global economy, and it is in the interest of the former imperial core and their formally white dominions to maintain other states in the periphery, in a relationship of domination that allows them to profit from their resources – and inhibit them from developing their own productive industries through various means (see also Selwyn, 2014).

One can recognize in these basic claims the perspective that informs much of Pogge's concern with institutions such as the International Monetary Fund (IMF) and World Bank, rules and regulations concerning the global economy, borrowing and intellectual copyright, and the need to address inequalities and imbalances through concrete policies. Unless we reform the system and provide the conditions for democracy to flourish and national economies to develop modern industries, then the chances of states reforming for the better and addressing poverty remain slim. Again it helps us recognize the origins of these ideas in recognizing how nominally philosophical debates recalibrate debates in other empirical fields, and as readers this can spur us on to question whether this undermines some of the moral position put forward, and to what extent philosophical discussion can extract itself from the various theories and ideas that help us organize and account for the empirical world.

The demand for the redistribution of resources that is so central to Beitz's arguments – and is emulated by many other global justice philosophers – cannot be linked so easily with any particular political or ideological precedent (it could be suggestive of either a state or system based interpretation, which regards financial redistribution as a means for addressing the problems identified by either). However, we may helpfully link it to concerns with 'welfare state capitalism' as a means to show how philosophically grounded principles may become embroiled in political controversies.

It is possible to view a 'resources' solution as an attitude which compensates or ameliorates a problem but does not eradicate it or solve the root causes. Welfare state capitalism allows for a small class to dominate and profit from the economic system, while compensating others through possibly quite generous welfare provisions, but doing nothing to challenge the basic inequality that maintains an underclass that are exploited and marginalized – if perhaps materially comfortable. This critique can be borne in mind when thinking about the value of instituting a global distributive principle as the primary form of addressing issues of global poverty. Can financial resources address the problem without systemic change, or more direct intervention – or does this breed dependency in the manner that sceptics such as Moyo suggest?

***

The temptation in drawing together some of the points and arguments raised in these two prior sections is to offer the kind of response that is all too often seen in undergraduate essays: well, it's a combination of all of the above, isn't it? It is probably true that there is an element of this in the discussion. That is to say, philosophers with various views, and those involved in more empirical theorizing and analysis of development would all recognize that in reality, there is an overwhelmingly complex set of issues that relates to underdevelopment and that they all play some role in accounting for poverty and ways of addressing it. However, what philosophers and academics are aiming for is to provide some way of grasping these impossibly difficult issues in ways that allow us to order our thinking and address the issues, in whatever ways we can.

This leads, of course, to the 'silver bullet' tendency of identifying one factor, or one set of factors, that need to be addressed above all others. With respect to key figures in the mainstream debate such as Beitz, Miller, Pogge and Rawls, it is fair to say that they are largely somewhere in between, inasmuch as they all recognize a range of factors that are significant, but they all have a tendency to prioritize some ideas over others. Emphasizing specific causes of poverty and identifying certain remedies in their case is particularly important because ultimately their discussions lay the basis for identifying the prior, more fundamental question of duties and obligations.

That is to say, philosophically and practically what is most important about Pogge's emphasis on the global economy and the various policies identified is that they lay the ground for the moral claim that it is the global rich who are largely responsible, and it is those that hold the levers of power in global institutions that carry the major responsibility. These are the people politicians, activists and ordinary people should point the finger at – and Pogge justifies us doing so. Miller, conversely, suggests that while there is work to be done by these people, the more important moral responsibility falls on politicians and groups within nation-states, which may undercut to some extent those who direct their wrath at global actors such as the International Monetary Fund, World Bank and G8.

It is noteworthy in this respect that, as we have seen, some philosophers such as Young and Jaggar argue that this kind of finger pointing exercise is ultimately thankless and fruitless. Such are the historical complexities it is not possible or coherent to try and identify one set of factors, or one group of actors as the most 'responsible'. Rather than seek a relationship between responsibilities and duties in this manner, it is more constructive to acknowledge the complex histories, the various immoral actions of those parties involved, but seek solutions through whichever means are effective and morally defensible. In fairness, such a view – where the link between the causation of poverty and the means to alleviate it is broken or discounted – can be identified in some of the key thinkers alluded to here. Miller, for example, refers to the most capable actors taking on remedial responsibility where outcome responsible does not lie with any specific agent, or with an agent unable to fulfil their duty (2007: 254–5), while Rawls' duty of assistance might be interpreted as forward looking in the same vein as Young's structuralist approach (Williams, 2014: 220).

As individual and independent thinkers, we can at best seek clarity in these works, and more important than seeking out ideas that buttress our own views, we should perhaps consider those arguments that challenge us most. In the rest of this chapter, we will look at two particular policies and initiatives which have been deployed to tackle global injustice, and consider how they claim legitimacy based on some of the theoretical and philosophical arguments explored so far in this book. Global justice, as we have repeatedly stressed, is not just about abstract philosophical debates. These debates have shaped how people think about and act in the world, and highly significant areas of global public policy have emerged from the work of thinkers like Nussbaum, Pogge and Rawls. We start by looking at one of the most influential global initiatives to end poverty, the Millennium Development Goals.

THE MILLENNIUM DEVELOPMENT GOALS

In 2000 the United Nations agreed a set of eight goals to tackle poverty and deprivation. These goals were explicitly set within the framework of the struggle for global justice. The Millennium Declaration which accompanied the Millennium Development Goals (MDGs) was signed by the member states of the United Nations as they gathered, 'at the dawn of a new millennium, to reaffirm our faith in the Organization and its Charter as indispensable foundations of a more peaceful, prosperous and just world' (UN, 2000). The MDGs structured the priorities for international development for over a decade and a half, and encapsulated a kind of contract between the rich world and the poor: the rich world would provide higher levels of official development assistance (ODA), aiming for a target of 0.7 percent of gross national income, in return for which the governments of the developing world would prioritize the MDGs, i.e. tackling hunger, sanitation, education, health, and so on. For the most passionate advocates of the MDGs, they represented the defining challenge of our generation: Jeffrey Sachs (2005: 368) concludes *The End of Poverty* by deliberately echoing John F. Kennedy: 'let the future say of our generation that we sent forth mighty currents of hope, and that we worked together to heal the world'.

The eight MDGs were:

1 Eradicate extreme poverty and hunger.
2 Achieve universal primary education.
3 Promote gender equality and empower women.
4 Reduce child mortality.
5 Improve maternal health.
6 Combat HIV/AIDs, malaria, and other diseases.
7 Ensure environmental sustainability.
8 Global partnership for development.

Each goal contains numerous targets. So, for example, MDG1 has a target of halving, between 1990 and 2015, the proportion of people whose income is less than $1.25 per day. This target was met by 2010, largely due to the rising economies of China and India which lifted millions of people out of extreme poverty in the 1990s and 2000s. Details on all the MDGs and the progress achieved by 2015 can be found at http://www.un.org/millenniumgoals/

The only goal without specific, measurable targets is MDG8, although it was this goal which entailed particular responsibilities for the rich countries. Its targets are more vague and open-ended: 'develop further an open, rule-based, non-discriminatory trading and financial system'; 'deal comprehensively with the debt problem of developing countries'; 'in cooperation with pharmaceutical companies, provide access to affordable essential drugs in developing countries'; and 'monitor aid delivery'. This goal is often associated with the aim to increase levels of ODA to 0.7 percent of gross national income, although this goal has actually been agreed by most developed countries since a UN resolution as early as 1970. It was reaffirmed by the European Union and at the UN World Summit in 2005.

In light of the earlier discussions in this chapter, the MDGs are revealing because of the implicit diagnosis of the causes of poverty and injustice which they represent, and the vision of a just world which they promote. The overwhelming majority of the goals focus on policy and governance challenges within developing countries, in order to provide sufficient food and clean water, improve literacy rates, protect natural resources like forests and fisheries, and so on. These are largely presented as a question of political elites in the developing world making the right choices: better driving around the roundabout to ensure fewer crashes, in Miller's terms. In contrast, MDG8 does recognize the importance of systemic, structural features of the global economy: the trading and financial system, the control of medicines by big companies, debt, and so on. It is notable that – with a few exceptions such as the campaign for debt reduction (see Chapter 5) – these structural issues have proved some of the most difficult to tackle. Finally, the distribution of wealth in the world is largely ignored in the MDGs, and even the 0.7 percent goal of aid redistribution is not explicitly mentioned. The United

Nations does note on the MDG website that ODA from developed countries 'increased by 66 per cent in real terms between 2000 and 2014, reaching $135.2 billion'. Some countries have taken steps to enshrine the 0.7 percent commitment in law: in 2015 the United Kingdom became the first of the G7 countries to make it a legal obligation to spend 0.7 per cent of its gross national income on aid every year (Anderson, 2015). But the overriding message of the MDGs is that poverty can be solved by taking the correct development decisions within poor countries: as the Millennium Declaration (UN, 2000) states, 'Success in meeting these objectives depends . . . on good governance within each country'.

Part of the success of the MDGs, however, at least in terms of the extent to which they have become globally accepted as the defining vision of development in the twenty-first century, is their capacity to incorporate several different positions on the causes of injustice and the nature of a more just world. Thus a theorist like Pogge might focus his attention on reforming the global financial system and the regulation of the pharmaceutical industry (MDG8), whereas philosophers like Miller would stress the need for developing country leaders to get more of their country's children into school (MDG3).

Similarly, few would disagree that the goals espoused in the MDGs are important, or that achieving them would help create a more just world. Who does not think that eradicating extreme poverty and hunger, improving education and environmental sustainability, or reducing the chances of infant mortality or mothers dying in childbirth, are important? More critical theorists, however, have pointed out that these are quite minimal goals for global justice in the twenty-first century. Indeed, some have even dubbed the MDGs the 'minimum development goals' (see discussion in Death and Gabay, 2015). The absence of goals on democracy, civil rights, peace and security are notable. In fact, in this sense the MDGs are more Rawlsian in that they set out some of the minimum standards that we can all agree are necessary for a good life, without dictating the type of society in which the good life should be pursued.

There is a discrepancy here between the language of the MDGs, which was specifically intended to be brief, to-the-point and easily comprehensible, and the language of the Millennium Declaration (UN, 2000) or some of the most prominent academic voices on poverty eradication and global justice (Sachs, 2005). The MDGs were designed to be as politically effective as possible in raising support for a clear and uncomplicated vision of development (with a set of goals that could be printed on a credit card-sized piece of paper). Others have put forward a fuller and more robust defence of a liberal vision of global justice centred on poverty eradication, democratization and modernization. Jeffery Sachs is one of the most well-known of these.

Sachs is a Harvard-trained American economist and director of the Earth Institute at Columbia University. He is well-known for two, deeply contradictory phases of his academic and public policy career. The first was as a neoliberal architect of shock therapy in Latin America, Eastern Europe and post-Soviet Russia in the 1980s and 1990s. During this phase he was deeply committed to 'internal' solutions to economic stagnation: proper financial and economic policy in the form of the removal of trade protection, fiscal responsibility, the privatization of state-owned companies, and so on. In short, promotion of the Washington Consensus (Wilson, 2014). In later years he has distanced himself from this record and now campaigns on more 'external' issues, notably calling for rich countries to give more money to the world's poorest in ODA. In *The End of Poverty* he likens this project to the struggle for civil rights in the United States. He recalls Martin Luther King's 'I have a dream' speech in which he invoked the constitutional American promise that 'all men would be guaranteed the unalienable rights of life, liberty, and the pursuit of happiness' (Sachs, 2005: 363). The failure to deliver on that promise to blacks in America was, for Sachs, akin to the current failure by the international community to deliver on the eradication of extreme poverty.

> Our assertion today must be like King's forty years ago. The bank of international justice is not bankrupt. The world's poor cannot accept a bad check marked insufficient funds, especially when it is painfully clear that the funds are ample and even residing in the accounts of a few hundred of the U.S.' superrich, not to mention the four million or so American households with net worth in excess of $1 million, or the eight million or so households worldwide, or the one billion people in total who live in the high-income countries with a combined annual income of some $30 trillion.
>
> (Sachs, 2005: 364)

For Sachs the achievement of the MDGs is a matter of global justice. Of course, there is a strong case that some of his earlier policies in advocating neoliberal shock therapy in vulnerable economies like Poland and Russia contributed to poverty and injustice. To go even further, some would argue that the current policies promoted by Sachs, which include funnelling money and development assistance into selected Millennium Villages in Africa, exacerbate unjust and unequal conditions (Wilson, 2014; cf. Moyo, 2009). Both these charges are vigorously rejected by Sachs, who continues his quest.

The MDGs officially came to a close in 2015, the target year by which point some of the goals had been met and others missed. They have now been replaced by a new set of 17 Sustainable Development Goals (SDGs), regarded by many as a much more ambitious set of targets which prioritize environmental issues including consumption of resources, as well as inequality, and peace and justice. The SDGs can be found at http://www.un.org/sustainabledevelopment/. While MDG1 sought to halve extreme poverty, SDG1 aims to 'end poverty in all its forms, everywhere'. Opinion is divided on whether this is a sign that the international community is rising to meet the challenge of global justice, or whether this is hubris on a planetary scale (Death and Gabay, 2015). These debates about the means and ends of global justice are not easily concluded, and they may be essentially contested and thus fundamentally irreconcilable. But as noted above it is important for philosophers of global justice to consider arguments, examples and policies which challenge our view of the world. Most observers can find something to challenge them in the debates around the MDGs and SDGs.

Another challenging set of issues are raised by policies pursued in the name of global justice during times of war and conflict. The next section turns to the invasion of Afghanistan and post-conflict attempts to build a stable and just state and society.

STATEBUILDING IN AFGHANISTAN

On 7 October 2001, the United States officially launched Operation Enduring Freedom with the assistance of the United Kingdom and invaded Afghanistan, quickly driving the Taliban regime from power. This was in direct response to the 9/11 attacks in the United

States, in which four commercial passenger jets were hijacked by al-Qaeda and crashed into the twin towers of the World Trade Center and the Pentagon. The refusal of the Taliban regime to extradite Osama Bin Laden for his role in the attacks precipitated the invasion of Afghanistan, first by special forces troops, then later by troops authorized by the United Nations and, after 2003, NATO. The involvement of NATO lasted until 28 December 2014, becoming one of the longest conflicts in US history. Tens of thousands of people have been killed in the conflict, the majority Afghan civilians.

Global justice philosophers have a number of criteria for determining whether a war is just or not. These are usually categorized as concerning *jus ad bellum* or the right to go to war, and *jus in bello* or the right conduct within war. The criteria for *jus ad bellum* include just cause, right intention, probability of success, and last resort. Opinions on the 'justness' of the Afghan invasion are varied, but many would accept that the aim of holding Bin Laden responsible for his role in 9/11 constituted a just cause. The stated intentions of the allies shifted between obtaining justice for 9/11, destroying a hated Taliban regime, and improving the conditions of the Afghan people, particularly women. Many doubted the probability of meaningful, lasting success, given the long history of unsuccessful superpower conflicts with Afghanistan, but the overwhelming force and technical superiority of the NATO forces did seem to suggest that defeating the Taliban and finding Bin Laden was possible. The speed of the invasion in the aftermath of 9/11 meant that few accepted the invasion was a 'last resort'; President Bush and Secretary of Defence Donald Rumsfeld were well known to have demanded a quick intervention to demonstrate a strong response to an attack on US soil. The sanction of the war by the United Nations indicated that the international community accepted the US case for war, at least to some extent.

The criteria for *jus in bello* include a distinction between combatants and non-combatants, proportionality, military necessity, fair treatment of prisoners of war and the avoidance of 'evil' weapons such as mass rape or biological warfare. On these criteria many criticisms have been made about the conduct of NATO in Afghanistan, including the targeting of civilians, as well as broader allegations about the conduct of the global war on terror, including the use of torture and detention without trial in Guantanamo Bay. These debates – encompassing both ethical principles and strategic considerations of national interest and efficacy – have repeatedly resurfaced throughout the war and the accompanying statebuilding project.

For the purposes of our discussion, the statebuilding project in Afghanistan raises some of the most interesting questions of justice. Many global justice philosophers, including figures like Rawls and Miller, argue that basic conditions of justice include the rule of law, political and civil rights, and a state able to ensure security for its population. These have been precisely the terms in which attempts to build a secure state in Afghanistan after the fall of the Taliban regime in late 2001 have been justified. As Francis Fukuyama (2004: 3) argues, 'The problem of weak states and the need for statebuilding have thus existed for many years, but the September 11 attacks made them more obvious'. The war in Afghanistan quickly evolved to become a counter-insurgency operation, and an attempt to promote both development and security in a war-torn region. Some justified this in terms of United States or western security: a stable Afghanistan made the world a safer place. For many, however, the argument quickly became couched in civilizing terms: Afghanistan under the Taliban had been a terrible place to be a women, to be gay, or to be secular or a religious minority, and the regime had struggled to achieve basic standards of living for its population. The invasion therefore offered a chance for security, development, and justice; dealing with an 'outlaw state', in Rawlsian terms. As Laura Bush explained in her radio address to the American people on 17 November 2001: 'Civilized people throughout the world are speaking out in horror—not only because our hearts break for the women and children of Afghanistan, but also because in Afghanistan, we see the world the terrorists would like to impose on the rest of us' (in Hirschkind and Mahmood, 2002: 341–2).

There are some obvious flaws with this argument, most notably that there are many other regimes around the world which also oppress their populations but do so with western support rather than invasion and statebuilding. Saudi Arabia and the Israeli occupation of Palestine are two obvious examples, but there are many others. The invasion of Afghanistan was clearly motivated primarily by the US desire for retributive justice after 9/11, and broader civilizing, developmental narratives only grew stronger at a later stage. The probability of achieving meaningful development by military means can also be debated, and the empirical efficacy of the occupation of Afghanistan is also contested by many. As put vividly by Hirschkind and Mahmood (2002: 341), writing at the very early stages of the conflict:

> In the crusade to liberate Afghan women from the tyranny of Taliban rule, there seemed to be no limit of the violence to which Americans were willing to subject the Afghans, women and men alike. Afghanistan, so it appeared, had to bear another devastating war so that, as the *New York Times* triumphantly noted at the exodus of the Taliban from Kabul, women can now wear *burqas* 'out of choice' rather than compulsion.

One of the empirical points made in an article in the *New Yorker* was that despite the rhetoric about the US invasion saving Afghan women from an oppressive regime, when it came to rural, uneducated Afghan women, Taliban rule reflected broader social norms. Thus, 'the Taliban has scarcely altered the lives of uneducated women, except to make them almost entirely safe from rape' (in Hirschkind and Mahmood, 2002: 346).

It is certainly hard to argue that Afghanistan presents a compelling case of the success of international statebuilding in action. Despite the election of Hamid Karzai as president in 2004, the Taliban insurgency continued and required an increase of international troops in 2006. Following the assassination of Bin Laden in Pakistan in 2011 international troops began to withdraw, but the state they left behind has been described as a 'phantom state' (Chandler, 2006: 43–4), with international legal sovereignty but lacking domestic legitimacy, and having largely ceded policy control to international institutions. The Afghan government under Karzai acquired a reputation for being one of the most corrupt in the world, and in 2015, after over a decade of international occupation, Freedom House (2015) rated it 6 out of 7 for civil liberties and political rights (where 1 is the best and 7 is the worst). Deadly attacks against journalists were on the increase and women's rights were on a downward spiral.

Despite the manifold difficulties of statebuilding as illustrated in Afghanistan, there are those who argue that societies have a duty to help other populations elsewhere in the world, and this should be done by force if necessary. At the UN World Summit in 2005 the international community unanimously approved the concept of the 'Responsibility to Protect', or R2P, which held that sovereignty entailed not only rights but also responsibilities, specifically a state's responsibility to protect its people from *mass atrocities* and in particular *genocide, war crimes, ethnic cleansing, and crimes against humanity* (Orford, 2009; Pattison, 2010). Where a state was unable or unwilling to protect its people, it was argued, the responsibility should shift to the international community to assist. This could be with the consent of the recipient state or, ultimately, the principle of non-intervention (a basic tenet of the United Nations and the international community) could be supplanted by the international responsibility to protect.

While the invasion of Afghanistan was not justified in these terms the invasion of Libya to overthrow Colonel Gaddafi in 2011 was. Moreover, some theorists of development have expanded upon Rawls' notion of a duty of assistance to argue for the role of military intervention in a developmental context. One of the most well-known is Paul Collier, an Oxford-educated economist who worked in the World Bank and has advised governments and international organizations. In *Bottom Billion: Why the Poorest Countries Are Failing and What Can Be Done about It*, he makes the case that while aid can help some countries at some times, it is not the panacea for development. It can also make some problems worse, such as corruption and bad governance. Collier tends to explain underdevelopment more through 'internal' than 'external' causes: bad governance, bad policy-making, greedy, ignorant or psychopathic political elites (2007: 4). So what can 'we' do if we want to help those countries at the bottom when their own leaders are usually one of the reasons they are in so much trouble? Collier considers a number of options, including aid, legal reforms, and trade policy. But one option is military intervention; in fact he devotes a whole chapter to it.

Writing in 2007, Collier admits that the legacy of the invasion of Afghanistan and Iraq in 2001 and 2003 make it hard to defend the prospect of military intervention for developmental purposes. Both societies remained violent and unstable despite years of statebuilding after the initial military victories. But he points to other examples which show the potential of well-targeted military intervention. His key case is Sierra Leone, in which a long-running and very violent civil war was ended by British military intervention in 2000 and subsequent peacebuilding which has prevented a recurrence of armed violence, at least so far. For Collier, 'Operation Palliser was brilliant, and the British army can be proud of its contribution to the development of Sierra Leone' (2007: 128; cf. Denney, 2011). Moreover, he suggests that the absence of international military intervention in 1994 during the Rwandan genocide, when 800,000 to one million people were slaughtered at the direct instigation of the Hutu regime, was one of the disasters of the twentieth century and a clear case of international injustice (Collier, 2007: 126). Thus, he concludes, despite the cases of Afghanistan and Iraq, the other examples show 'we should intervene, but not necessarily every-where' (2007: 128).

The merging of development and security narratives here is simul-taneously enthralling and troubling. In moments like the months post-9/11 it seemed as though both liberals and conservatives could agree that a US invasion of Afghanistan was justified. It would make the west safer (so appealed to self-interest) and it would help to free and empower a downtrodden population (so appealed to concep-tions of justice). The geopolitics and emotion of the period meant objections to either logic were hard to voice. It would later emerge that the success in both developmental and security terms was ques-tionable at best, and some profound injustices certainly occurred during the decade and a half (and ongoing) global war on terror. In this light it is easy to see how critical theorists have castigated liberals for allowing developmental interventions to become simply a means of 'securing the Western way of life' (Duffield, 2007: 2; see also Chandler, 2006; Denney, 2011).

A CRISIS OF GLOBAL JUSTICE?

These two examples are some of the most high-profile public policy issues which raise fundamental questions of global justice: what duties do we have to help distant strangers? The MDGs have dominated the discourse and practice of development since the year 2000, and have determined how aid money is spent, and how people think about the causes of poverty. The MDGs have attracted criticism for both the aggressive promotion of a liberal conception of development, and for failing to tackle issues of inequality, climate change and environmental degradation, corporate crime and corruption, and so on. International efforts to build stronger states can claim some (partial) successes in places like Sierra Leone and East Timor (see Denney, 2011; Orford, 2009), but the legacy of western intervention in Afghanistan, Iraq and Libya is more troubling.

As such, do these cases signal a crisis in and for global justice? This question can be addressed in a number of ways. First, the continued existence of injustice, and the failure of political measures to achieve greater justice, are hardly a crisis for theorists and philosophers. The existence of injustice makes the need for continued thought about what justice is and how it might be best realized even more necessary. Similarly, the problems associated with particular policies such as the MDGs or statebuilding in Afghanistan might arise for a number of reasons. These policies may have been motivated by other considerations which ultimately took precedence over questions of justice. They may have been implemented badly or unwisely, and so failed in their aims. Or other factors could have intervened, making their success more complex than initially hoped.

As such it is clearly a stretch too far to lay the problems in world politics at the door of the philosophers of global justice. However, as noted at the start of this chapter, moral principles are no good if they do no good. Theorists of global justice have always made claims about effectiveness as well as moral principles. So it is important to make enquiries both into whether policies were informed by or espoused principles of justice, and whether they did any good. Have the MDGs made the world a better place? Did attempts to promote democracy and women's rights in Afghanistan have a positive or negative effect? These questions are empirically complex and involve counter-factual assessments: what would have happened if the intervention had not happened, or had taken a different form? It is normatively complex too: what do we mean by better, and better for whom? Ultimately, perhaps, many advocates for global justice – liberals and radicals, theorists and activists, politicians and citizens – may conclude that for all sorts of reasons the optimism that characterized the 1980s was replaced by a resurgence of self-interested realism in the 2000s. The decade of democratization, good governance, and multilateralism was replaced by a decade of war, terrorism, economic crisis, fragmenting governance and new looming problems such as climate change. From this perspective, perhaps global justice is in crisis?

Finally, a third way to think about a possible crisis in global justice concerns the intellectual sphere of academic debate and inquiry. To put things very crudely indeed, one way of telling the story of the last fifty years of political theory is that from the 1950s to the 1980s the liberal philosophers of global justice were often aligned against political realists and conservatives, marching alongside radical movements in civil society and the struggles for decolonization, post-racialism and women's liberation. By the 1980s the ideological 'end of history' had arrived, pluralist democracy and human rights had triumphed, and philosophically-speaking everyone was a liberal. The new orthodoxy gave rise to new challenges, however, and new social movements emerged that were deeply critical of liberal assumptions about individuality, rationality and truth. Postcolonial and poststructuralist theorists pronounced the 'death of the subject' and the need to provincialize Europe. In the new millennium it is less clear that liberals are on the side of the radical, counter-cultural struggles. In the hands of some of those profiled in this chapter – Jeffrey Sachs, Paul Collier, Francis Fukuyama – liberal political theory has been used to justify wars, dislocation of rural populations in the name of modernization, and vicious cultural denunciations of other religions and other ways of life. These writers, all western, English-speaking men, are passionate believers in the truth of their values and their analysis. They do not take kindly to criticism. When questioned about his policies in Africa at a lecture in 2011, Sachs responded that such criticism was a sign of 'immoral ignorance because . . . issues of life and death carry a moral burden to know what you're talking about' (in Wilson, 2014: 68). Collier (2008) has dismissed criticisms of commercial industrial agri-culture and genetic modification as romantic populism symptomatic of western privilege, with little time for the many indigenous and rural movements campaigning against the control of seeds and land by international agro-corporations (see Chapter 6, and Clapp, 2012).

For some observers, therefore, there is a curious and frustrating lack of diversity within both the global justice debates in philosophy, and within the policy debates informed by liberal theorists. To many activists, as well as theorists from other traditions, there seems to be an unwillingness to debate or fundamentally question some of the basic assumptions of the liberal worldview (despite the robust debates we have already explored in earlier chapters). If true – and for the moment we merely raise this as a question rather than claim it to be an accurate portrayal of the field – then this would also constitute a type of crisis for global justice theory. For this reason the next two chapters explicitly seek to broaden the conversation about global justice, while also building upon and extending many of the debates already broached in previous chapters. The next chapter does so by considering some of the charges against mainstream global justice philosophy, and then looking at some activist campaigns for global justice whose inclusion has the potential to admit more diversity to the discussion. Chapter 6 then considers how theorist-activists engage with questions of global justice which start from very different normative positions to the liberal theorists predominantly discussed so far in this book.

5

GLOBAL JUSTICE IN MOVEMENT AND PRACTICE

THIS CHAPTER . . .

. . . explores the charge that the dominant philosophical and empirical traditions of global justice theorizing – as explored in the preceding chapters – are parochial and even Eurocentric and do not adequately reflect the concerns of the Majority World. The chapter then considers one line of response to such a critique, which is to consider more closely some of the most prominent activist movements and struggles around the world which are campaigning on the basis of global justice. This includes movements for historical reparations and debt forgiveness, climate and environmental justice, anti-racist movements, divestment and empowerment campaigns. These movements are interesting because few would describe themselves as part of the liberal political tradition, yet, their struggles have many points of connection with the global justice debates discussed in earlier chapters. Examining their interpretations of global justice and exposing these points of connection and tension with the mainstream theories of global justice, will help reflect on the degree to which these theories really are parochial or Eurocentric.

EUROCENTRIC THEORY?

For philosophers and theorists of global justice, it is important to show that their conceptions of justice are universal rather than partial; indeed it is a central claim of most theorists of justice that all people should be treated fairly and the right to justice does not depend on where you happen to be born or what religion you are. As discussed above, Rawls' veil of ignorance is intended precisely to overcome the limitations and constraints of rank, geography, wealth, gender and so on. Despite this, many theorists have argued that the dominant traditions of global justice theorizing are parochial, i.e. they are focussed on a narrow and exclusive set of concerns, they speak in a language only understood by a small group of English-speaking western academics, and their principles are inherently biased or prejudiced against whole swathes of the global population (see, for example, Inayatullah and Blaney, 2004; Ling, 2014; Shilliam, 2011; Spivak, 1988). Indeed, some argue that dominant traditions are Eurocentric in that they assume European values are global values and that European models of politics, society and the economy are either superior to or foreshadow the rest of the world. John Hobson (2012: 1), for example, argues that much of international political theory tends to 'parochially celebrate and defend or promote the West as the proactive subject of, and as the highest or ideal normative referent in, world politics'. These are serious allegations which require careful consideration, study and unpacking. While there are no easy answers, doing so can enrich the broader global justice debate.

One of the first objections to much academic theorizing about global justice is that it is written in a language most people cannot understand and that it is removed from the day-to-day concerns of most of the global population. While English is one of the most widely spoken and read languages worldwide, it is the native language of only 5.5 per cent of the world's population. Mandarin and Spanish have more native language speakers than English, and native speakers of Hindi, Arabic, Portuguese and Bengali combined outnumber native English speakers by a ratio of almost 3:1. However, in order to participate in the mainstream global justice debates discussed so far in this book (and, of course, to read this book), you need to be pretty fluent in English. Moreover, the register and level of the debate requires more than a conversational command of the language; most texts on global justice expect a university education in the humanities or social sciences and a familiarity with a canon of authors ranging from Greek antiquity to contemporary (western) politics and philosophy. For the 67 per cent of the global population without higher education in 2013, or even the 80 per cent of the global population whose average individual wealth is $3,851 per adult, the debates of global justice philosophers appear almost completely inaccessible, confined to a tiny circle of almost entirely western-educated, English-speaking, university academics (many of whom seem to be white and male). It is evident that global justice philosophers cannot claim to be representative of what some people refer to as the 'Majority World' (Chaturvedi and Doyle, 2015; Munck, 2013) or the 78 per cent of the global population who live outside the OECD.

This criticism, while an important reminder of the privilege reflected in the fact that we are able to read (and write) this book, is not generally regarded as a serious philosophical weakness for global justice theorizing itself. It does not make global justice theory Eurocentric, except from the standpoint of the identity of most of its authors (see Longhurst, 2015). The inaccessibility of the academic debates is rather seen as a regrettable feature of the unjust and unequal world in which we live, one which global justice philosophers seek to redress (or provide guidance on how to redress) in their work. Writers like Rawls, Nussbaum and Pogge would love more people to be able to engage with and critique their work. Indeed, Thomas Pogge has led the work of Academics Stand Against Poverty that seeks to promote greater access to education and progressive policy reform on poverty and development goals.

LINGUISTIC JUSTICE

The question of linguistic justice is in many respects peripheral to the global justice debate, while in the context of the wider field of (international) political theory it tends to be arguments about language

(Continued)

(Continued)

speakers' rights that are given most attention – often as part of a wider discussion about multiculturalism. One of the most significant, recent contributions to this field comes from the Belgian philosopher Philip Van Parijs (2012), and he is particularly concerned with issues of equality around the English language. He supports the proliferation of English as the global lingua franca because of the benefits accrued by global society in having a common language, such as increased solidarity. However, he is concerned with the way in which this will unfairly benefit native English speakers. Therefore, much of his work is given to detailing policies that can make good for this unfair distribution, encouraging opportunities for non-native speakers to acquire the language and ensure greater equality of opportunity in the global context.

Van Parijs recognizes the problem that languages carry with them symbolic value that can lead to linguistic conflicts where equality of dignity is at stake, and his response is to support the principle of linguistic territoriality, by which means official languages are respected on the basis of reciprocity. In this regard he has little to say to speakers of minority languages, whom he considers to be facing the inexorable forces of vanishing linguistic diversity. This attitude reflects a prevailing current in these debates that languages are instrumental in value, a good that is separable from the individual, and that special status is to be accorded to the languages of political communities – in particular states. Indeed, few scholars have made the case for conserving minority cultures and languages because of their intrinsic value; important exceptions include Albert Musschenga (1998) and Ngũgĩ wa Thiong'o (1986). Those who campaign for the protection of the world's 7,000 languages see the relationship very differently, comparing endangered languages to endangered species (Campbell, 2012) and lamenting the possibility that between 50 per cent and 90 per cent of these languages could be extinct by the end of the century (it is estimated a language 'dies' once every 3 months).

Although the majority of those languages that tend to be under threat or nearly extinct are in the Global South, the case of linguistic justice is particularly interesting as it cuts across what we might call the traditional in-out divide in the global justice debate – where global injustice is largely if not exclusively seen as something that occurs outside the developed world. This is because there are many minority languages within states in the Global North which also face a perpetual struggle for equal recognition and status. The United Kingdom is no exception in this case, with English on one count being one of 11 'indigenous' languages. There have been innumerable activist campaigns defending some of these languages, some of the most high-profile being those that started in earnest in Wales in the early 1960s with the group *Cymdeithas yr Iaith* (The [Welsh] Language Society).

One of the most interesting aspects of their campaigning with respect to this chapter is the manner in which it was inspired directly by certain philosophical arguments, particularly those put forward by a well-respected academic of the period, J.R. Jones. He was the head of philosophy at Swansea University, world-renowned as one of the foremost centres for Wittgensteinian philosophy, and Jones' philosophical perspective on language took a different approach to the liberal view, reminiscent to some degree of Wittgenstein's emphasis on language as delineating the limits of our world. Jones conceived of language as constitutive of identity and also constituting what we might describe as a 'lifeworld' (*bychanfyd*). Rather than being symbols for objects already complete with meaning, language is seen as creating and defining one's reality through communal and historical processes of linguistic development – in Jones' view interpenetrating with the material, geographical surroundings (1966). Language death on this account is interpreted as the death of a 'lifeworld' or a way of being – something to be lamented and guarded against in a similar fashion to the weakening of biodiversity due to species extinction, for example.

This view of the intrinsic value of language has very different philosophical roots to the kind of instrumental view of language – as a means of communication – that is often implicit in some liberal perspectives and which can be traced back to John Locke (Phillips, 1993: 5–8). Language activists in many societies will face these sorts of philosophical and ideological objections to their campaigns. For example, 'protectionist' policies to guard against the dilution of a language community – with impacts for various issues including housing policy – are accused of being illiberal and anti-capitalist. Moreover,

(Continued)

(Continued)

certain prejudices in favour of the assimilatory requirements of the nation-state run deep – often connected to the colonial impulse – with priority given to the need to absorb certain languages and cultures in order to promote unity over minority concerns (Mill [1862] 1991: 314).

A far more serious philosophical critique is that the ideas and values themselves which run through global justice debates are inherently parochial or Eurocentric. Some frame this in terms of the problems left undiscussed or invisible. Aakash Singh Rathore (2012: 164) notes that Indian untouchables (or Dalits) constitute some 10 per cent of the global chronic poor, and thus should be a central problem for global justice philosophers. But few theorists discuss or even mention them, even in Amartya Sen's 500-page book *The Idea of Justice*. Feminist theorists like Cynthia Enloe (2014), Catherine Eschle (2001), Marianne Marchand (2005) and Spike Petersen (2005) have asked 'where are the women' in discussions about global justice and argue that patriarchal structures and knowledge practices have rendered many women's issues and concerns marginal in mainstream global justice philosophizing (notwithstanding the contributions of thinkers like Nussbaum, Fraser and Jaggar, discussed earlier). Theorists interested in indigenous peoples and other historically marginalized communities – such as Australian Aboriginals or the Basarwa (also known as San Bushmen) in Botswana – have made similar claims that the sorts of concerns and issues which animate their communities are largely invisible in global justice theorizing.

This is a powerful criticism, and the evidence is often there in black and white. Rawls mentions sexual discrimination only once in *TJ*. Pogge does not mention any world religion apart from Christianity in *World Poverty and Human Rights*. Nussbaum fails to mention indigenous peoples in *Frontiers of Justice*. Of course, not every thinker can cover every topic, but still the field as a whole is remarkably dominated by the sorts of concerns which have traditionally absorbed the attention of white English-speaking professors: war, taxation, wealth redistribution, political rights, freedom of speech, and so on. On the other hand, this critique has an easy response. 'Well, I may not have discussed it yet', the (white, male) global justice theorist can respond, 'but you certainly should, and my theories will help you to think about it'. This response argues that there is nothing inherent in theories of global justice which prevent them from being applied to cases of injustice involving women, indigenous peoples, or Dalits. Moreover, as we have seen in previous chapters, increasingly many philosophers from within mainstream traditions have considered these questions in some depth.

The most powerful, and most fiercely resisted, line of critique is one which argues that the mainstream traditions of global justice theorizing are inherently (and perhaps irretrievably) parochial and Eurocentric. For Rathore, for example, the real problem is not that Sen doesn't discuss untouchables. This is just a symptom of how Sen, and other philosophers as well, define the concerns of *global* justice and *local* politics. Rathore suggests that the distinction between global justice issues and local/social justice issues is 'unstable', and theorists might be more useful if they ceased their 'romantic' search for grand universal formula and solutions and started working on specific and local problems like the status of untouchables in India. Dipesh Chakrabarty (2000: 7) has argued that the basic intellectual building blocks of modernity, the ideas of progress and development, are characterized by deep-seated assumptions of the dictum 'first in Europe, then elsewhere'. In both liberal and Marxist intellectual traditions, he argues, these concepts are seen as essentially universal, but they begin in Europe and 'thence' spread to the rest of the world.

THE ICC AND AFRICAN JUSTICE

In October 2015 the African National Congress (ANC), South Africa's ruling party, the party of Nelson Mandela, the Freedom Charter, and the hero of global justice activists during the anti-apartheid struggle, voted to leave the International Criminal Court (ICC) and lead an African walkout. Why is one of the world's most famous liberation

(Continued)

(Continued)

movements, who crafted a Bill of Rights recognized as one of the most progressive in existence, so at odds with one of the premier institutions of international criminal justice? The answer is connected to allegations that the institutions of global governance are racist and Eurocentric (Clarke, 2009).

Although the Rome Statute which founded the ICC was signed by 22 African nations, South African leaders spoke for many others in Africa when they accused the court of having 'lost direction' and disproportionately targeting African leaders (Pizzi, 2015). The court has only ever managed successful prosecutions against African citizens, and has brought charges against a number of sitting heads of state, including Omar al-Bashir (Sudan) and Uhuru Kenyatta (Kenya). African critics of the court note that many other individuals and leaders worldwide flaunt human rights and abuse their populations, and leaders of powerful countries like Israel, the United Kingdom and the United States have broken international law. But the United States does not recognize the ICC and western nations baulk at holding US citizens to account.

Defenders of the court argue 'it is only elites on the continent who have reason to fear the proper implementation of the rule of law' and suggest African countries should take pride in being willing and able to call on international courts to enforce human rights (Hoffman, 2016). In fact, all the ICC's investigations in Africa have occurred at the request of African states or courts, or the UN Security Council, and the appointment of Fatou Bensouda's as Chief Prosecutor of the ICC was seen to reflect the court's commitment to represent African voices for the victims of crimes committed in the continent (Lamony, 2013). Until a prosecution of someone other than an African takes place, however, it is likely than many will continue to associate international justice with white man's justice.

One of the most recent and thorough critical arguments that most international political theory is Eurocentric is presented by Hobson (2012), in a book which takes on a whole range of thinkers from Immanuel Kant, Adam Smith and Karl Marx, to John Rawls, Immanuel Wallerstein and Anne-Marie Slaughter. His argument is, first, that Eurocentrism is more than just racist imperialism. Rather, it can take racist or institutionalist forms, and be pro- or anti-imperialism (ibid.: 5). Thus, Eurocentrism can be paternalist or anti-paternalist, and has offensive or defensive variants. The core of Eurocentrism for Hobson is an implicit or explicit belief that western civilization is superior and its values are universal; the differences between thinkers in liberal or realist or radical traditions often come down to whether other civilizations and cultures are thought to be capable of following the example of the west, and how best to encourage or permit their development. The second strand of his core argument is that over the last 250 years international theory has largely constructed 'a series of Eurocentric conceptions of world politics' (ibid.: 1).

Hobson castigates US President Woodrow Wilson for his racist attitudes to the Japanese and black Americans, and realist theorists of international relations like Kenneth Waltz for his ethnocentrism and paternalism (and apparent failure to notice the violence caused by the so-called Cold War in Africa and Asia). But it is worth considering his critique of Rawls in more depth given its relevance for contemporary global justice debates. To Hobson, Rawls is a western-liberal who seeks to make everyone in the world more western and more liberal (ibid.: chs. 11 and 12). However, Hobson recognizes that Rawls is committed to articulating a genuinely universal theory of justice which does not impose European values on other peoples (ibid.: 287). Rawls does this, as we already know, by erecting a four-fold picture of world society: western, liberal societies; 'decent hierarchical societies' which are non-western; 'outlaw states' which are violent and autocratic; and 'burdened societies' which are anarchic and require assistance. Hobson is not convinced by Rawls' protestations that the second category of decent societies is a genuine alternative to western liberal societies. For Hobson, it is clear that Rawls sees the liberal West as the ideal type, and these other well-ordered societies are at best marginal examples which copy from and emulate liberal democracies in aspects of their tolerance and respect for law (ibid.: 288).

Moreover, on Hobson's reading, Rawls remains Eurocentric in five further ways (ibid.: 292–5). First, he demands that decent societies must separate church and state, throwing into doubt his tolerance of other major faiths like Islam, and there seems to be little requirement for western liberal societies to jettison their religion. Second, Rawls demands the imposition of free (and hence fair) trade. Hobson rejects the argument that free trade (i.e. reduction of tariffs and protection) is fair, especially in a context where western societies have benefitted from centuries of protection. Third, Rawls' Eurocentrism is paternalist because western liberals must work to bring eastern peoples into the sphere of civilization, either through duties of assistance (to burdened societies) or more forcible sanctions or armed intervention (against outlaw societies). Moreover, and this is Hobson's fourth point, there is a double standard in the treatment of outlaw states. While Rawls acknowledges that western states can behave in ways which are outside the law (such as the US and UK invasion of Iraq in 2003), other liberal states are not permitted to punish them or intervene. This stands in direct contrast to the duty to punish non-western outlaw societies. Finally, Hobson observes the similarities between the League of Nations Mandate System in the 1920s and 1930s, and Rawls' duty of assistance to burdened societies which ends when those societies are able to 'stand on their own feet'. This is, for Hobson, a quintessentially paternalist and Eurocentric view of world politics.

Rawls' advocates would no doubt rail against Hobson's arguments, and the debates between them and Rawls' critics, and between the global justice mainstream and those who have accused them of parochialism and Eurocentrism, are heated and ongoing. They will not be solved or concluded here. However, these debates raise interesting and important questions which will be discussed in two main ways in the remainder of this book, both of which aim to open up the field of global justice philosophy to new discussions, new participants, and new issues. The first direction to take in opening up this debate is to bring in the perspectives and concerns of actual movements and activists engaged in real struggles under the banner of global justice, while the second direction (in Chapter 6) is to consider alternative theories of justice. Following the first of these avenues, the rest of this chapter discusses what has become known as the global justice movement in the twenty-first century, and shows the points of connection to theoretical and philosophical debates on global justice. Some of the prominent concerns of these movements revolve around issues of coloniality and history, identity and subjectivity, and solidarity and recognition (and as such picks up some of the themes discussed in earlier chapters). Simply by engaging with and recording the struggles of people on the frontlines of campaigns against injustice, the conversation can become immediately more receptive to issues of gender, sexuality, race, religion, class and the multiplicity of types of violence. Opening up the conversation in this way helps to mitigate against presenting a parochial or Eurocentric view of the global justice debates.

THE GLOBAL JUSTICE MOVEMENT

The best way to introduce the movements for global justice is through two snapshots of protests in 2015. On 22 March 2015, students at the University of Cape Town (UCT) in South Africa occupied a building in which the UCT vice chancellor, Max Price, was addressing an audience on the subject of the statue of Cecil Rhodes on the campus. Rhodes, a nineteenth-century British business magnate and ardent imperialist who founded the colony of Rhodesia (which became Zimbabwe after independence), had become the target of contemporary student ire related to the treatment of black pupils, staff, and black history and culture at UCT. The statue had become a symbol of continued institutional racism in South Africa, and despite the UCT senate voting to remove it on 27 March, protests continued throughout the rest of the year over issues of racial justice, higher education fees, and the curriculum.

The second snapshot comes from 9 November 2015, when a march in Washington DC brought together hundreds of young people – the millennial generation – from the movements for climate justice, for black lives, for prison and fossil fuel divestment, for immigrant justice, and many other campaigns. It included civil disobedience by those who defined themselves as living 'at the intersection of the most pressing problems today' (see http://ourgenerationourchoice.org/). One organizing group, the Million Hoodies Movement, formed after a neighbourhood watchman shot and killed unarmed Black teenager Trayvon Martin on 26 February 2012 in Sanford, Florida, because he 'looked suspicious'. It describes itself as a Black and Brown-led racial justice network that builds next generation leaders to end mass criminalization and gun violence. We are a mass organization of human rights leaders confronting anti-black racism and systemic violence through grassroots organizing, advocacy, and education.

(http://millionhoodies.net/who-we-are/)

The march in Washington on 9 November 2015 was regarded as significant by activists from the participating movements because of the difficulties they had previously faced in overcoming their differences on issues like class, race and gender.

These two snapshots reveal much of the creativity and energy, as well as the tensions and problems, which characterize what is sometimes known as the global justice movement. First and foremost, they are examples of actual movements campaigning against lived injustices. Immanuel Wallerstein described the emergence of the global justice movement as the most significant counter-systemic political development since the end of the Cold War (in Routledge and Cumbers, 2009: 1). Theories of global justice should be able to help us understand them and their claims. Second, both involve intersecting concerns related to history, identity, and solidarity: who we were, who we are, and how we relate to each other. These concerns recur across many of the campaigns and movements under the global justice umbrella and the sections below will show how they link to and illustrate key problems in the global justice debates, such as recognition, structural injustice, and rectification. Third, both protests highlight the importance of questions of parochialism and Eurocentrism. The UCT protest took place in a traditionally white, English-speaking university at the tip of Africa, and involved mainly black students demanding the removal of a statue of a white European man from their campus: #RhodesMustFall. In its tactics and language it evoked the global Occupy! protests against inequality, neoliberalism, privatization and austerity which had sought to seize public spaces in 2011. The Washington DC protest took place at the seat of US government, but in a city to which Martin Luther King led his march on Washington and delivered his 'I have a dream' speech. The march in 2015 drew attention to the divided, unequal and unjust society within one of the riches countries on earth, in which the dream that all people 'will not be judged by the color of their skin but by the content of their character' has not yet been achieved.

The global justice movement is often described as a 'movement of movements' or a network of organizations and campaigns who loosely coalesce around opposition to war, neoliberal globalization, and the global governance of the World Trade Organization, International Monetary Fund, World Bank, and so on. The term has tended to replace others like the anti-globalization movement or the alternative globalization movement, but in truth there is no one singular or unified 'movement' (Klein, 2005; Monbiot, 2005). Routledge and Cumbers (2009: 18) suggest that the 'global movement' is 'composed of a diversity of struggles that are still territorially based, but are increasingly upscaling their actions to become involved in broader spatial networks'. Those who mobilize under the banner of global justice tend to have a radical political outlook, and protest repertoires include marches, sit-ins and occupations, petitions (increasingly online), and mass gatherings such as at the World Social Forum (WSF; Della Porta *et al.*, 2006). Describing the history and key elements of the movement is highly political however, and revives some of the concerns about identity and Eurocentrism discussed above. Assuming that global justice struggles began with civil rights in the United States, or the anti-globalization movement was launched in Seattle in 1999 in protests against the World Trade Organization, could be seen as a form of Eurocentrism. The tendency of groups from the Global North to attract more attention for their campaigns is often resented as a form of injustice by groups and activists from the Global South (Starr, 2005: 10). Certainly, it is true that anti- and postcolonial movements have provided the traditions, language, ideology, numbers and impetus for much of the contemporary global justice movement, with prominent examples including landless peoples' movements (e.g. MST in Brazil), liberation struggles (e.g. the anti-apartheid movement in South Africa), ecological movements (e.g. the Indian Chipko movement), indigenous and territorial struggles (e.g. the Zapatistas in Mexico), democracy movements (such as the National League for Democracy and their president Aung San Suu Kyi in Burma), and trade union federations (e.g. the Congress of South African Trade Unions).

THE WORLD SOCIAL FORUM

The first WSF was held in Porto Alegre, Brazil, in January 2001, and was organized by groups including the French Association for the Taxation of Financial Transactions for the Aid of Citizens (ATTAC) and sponsored in part by the Brazilian Workers Party. It was intended to provide a space to meet, build solidarity, and discuss alternatives under the banner 'another world is possible'. It was conceived as a grassroots alternative to the World Economic Forum, an elitist and restricted event for the wealthy and powerful held in January each year in Davos, Switzerland.

The WSF does not play a representative role, and it makes no recommendations or formal statements on behalf of participants. It does require 'that participants adopt a general opposition to neoliberal globalization and a commitment to non-violent struggle' (Smith, 2004: 414). These points are themselves contested though, as many participants have called for consensus positions in opposition to the 'Washington Consensus' on free trade or neoliberalism. Others have questioned the commitment to non-violence, arguing that anti-colonial resistance groups who use violence against oppressors, or against capitalism, should be embraced. Many of these tensions emerged at the Mumbai meetings of the WSF in 2004, which was dominated by opposition to the Iraq War and discussed to need to take a coordinated policy stance in response (Smith, 2004). Indian activists in Mumbai also spent much time educating other activists about the inequalities within India, including the problem of the status of Dalits.

After Mumbai the WSF returned to Brazil in 2005 and was then held simultaneously in Bamako, Caracas and Karachi in 2006. In 2008 and 2010 it was not held in any specific location but took place through a Global Call to Action heeded by thousands of autonomous local organizations, on or around 26 January. In 2013 and 2015 it was held in Tunis, reflecting the upsurge of popular movements known as the Arab Spring which toppled autocratic regimes in Tunisia, Egypt, Libya and Yemen from December 2010 to mid-2012.

The WSF has had a Charter of Principles since 2001, which include the following statements:

- #1: The WSF is an open meeting place for reflective thinking, democratic debate of ideas, formulation of proposals, free exchange of experiences and interlinking for effective action, by groups and movements of civil society that are opposed to neo-liberalism and to domination of the world by capital and any form of imperialism, and are committed to building a planetary society directed towards fruitful relationships among Mankind and between it and the Earth.

- #4: The alternatives proposed at the WSF stand in opposition to a process of globalization commanded by the large multinational corporations and by the governments and international institutions at the service of those corporations' interests, with the complicity of national governments. They are designed to ensure that globalization in solidarity will prevail as a new stage in world history. This will respect universal human rights, and those of all citizens – men and women – of all nations and the environment and will rest on democratic international systems and institutions at the service of social justice, equality and the sovereignty of peoples.

Global justice movements are usually characterized by a strong commitment to democracy, but in opposition to the narrow forms of participation and representation on offer in liberal democracy and through political parties (Young, 2001). Public assemblies have provided opportunities for experimentation with alternative forms of political expression and more direct models of democratic deliberation. In Occupy! this was achieved – even if only in a limited and still problematic way – through techniques like the human mic and the stack system. Such techniques are often designed to prevent the domination of traditionally privileged groups (educated, articulate, experienced activists; often white men; sometimes global justice philosophers) and allow a greater plurality and diversity of views. Such diversity does not need to end in consensus or decisions being taken (Pleyers, 2004). Critics have sometimes accused the global justice movement of being anti-political for not forming or supporting political parties, and not articulating manifestos for government (cf. Gill, 2005: 156–7; Klein, 2005: 162). Rather than being anti-political, however, such movements can be better conceived as pursuing a different model of politics than is the norm within liberal democracy. This alternative model is sometimes described as anarchic, prefigurative, popular or from the grassroots (Della Porta et al., 2006: 231; Holloway, 2005).

TIMELINE: KEY EVENTS FOR
THE GLOBAL JUSTICE MOVEMENT

1 January 1994 – the North American Free Trade Agreement (NAFTA) came into effect and on the same day the Zapatista Army of National Liberation went public and declared war against the Mexican state. It sought to create, with some success, a liberated zone in Chiapas.

10 November 1995 – execution of Ken Saro-Wiwa and the Ogoni 9 in Port Harcourt, Nigeria, by the military regime after being involved in protests against the exploitation of the Niger Delta and its oil reserves by Shell.

30 November 1999 – at least 40,000 people protest against the WTO in Seattle, over the unjust impact of free trade policies, and clash with police forcing the suspension of the WTO meeting.

25 January 2001 – first WSF opens in Porto Alegre, Brazil, organized by groups including the French Association for the Taxation of Financial Transactions for the Aid of Citizens (ATTAC) and sponsored in part by the Brazilian Workers Party. It was attended by around 12,000 people.

20–21 July 2001 – 200,000–300,000 people march in Genoa in protest against the G8 meeting, with tempers fraught after the death of protestor Carlo Giuliani the previous day at the hands of the Italian police.

15 February 2003 – protests against the US and UK invasion of Iraq took place around the world, with some of the largest public demonstrations ever in cities like London and Rome.

26 January 2005 – opening of the largest WSF held in a single location took place, again in Porto Alegre, with 155,000 registered participants.

12 December 2009 – more than 30,000 demonstrators marched at the UN climate conference in Copenhagen calling for climate justice and stronger international action on greenhouse gas emissions. Danish police took nearly 1,000 protestors into custody and the conference ended in disappointment.

25 January 2011 – the 'Day of Revolt' in Egypt as thousands of people spill into the streets and head to Tahrir Square in opposition to the Mubarak regime, forcing his resignation less than three weeks later.

17 September 2011 – Occupy Wall Street begins in Zuccotti Park, New York. A month later there were Occupy! protests underway in more than 80 countries and nearly 1,000 cities, all calling for greater democracy, equality and global justice.

Discussions of the global justice movement from more activist and social movement literature, as well as traditions of radical or continental political theory, have tended to emphasize the aesthetic, expressive and emotional dimensions of the movement. Questions concerning democracy, voice, identity and violence are more prominent than in most mainstream liberal variants of global justice philosophy. Stephen Gill, reflecting on the Seattle protests in 1999, sees the emergence of new forms of political agency involving new beliefs and values about human society. He concludes that

> the anonymous, unaccountable, and intimidating police actions seemed almost absurd in light of the fact that the protests involved children dressed as turtles, peaceful activists for social justice, union members, faith groups, accompanied by teachers, scientists, and assorted 'tree huggers' all of whom were non-violent.
>
> (2005: 154)

In fact, much academic reflection on these movements has devoted itself to questions such as 'who is the global justice movement?' This goes well beyond simply trying to identify the individuals involved in protests. Rather, theorists of these movements tend to reject the individualist approach of liberal theorists, and focus on collective categories like class, race, gender, religion and coloniality. This means that there is a more prominent focus on concepts like recognition and identity, as we have seen in some of the philosophers discussed in Chapter 3, rather than limiting questions of justice to distribution of goods between individuals (Burns and Thompson, 2013;

Fraser and Honneth, 2003; Fraser, 2008; Schlosberg, 2004). A basic concern for many of these movements – as seen in the examples of the 2015 protests in Cape Town and Washington with which this section started – is 'who counts as a legitimate political actor, or bearer of rights?' This concern arises because, whatever liberal theorists might say about the equality and universality of rights, in practice even liberal regimes have tended to exclude certain voices, or certain forms of expression (often deemed too emotional, irrational, uninformed, or unreasonable), from the domain of civil society (Young 2001). Children, people with mental illness, women, racialized groups, homosexuals, labourers or peasants, and many other groups have all been historically denied full rights of expression or political status, and in many cases these injustices continue albeit in more subtle forms. In this respect the concerns of many activists within the global justice movement reflect the issues raised by philosophers like Nancy Fraser (2008) or those within the dialogical cosmopolitan tradition (such as Culp, 2014).

The global justice movement, in practice, has been concerned with many very similar issues to those which have animated global justice philosophy. War, poverty, states, responsibility, harm, capabilities and so on are all issues that activists as well as philosophers think hard about. But the activists and philosophers involved in the various forms of the global justice movement raise some further issues which sometimes (not always) receive less attention in the academic discussions. Who gets to participate, and on whose terms? Who sets the rules? What forms of expression are permitted or valued? In what language? How did we get here? And how will we act together in the future? These questions can be grouped under the categories of history, identity, and solidarity, and the rest of this chapter uses these categories to explore a number of branches of the global justice movement in a little more detail.

HISTORY

The stories people tell reveal a lot about them, and certain stories crop up time and again (Ling, 2014). In the philosophical debate about global justice some of the most frequent stories date from classical Antiquity, such as Plato's cave, or medieval history, such as Rousseau's stag hunt. Contemporary philosophers of global justice such as Rawls and Singer, often use abstract thought experiments to simplify dilemmas and isolate crucial issues. Thus we are told simple parables about the cutting of cake (see Chapter 1) or traversing roundabouts (see Chapter 4).

In contrast, activists and theorists within the global justice movement might be more likely to tell stories about ancestral gods (Ling, 2014), colonialism (Césaire, 1972; Chakrabarty, 2000), racism (hooks, 1994), the late Victorian holocausts (Davis, 2001), or the genocidal wars of the twentieth century (Fanon, 2004). These stories might be more complex and contested, but they also have an immediacy and relevance that is sometimes not as clear in the more abstract philosophical thought experiments. Influenced by theorists of colonialism and postcolonialism, many activists in the global justice movement see our world not in terms of the gradual spreading of European civilization, liberal values and Enlightenment out towards the rest', but rather as the product of a violent clash between hitherto mutually coexisting and interrelating societies (Fanon, 2004; Loomba, 1998; Shilliam, 2011: 4). In this view, we are all postcolonial because the world in which we live is a product of colonial and imperial violence, as well as the legacies of political independence, economic dependency, colonialism of the mind, and so on (see Butt, 2009; Collste, 2015; Lu, 2011; Spivak, 1988; wa Thiong'o, 1986).

The starting point for many global justice movements, therefore, is not an abstract thought experiment or an attempt to determine true or reasonable principles of justice. Instead, the starting point is actually existing injustice: violence, harm, exploitation, dispossession, and cultural subjugation at the hands of a civilization and ideology which proclaims itself superior. Before we can even begin to talk about principles of justice or ideal theory, some restitution or recompense for the miseries caused in the process of the European Enlightenment is required. These concerns directly echo the discussions in Chapter 3 about theories of rectificatory justice (see Butt, 2009; Collste, 2015; Lu, 2010), as well as the notion of structural injustice associated with Iris Marion Young (2006).

One significant movement and campaign within the global justice movement which encapsulates some of these concerns is Jubilee 2000, an international coalition which called for the cancellation of Third World debt by the year 2000. It started from the perspective that the debt owed by the countries of the Global South to the North was unfair, 'odious' even, considered in the light of the history of the slave trade and colonialism. These crimes had never been compensated (awards of compensation at the abolition of slavery in the British Empire went to the slave *owners*, not to the slaves). These odious debts were also unreasonable given the coercive conditions under which loans were made, the high rates of interest imposed, and the fact that loans were often given to brutal dictators in reward for their support during the Cold War. Dictators – such as Mobutu Sese Seko in Zaire, or General Suharto in Indonesia – used the funds to arm their regime and suppress their people. Holding later democratic governments liable for the repayment of these debts seemed patently unfair to many activists and philosophers.

Early activism was often strongest in religious groups, and the name Jubilee 2000 came from the Biblical idea that the jubilee year, the fiftieth anniversary, is one in which debts are forgiven and lands are restored. Pogge has been a prominent voice in this campaign, deploying philosophical arguments to have an impact on real world politics. The movement gathered wider support, particularly from celebrities and musicians (famously Bono from Irish band U2, and Bob Geldof who had campaigned for food relief during the Ethiopian and Somali famines), and drew in a number of activist groups in countries around the world. At the meeting of the G8 in Birmingham in 1998 between 50,000 and 70,000 demonstrators participated in a peaceful protest to put debt relief on the agenda of Western governments. A worldwide petition received 24 million signatures, and G8 leaders committed themselves to cancelling more than $110bn of the debt of the 42 heavily indebted poor countries (HIPCs). Goal #8 of the Millennium Development Goals included targets of making 'debt sustainable in the long run' (8D) and cancelling official bilateral debt for the poorest countries (8B). Despite some successes the campaign for the relief of odious debt as a matter of justice, not of charity, continues.

The pressing need for global justice to address historic legacies takes other forms. In July 2013 a coalition of 15 Caribbean countries and dependencies resolved to 'set up national committees on reparations, to establish the moral, ethical and legal case for the payment of reparations by the former colonial European countries, to the nations and people of the Caribbean Community, for native genocide, the transatlantic slave trade and a racialized system of chattel slavery' (Pears, 2014). Reporters noted that this came less than a month after a £19.9 million landmark court settlement of the Mau Mau case, brought by five elderly Kenyans who were tortured by the British during the 1950s and won their case against the British Government. In response to the Caribbean case, the British Foreign and Commonwealth Office said: 'We do not see reparations as the answer. Instead, we should concentrate on identifying ways forward with a focus on the shared global challenges that face our countries in the 21st Century. We regret and condemn the iniquities of the historic slave trade, but these shameful activities belong to the past. Governments today cannot take responsibility for what happened over 200 years ago'. In contrast, global justice activists and campaigners would argue that given the benefits which have accrued over centuries to societies and individuals in Europe and America, and the corresponding harms done to individuals and societies in Africa, Asia and Latin America, some measure of restitution is the only just course of action. These campaigns have been led by activists, but philosophers have both participated in them and reflected in some depth on their ramifications for global rectificatory justice (see Collste, 2015).

IDENTITY

All the protests discussed so far in this chapter have included a dimension concerned with identity, and recognition of their particular circumstances and the local form of that injustice takes. Whether it is the case of the Indian Dalits or #BlackLivesMatter in the United States, landless peasants in Brazil or #RhodesMustFall in South Africa, questions of identity and subjectivity are crucial to many branches of the global justice movement. These concerns arose in Chapter 3 under the theme of recognition, but in this section we briefly profile one revealing example from Botswana which raises big philosophical questions about the meaning of global justice, the universality of rights, and the ends of development.

Botswana, in southern Africa, is a large and sparsely populated country with an economy reliant on diamonds, cattle, and tourism. The country has a reputation for good governance, sound economic management and a stable liberal democracy: there has been an uninterrupted multiparty democracy since independence in 1966 although the ruling party has never lost an election. The Kalahari desert covers much of the country, and there is a large indigenou population known variously as Bushmen, San peoples, Basarwa N/oake or Kwe, or 'Remote Area Dwellers' (Odysseos, 2011 Saugestad, 2001). The Central Kalahari Game Reserve 'was created in 1951 by the colonial administration with a view to conserve wild life fauna and flora, as well as to create a sanctuary for the Basarwa to continue their traditional way of life, unfettered by the encroachmen of cattle farmers from the dominant Tswana groups' (Molomo, 2008 169). Yet the modernizing and developmentally orientated govern ment have not been satisfied with this situation. In 2004 President Festus Mogae declared that 'rural poverty, no matter how romanti cized, is a condition, not a culture', and there have been attempts to relocate the Basarwa outside the CKGR as it deems their settlement to have 'no prospect of becoming economically viable' (Odysseos 2011: 441–3). This case has caused international outrage, and the Basarwa have been supported by indigenous peoples' movements and organizations such as Survival International who have argued that the relocation policy is 'cultural genocide' (Molomo, 2008: 170).

The government position is that the Basarwa deserve a proper modern life with amenities and schools, and that the CKGR should be preserved as a pristine wilderness for foreign tourists. Following a High Court ruling in 2006 that the relocation of the Basarwa was unconstitutional, the government acquiesced, but in a somewhat perverse turn chose not to replace the facilities (including water supplies) on which the Basarwa depended. In a series of complex legal manoeuvres between government and Basarwa lawyers, this was upheld by the High Court in 2010, before being subsequently over turned by the Court of Appeal in 2011 which ruled that the denial of the Basarwa's right to water amounted to 'degrading treatment' (Odysseos, 2011; Molomo, 2008).

The Government of Botswana has emphatically denied it is per secuting an ethnic minority; instead it argues forcefully and cogently that it does not recognize ethnic differences and instead treats all Batswana equally (in distinction to what it sees as apartheid policies of separate development). Thus it 'justifies its relocations of the Bushmen from the CKGR as part of its wider program of development and modernization as a progressive and modern state' (Odysseos, 2011: 442; see also Saugestad, 2001: 30). Its programme of social empowerment 'involved the full exercise of the Bushmen's citizenship rights on a par with all other citizens, and their use of social and welfare services' (Odysseos, 2011: 442). This reflects broader discomfort with the status of 'indigenous groups' in many African states. As Dorothy Hodgson (2009: 3) was told emphatically and frequently when conducting research in Tanzania, 'we are all indigenous in Africa'. The legacy of colonial and apartheid policies of separate development, group rights, and ethnic divide-and-rule (which has played out with tragic consequences in places like Rwanda in the genocide of 1994) means that advocating special rights for special communities is often deeply unpopular with African intellectuals and political leaders (Mamdani, 2001). For these reasons, a group of African states led by Namibia delayed the progress of the negotiation of the UN Declaration on the Rights of Indigenous Peoples, and eventually managed to negotiate substantial amendments to the text before it was agreed by the General Assembly in 2007 (Hodgson, 2009). Complex debates over the meaning of indigenous versus minority groups, involving questions of migration, 'first peoples', settler colonialism, and lifestyle, have meant that 'justice for the Basarwa' is a slogan which can be used in support of any number of positions within Botswana and the wider transnational campaign. The most articulate campaigners challenged fundamental modern values like democracy and development. For Aron Johannes, spokesman for the community, speaking in 1994: 'Development is meant for people who are bundled up and put in settlements' (Saugestad, 2001: 215). Saugestad (2001: 235) concludes that 'Indigenous people everywhere represent an inconvenient category for the administrative apparatus, and Botswana is no exception'.

This case raises questions of identity that pose particular problems for theorists of global justice. Who are the Basarwa? The government claims they are a category defined by poverty measures, whereas community spokesmen claim they are an indigenous people with particular traditions and lifestyles. But in a community with gendered and age-related inequalities, the question of who is able to speak as an authoritative representative of the Basarwa is also political and sometimes contested. Perhaps even more profoundly, parties in the debate disagree over whether the Basarwa are modern rights-bearing citizens (whom the state has a duty to educate, support, police and tax) or non-liberal subjects constituted according to different cultural values and ideological worldviews. These issues – who are the subjects of justice? – are therefore very immediate concerns for many global justice movements (Schlosberg, 1999: 67–8).

Such cases also raise potentially profound issues for philosophical advocates of recognition (Burns and Thompson, 2013; Fraser, 2008; Fraser and Honneth, 2003; Schlosberg, 1999) and dialogic cosmopolitanism (Culp, 2014; Dobson 2006, 2007; Forst, 2005, 2007; Linklater, 1998) discussed in Chapters 2 and 3. How is it possible to enable and facilitate the voice and participation of those who are poor, marginalized, dispossessed and alienated? What institutions of justice could possibly incorporate the Basarwa successfully? This concern is discussed by philosophers such as Iris Marion Young (2001) who concludes that ideological structures always effectively prevent some groups from speaking, and Gayatri Chakravorty Spivak (1988: 308) who famously concluded that 'the subaltern cannot speak'. Reflecting on the power of hegemonic discourses to reincorporate and 'speak for' marginalized groups such as third world women, she concludes somewhat bleakly that 'There is no virtue in global laundry lists with "woman" as a pious item' (1988: 308).

SOLIDARITY

Closely related to who we are is the question of who we choose to support politically. The concept of solidarity is a key feature of many global justice campaigns: the fourteen principles of the WSF end with the aim of 'building a new world in solidarity'. Traditions of solidarity have a long history for both right and left political ideologies, but the global justice movement traces its origins to the French Revolutionary declaration of fraternity, as well as the 'friendly societies' or trade unions through which working-class labourers supported each other (often paying for members' sick pay or funerals) and bargained collectively on pay and conditions (Calhoun, 2002; Routledge and Cumbers, 2009; Tarrow, 1998: 4; Thompson, 1964). Networks within the global justice movement often place a high value on mutual solidarity. One example is Friends of the Earth International, a network of nationally based environmental groups with a horizontal rather than hierarchical structure. Forging a common position while allowing for national and cultural differences can be difficult within such groups, especially in the context of the historical and identity-based tensions discussed above. Different Friends of the Earth groups have different ideas and priorities over issues like attitudes towards capitalism, corporate power, technology, and democracy, as well as differing strategies and tactics. At a heated biennial general meeting in Abuja, Nigeria, in October 2006, as disagreements over the types of democracy the organization wanted to promote in the world threatened to lead to lasting fractures, a Nigerian delegate brought the discussion to some kind of consensus with an appeal for negotiation and deliberation rather than heated personal attacks. 'We are heavily in solidarity in this room', he said. 'Our solidarity in not in doubt' (in Doherty and Doyle, 2014: 94).

The principle of solidarity has been an important element of boycott, sanctions and divestment campaigns within the global justice movement, according to the argument that groups committed to democracy and social justice should not buy products, invest in, or otherwise support institutions, governments of corporations who are infringing the rights of others. The most famous and controversial of these movement is the Boycott, Divest, Sanctions (BDS) campaign against the Israeli occupation of Palestine. Other campaigns have urged divestment from and sanctions against the apartheid regime in South Africa, Sudanese atrocities and genocide in Darfur, and the Burma regime, as well as products like tobacco, pornography and landmines. Hotel chains with poor labour practices have been targets in the United States, and the prison-industrial complex is the focus of another campaign.

The BDS campaign includes a call to boycott Israeli academic institutions, and the combination of accusations of Zionism and anti-Semitism, and the tensions of Middle East geopolitics together with questions of academic responsibility versus freedom of speech, have led to an incendiary debate (Barghouti, 2011; McMahon, 2014). The campaign focuses on Israel's violations of international law, as recognized by the United Nations, and the atrocities committed against Palestinian human rights, while refraining from officially supporting a particular solution to the conflict (McMahon, 2014: 74). Prominent intellectuals such as Naomi Klein, Noam Chomsky, Martha Nussbaum and Stephen Walt, and politicians such as George

Galloway and Tony Blair have weighed in on one side or other, and all fervently believe justice is on their side. One of the first calls for a boycott of the state of Israel came in 1948 from the Arab League but even earlier Palestinian Arabs living under British colonialism had privately boycotted Zionist businesses (Bakan and Abu-Laban 2009: 33–5). The contemporary movement has drawn more parallels with the anti-apartheid struggle however, and South African public figures such as Archbishop Desmond Tutu have compared Israel's treatment of the Palestinians to that of blacks in apartheid South Africa. Bakan and Abu-Laban (2009: 39) observe that 'the most comprehensive call for a global campaign for boycott, divestment and sanctions was launched in July 2005, by 170 civil society organisations within Palestine itself'. The 2009 meeting of the WSF issued a statement supporting the BDS campaign, and universities churches, trade unions and political parties have also joined in solidarity. In response to the war on Gaza in 2009 both Venezuela and Bolivia severed diplomatic relations with Israel. Despite this attempts to portray Israel as a 'world pariah' – or what Rawls might term an 'outlaw state' – have had limited effect on either Israeli policy, or the foreign policy of its most important ally, the United States (Barghouti, 2011: 15). Perhaps more importantly for the purposes of our discussion here, however, the campaign has been more effective in ensuring that any individual, company or state with connections to Israel has to make a decision: act in solidarity with the global justice movement and support the boycott, or cross the line and engage with the Israeli state. This has led to vicious condemnations on both sides, for students who boycott speakers from Israeli universities; for academics who attend conferences in Israel; charities who refuse to work with Israeli NGOs; and for musicians who play concerts in Jerusalem. In January 2014 actress Scarlett Johansson had a 'fundamental difference of opinion' (or a public row) with the charity Oxfam, for whom she had been an ambassador for eight years after she participated in an advert for the company Sodastream, an Israeli company operating in the West Bank (BBC, 2014).

One of the fastest growing divestment campaigns since 2012 has been against fossil fuel companies, particularly those drilling for coal, oil and gas (Grady-Benson and Sarathy, 2016; Klein, 2014 402–3; McKibben, 2012). Activists are demanding that institutional investors divest, or sell their investments, from stocks or portfolios which include companies who extract or burn coal, oil and gas. Early campaigns ran in 2011 in Swathmore College, the University of North Carolina at Chapel Hill, and University of Illinois Urbana-Champaign, and gathered momentum after Bill McKibben published a widely read *Rolling Stone* article in July 2012. Organized by groups like 350.org and the Divestment Student Network, it has been promoted not only by environmental groups but also by the Guardian media group, the Papacy and other churches, schools, universities and scientists, and political leaders around the world. At the UN Climate Change Summit in September 2014 more than 800 institutions and individual investors with more than $50 billion in assets promised to divest from fossil fuels. Overall, the movement claimed in January 2016 that 499 institutions had committed to divest a total of $3.4 trillion (see http://gofossil free.org/commitments/). This is hardly insignificant, especially when considering that the ten largest listed fossil fuel companies (including ExxonMobil, Shell, Sinopec and BP) had combined revenues of about $2.9 trillion in 2013 (Ansar *et al.*, 2013: 53).

The movement aims to stigmatize fossil fuel companies for their direct contribution to environmental injustice and dangerous climate change, and activists intend to do to Shell and Exxon what was done to tobacco companies in the 1990s: expose their distortions of scientific evidence and their donations to politicians to ensure favourable regulation. The logic here is similar to that in the BDS Israel campaign, to make socially responsible actors decide whether they are on the side of climate justice, or not. Archbishop Desmond Tutu (2014) has thrown his moral authority behind the fossil fuel campaign, calling for an apartheid-style boycott and declaring that people of conscience need to break their ties with corporations financing the injustice of climate change'.

In 2016 the fossil fuel divestment campaign had two main aims: to escalate civil disobedience in cities and on campuses across the world, and to build the case not just for divestment but for reinvestment in low carbon forms of energy or community projects in areas affected by the fossil fuel industry. According to one activist with Fossil Free Yale, interviewed in October 2015, this is about replacing the 'extractive economy' with a 'regenerative economy', shifting current forms of ownership by promoting 'an oppositional economy that challenge systems of greed and violence by creating more just forms of energy food, education, exchange and self-governance'. Such aims illustrate what solidarity means to many global justice activists: that the wealth which has been extracted from the Global South and poor communities, and used for centuries to perpetuate unjust policies and systems should now be put back into those communities and used to build more just, secure and sustainable places to live and work. The essence of this campaign is not charity, or efficient or profitable investment but justice. In this it is similar to the campaigns for debt relief and reparations for slavery discussed above, and it illustrates the argument deployed by philosophers such as Caney (2005) and Pettit (2010) who emphasize the importance of activists in securing greater environmental and social justice, even extending to civil disobedience.

JUSTICE AND POWER, ON THE PAGE AND THE STREET

In December 2015, delegates from all countries around the world met in Paris to discuss an international agreement on climate change Outside, activists marched under banners which read 'Climate Justice. Peace'. The eventual agreement received considerable praise from negotiation-watchers, as it represented the first genuinely global multilateral agreement to reduce greenhouse gas emission and tackle climate change. Activists from more radical climate justice movements were disappointed however (e.g. Reyes, 2015): the pledges made were insufficient to halt dangerous climate change there was no way of holding countries accountable for their promises; progress on new funding from the richer to the poorer countries to help mitigate and adapt to climate change was slow in materializing; and while the text recognized the importance of addressing the 'loss and damage' already caused by climate change, it explicitly stated that this recognition does not 'provide a basis for any liability or compensation'. There will be no reparations for the climate chaos already caused by centuries of burning fossil fuels, and the text didn't even mention fossil fuel. The Annex to the agreement noted 'the importance for some of the concept of "climate justice", when taking action to address climate change' (UNFCCC, 2015). The was the only reference to justice in over 30 pages, hardly a stirring endorsement of the centrality of justice to the negotiations.

Despite these disappointments, thanks to the efforts of thousands of committed campaigners in the global justice movement, issues of global justice have been brought to the forefront of global politics in every country and on every topic imaginable. Critiques of injustice are available in print, online, on the TV and radio, and in academic presses. And although some of these may well be disputed or rejected, as a direct result of these arguments, companies, political parties, and governments are being forced to publicly account for their actions and defend their policies according to criteria of fairness and responsibility. It is thanks to these activists that the debates of global justice philosophers have any political power or traction at all. One book (or even a journal special issue) on climate justice is easy to ignore, but over 300,000 people marching through the streets of New York for the People's Climate March on 21 September 2014 tends to get more attention.

More than just getting wider attention and translating philosophical arguments into political power, these movements prevent global justice debates from becoming too parochial or Eurocentric. While a march in New York gets more media coverage than one in Accra or Mumbai, any consideration of the actual campaigns for global justice has to acknowledge the diversity and range of participants and issues and values, from many different cultures around the world. The movements bring global justice out of the classroom and from behind the pay-per-view scientific publications, and into the everyday lives of the majority world. And as shown in this chapter, the issues of history, identity, and solidarity they raise have the potential to challenge traditions of liberal democracy and individual rights, adding a far more critical and revisionist aspect to what some have termed the 'third wave' of global justice philosophy (see Chapter 3). Of course, many global justice campaigners around the world are fighting precisely for the same liberal democracy and human rights enjoyed in the west. At the very least, however, acknowledging these movements and their particular contexts and concerns broadens the conversation – a conversation in which the philosopher may well challenge the activist about their most deeply held values, but which can also help to reinforce and buttress the ideas that provide springboards for action.

6

CHALLENGES FROM
ALTERNATIVE VISIONS
OF GLOBAL JUSTICE

THIS CHAPTER . . .

. . . explores the theories and activism of those within the global justice movement who advance alternative normative conceptions of justice, or alternative value systems, to those which dominate mainstream debates within liberal global justice theory. Of course, in some respects there are considerable similarities to positions and debates within mainstream political theory; the point of this chapter is to expand the conversation and find points of connection rather than establish a binary between liberal and alternative perspectives. Three specific issues or themes are considered: food sovereignty movements, campaigns for degrowth and ecocentric theorists. As such this chapter picks up some of the environmental issues first broached in Chapter 3 through the work of Simon Caney. Here the discussion is expanded and elaborated to show the ways in which the campaigns and beliefs of environmental activists and thinkers suggest new and more radical directions for the pursuit of global justice theorizing.

MELTING POTS AND SALAD BOWLS

The previous chapter started by considering the charge that global justice theory is parochial or Eurocentric. One response to that charge is to broaden the conversation to include a more diverse range of voices and movements, and the previous chapter looked at various branches of the global justice movement including the World Social Forum, indigenous peoples movements, and campaigns for reparations and divestment. As suggested however, one response to this charge from liberal theorists could be: 'Welcome! These are important new issues for global justice theory. Our existing frameworks, concepts and value systems will help you understand your struggles.' And, indeed, many social movements and radical struggles have found liberal theories of justice hugely empowering and liberating: campaigns for equal rights, freedom from state oppression, duties of responsibility to others, freedom of expression and religion, and so on, have been crucial tools in popular struggles for centuries (Clark, 2007; Keck and Sikkink, 1998). The work of the philosophers discussed so far in this book – Rawls, Pogge, Nussbaum, Sen, Fraser, Young and others – have contributed directly and indirectly to many radical movements.

Some theorists and activists, however, resist being incorporated so quickly into broadly liberal frameworks and discourses. From this perspective, rather than subsuming all struggles into a wider crusade for (liberal) justice, it is necessary to acknowledge the radical pluralism of competing, contrasting, sometimes overlapping campaigns for different forms of justice. Instead of viewing all new movements as additions to the melting pot, for example 'adding gender and stirring' (a charge which some might make against Nussbaum and even Jaggar's brands of liberal feminism), advocates of radical pluralism prefer to use the metaphor of the salad bowl: where differences could be interlinked, interwoven, without being fused or collapsed (Schlosberg, 1999: 94). Schlosberg (1999: 60) draws on traditions of pluralism in political theory – encompassing thinkers as diverse as Harold Laski, Michel Foucault, Richard Rorty, Chantal Mouffe, William Connolly and Iris Marion Young – to emphasize how 'contingency and the "plurality of reals" open up uncertainty and variability' in basic questions about the subjects and nature of justice. His version of critical pluralism has four starting principles. First, an agonistic respect for difference and multiplicity, together with the reciprocal assumption that 'we need not suffer fools, fascists, nor those who refuse to grant us recognition, gladly' (Schlosberg, 1999: 75). Second, the principle of intersubjective communication, or a process of communication and engagement which need not end in a Habermasian or rational consensus. Third, a form of deliberative or discursive democracy which allows for multiple meanings and value systems to be voiced and heard. Fourth, an extension of politics beyond the state and the public sphere, driven by social movements that continually open up new spaces for political engagement and contestation (Schlosberg, 1999: 91; see also Dryzek, 2006; Mouffe, 2005).

A key idea here, developed in a powerful article by Iris Marion Young (who we discussed in some detail in Chapter 3), is that processes of rational debate and reasonable deliberation may not exhaust the scope of valid politics or ethical engagement. Young stages a debate between a deliberative democrat and an activist. Activists engage in activities like 'picketing, leafleting, guerrilla theatre, large and loud street demonstrations, sit-ins, and other forms of direct action, such as boycotts. Often activists make public noise outside when deliberation is supposedly taking place on the inside' (Young, 2001: 673). The deliberative democrat is frustrated by this: the activist seems to be unreasonable. If they would just be quiet and respectful and join an intelligent debate, then rational deliberation will surely be able to resolve the concerns and come to a sensible consensus between all parties?

Young defends the activist stance of non-engagement on these terms in four steps. The first is that deliberative politics ignores the real world of structural inequality and power relationships, in which the powerful can manipulate institutions and debates. The activist points out that 'deliberation is primarily an activity of political elites who treat one another with cordial respect and try to work out their differences' (2001: 677). Such closed deliberations are not really democratic at all. To which the deliberative democrat must agree, and try to design institutions which are open to the widest range of potential participants, as Forst and Culp would advocate (see Chapter 2). At this point the activist raises another objection: in societies structured by deep social and economic inequalities, as in contemporary global politics, 'formally inclusive deliberative processes nevertheless enact structural biases in which more powerful and socially advantaged actors have greater access to the deliberative process and therefore are able to dominate the proceedings with heir interests and perspectives' (Young, 2001: 679). At this point, whereas some may disagree over the extent to which we have a duty to engage with unfair institutions and try to reform them, there s broad agreement that greater democratic access and openness to genuine deliberation is necessary.

But the activist has two further objections to participating in 'rational deliberation', even within open and inclusive institutions. First, the activist asserts that the institutional and political premises on which such deliberation takes place is inevitably biased towards existing power arrangements. The 'problem is not that policy makers and citizen deliberations fail to make arguments but that their starting premises are unacceptable' (Young, 2001: 683). Finally, even if deliberation could take place over issues which constitute the basic foundations and assumptions of society, the prospect of a free and level playing field for debate is blocked by the existence of, in Gramscian terms, 'hegemonic' beliefs which are largely unquestioned – forms of 'common-sense' which work to stabilize the status quo. Where such 'hegemonic discourse operates, parties to deliberation may agree on premises, they may accept a theory of their situation and give reasons for proposals that the others accept, but yet the premises and terms of the account mask the reproduction of power and injustice' (Young, 2001: 685). Ideological or discursive power, which structures the very terms of what can be thought possible, can ultimately prevent activist goals and agenda from being thought reasonable or permissible. In such a situation the activist has a right to protest and to disrupt and discomfort those defending the established order of things. Ultimately, for Young (2001: 687), 'one of the activist's goals is to make us wonder about what we are doing, to rupture a stream of thought, rather than to weave an argument'.

Some might see this as activists engaged in a certain type of philosophical reflection about the most efficacious way of carrying out their moral aims. Others, however, might regard this line of argument as philosophically unacceptable. If there are no solid foundations on which to adjudicate between truth and falsehood, then are we left in a terrifying situation overlooking the void of relativism: anything goes, and you can choose your truth and I'll choose mine (for a discussion of the 'perils' of relativism, see Geuss, 2015: 13–14; Jackson, 2015). In contrast, if there are universal criteria – such as reasonableness and coherence – then we might be able to agree on universal standards of justice. Rawls' conception of justice as fairness, determined from behind the veil of ignorance, is often stereotyped as a universal conception of justice, although as we have seen his commitment to pluralism between peoples who espouse different value systems means it is hard to sustain a charge of straightforward universalism against him. Fundamentally, therefore, this debate appears to boil down whether we think concepts like rationality, truth and justice can be universally valid, or whether they are only ever partial and particular. As discussed in Chapter 5, many of the critiques of liberal global justice theory have alleged that their claims to universal truths and values are merely the extension of parochial European, class-based, gendered truths and values (Chakrabarty, 2000; Hobson, 2012; hooks, 1994).

These are big questions which have absorbed many political theorists and filled pages of books and articles, ever since Plato's famous analogy of prisoners viewing the flickering of shadows on the cave wall (e.g., Erskine, 2008: 124–125). Public and private debates between figures like Foucault and Habermas, Rorty and Scruton, and Sartre and Derrida have often revolved around the question of universal values and transcendental truth. These debates will not be reconciled in this book! However, an interesting line of contemporary research within global justice theory is being articulated in the form of what is termed the practice-dependent approach to global justice, which takes existing social and institutional practices – rather than universal truths – to be constitutive of principles of justice (Banai *et al.*, 2011: 46). One of the most interesting and coherent articulations of this position has been advanced by Toni Erskine (2008) in her notion of embedded cosmopolitanism.

Erskine starts with exactly the problems with which we have been wrestling. The cosmopolitan claim to impartial neutrality and universality, the 'god's eye view' of the world, has been simultaneously the basis of its appeal, its inclusive and critical moral purview that lends robust support to appeals to duties beyond borders, as well as the terms on which philosophical critique has been launched against it, in the form of a parochialism and Eurocentrism which claims particular values to be universal. Erskine (2008: 2–4) argues for an alternative, qualified cosmopolitanism, 'a cosmopolitanism that would sustain an account of moral agency, judgement, and value as radically situated in particularist associations'. Her position rejects the prospect of impartiality, but continues to assert the equal moral standing of everyone. She locates this in a longer tradition of 'constitutive theory', drawing on Hegel, Mervyn Frost, and Michael Walzer, as well as feminist literatures on communities of place and ethics of care. These enable her to argue for duties to distant strangers, not on the basis of universal rights or values, but instead the existence of 'a wide range of overlapping, transnational, territorial and non-territorially defined communities' which enable 'reciprocal respect for the equal moral worth of those on respective sides of communal boundaries, political borders, and, even, enemy lines' (Erskine, 2008: 240). We all have roots, grounded in particular communities and places and histories, and these roots need protection and care. They should also be extended and overlapped to encompass distant others as far as possible, in Erskine's view.

These debates stretch the boundaries of liberal political theory, and raise the prospect of considering forms of politics and deliberation which are not 'rational' or 'reasonable', at least not in the same way as we understand these terms, and recognizing claims by others with whom we seem to share few points of connection. Recognizing the degree to which these issues are politically and philosophically contested, however, does permit a further opening up of the conversation, extending to groups and movements which start from very different moral values and different notions of justice. Three particular examples or issues will be explored in the rest of this chapter. The first concerns the right of particular communities to control their own food. The second brings into question what is meant by development, or what the substantive content of justice is. And the third extends the scope of the subject of justice, and of politics itself, in a radical way.

FOOD SOVEREIGNTY

Famine and hunger are quintessential problems of global (in)justice. There is enough food in the world to feed everybody, yet a substantial minority (currently around 750,000 to 1 million) are short of food, and at the other end a substantial minority are overconsuming and creating a range of health and social problems. Moreover, the image of a starving child or emaciated mother was the impetus for some of the major figures in political theory to consider questions of global justice (Singer, 1972; Sen, 1983; cf. Edkins, 2000: 4; Escobar, 1995: 103). These issues have not gone away. A food crisis was declared in Zimbabwe in early 2014 (although denied by the government), with 2.2 million people in need external assistance. In July 2012 at least 120,000 people in Somaliland required emergency food aid; southern Somalia faced a 'fresh hunger emergency'; and charities warned that the world's largest refugee camp at Dadaab, Kenya, had a looming combined crisis of funding shortages, insufficient food, water and sanitation, and an influx of Somali migrants. During the first decade of the twenty-first century 'three famines, all in Africa, have claimed at least a hundred thousand and possibly a quarter of a million lives' – confounding hopes that the era of mass famine mortality might have passed (Devereux, 2009: 25).

Most people accept that in the face of these humanitarian catastrophes, those who are able to act to alleviate suffering should do so (Edkins, 2000). Even critics of aid like Dambisa Moyo (2009; see Chapter 4) acknowledge that short-term humanitarian aid is sometimes necessary. The bigger debates arise over what the longer-term policies to ensure a just and sustainable food system should be, and who should have control over it. Those in favour of faster and greater modernization put their faith in the processes which have largely ended famine in developed societies: economic growth, liberal democracy, technological progress, and cheap transport and mass-produced food. Sen (1983, 1999: 16; cf. Edkins, 2000) is famous for showing that famines occur even when plenty of food is available, it is market distortions by greedy landowners and grain merchants that precipitate crisis. Economic freedoms (efficient food markets) and political freedoms (democracy) are therefore the principal ways to prevent famine. Sachs and 24 co-authors (2010) produced an editorial in *Nature* calling for a new 'global data collection and dissemination network' on food production and farming practices, helpfully offering the Centre for International Earth Science Information Network at Sachs' own Earth Institute, Columbia University, to host the network. Collier (2008) called for industrial agriculture on the Brazilian model of high-productivity, large farms to be rolled out by multinational corporations across the developing world, and more genetic modification to produce disease-, drought- and pest-resistant crops.

In contrast, new movements are emerging calling for 'food sovereignty': the control over the production and consumption of locally appropriate food by local communities, on a small scale. The concept of food sovereignty was first articulated by La Via Campesina, a global alliance of farmers', farmworkers', and rural peoples' movements, at the Rome World Food Summit in 1996. They argued that the right of peoples and countries to shape their food systems, food markets, and use of natural resources, rather than being left to corporations and market forces, was crucial to food sovereignty. Often this is accompanied by demands for the right to have GM-free food and organic agriculture. This is not simply a demand for resources or wealth to be redistributed. It is also more than a demand for consumer freedom to choose particular products. It is rather a demand for the collective right to a way of life which is threatened by the global food system, and which manifests in very different ways in different places. Thus poor famers in Malawi might occupy land, whereas French farmers resisting the encroachment of McDonalds and GM crops might launch legal campaigns or protest outside government buildings (Chinigò, 2016; Clapp, 2012; Lee, 2013; McMichael, 2008; Steward *et al.*, 2008).

This opposition to contemporary industrial agriculture was artic- ulated by movements who gathered in Nyéléni Village, Sélingué, Mali, in February 2007, and produced the Declaration of the Forum for Food Sovereignty, or the Nyéléni Declaration (see http:// nyeleni.org/). It begins with an important statement of identity, and a claim to local, communal values rather than a universal appeal:

> We, more than 500 representatives from more than 80 countries, of organizations of peasants/family farmers, artisanal fisherfolk, indigenous peoples, landless peoples, rural workers, migrants, pastoralists, forest communities, women, youth, consumers and environmental and urban movements have gathered together in the village of Nyéléni in Sélingué, Mali to strengthen a global movement for food sovereignty. We are doing this, brick by brick, as we live here in huts constructed by hand in the local tradition, and eat food that is produced and prepared by the Sélingué community. We give our collective endeavor the name 'Nyléni' as a tribute to and inspiration from a legendary Malian peasant woman who farmed and fed her peoples well.

The argument of these food producers was that their heritage and capacities to produce healthy, good and abundant food was being threatened and undermined by neo-liberalism and global capitalism, and that in response they asserted the right to food sovereignty. This is 'the right of peoples to healthy and culturally appropriate food produced through ecologically sound and sustainable methods, and their right to define their own food and agriculture systems'. In so doing they articulated a value system which put food producers and local communities at the centre, rather than transnational corporations or global trading links, and asserted the right of people to be treated differently, according to local norms, rather than a homogenous, universal system in which everyone buys and eats the same food. If 'we are what we eat', then food sovereignty movements have asserted that communities around the world produce and eat differently, and thus have the right to be treated differently and even identified differently. At the same time as the Nyéléni declaration invoked universal discourses of 'basic rights' and equality, they also rejected the privatization and commodification of food (contesting notions of private property) and asserted the special status of women and indigenous communities, 'who are historical creators of knowledge about food and agriculture and are devalued'. Whilst not explicitly framed in these terms, it is certainly possible to see connections in these campaigns to the ideas of some global justice philosophers, such as Nussbaum's rendering of the capability approach (see Chapter 2) in which she emphasizes the importance of living with a concern for nature, recreation and play, and control over one's environment including political participation.

However, food sovereignty campaigns also draw more explicitly and directly upon much older traditions of food protests and riots, and the concept of a moral economy. The idea of a moral economy is an explanation for why protest or resistance emerges which is not primarily based on the rational calculation of individual costs and benefits, but rather the transgression of shared, social norms or limits. E.P. Thompson (1971) famously discussed the moral economy of the English crowd when food price rises and taxation threatened subsistence, and James C. Scott (1977) contrasted a 'subsistence ethic' amongst the peasantry of South East Asia to classical Marxist conceptions of exploitation. This is a form of resistance emerging out of a basic claim that existing economic practices are violating current social values and cultural conceptions of what is legitimate. It is an appeal to 'stop doing this', or to stop causing harm. It is a 'safety first' movement, in Scott's terminology (1977: 5). Yet such movements do not have to be seen as conservative or anachronistic. As Arnold (2001: 94) argues, contemporary moral economies are embedded in concrete, ongoing social relations, not in generalized, mechanical moralities or romanticized pasts'.

Scott's study of why peasants were dissatisfied with the food, taxation and land-owning systems in South East Asia led him to reflect upon the different conceptions of justice that communities (or activists, or even academics) might deploy. He began with a Marxist conception of justice, in which value is determined by the socially necessary labour time that goes into producing a commodity. Under capitalism, according to Marx (1867), the worker is exploited because their wages do not reflect the surplus value which accumulates in the hands of the owner of the means of production (see also Selwyn, 2014). But, he observed, the degree of exploitation did not seem to capture all the ways in which peasants thought about justice. From a peasant perspective, he concluded that there are four potential standards of justice (Scott, 1977: ch. 6):

The comfortable standard of living. An absolute standard, which if violated is regarded as unjust.

The next best alternative. A relational standard, which is accepted as just if the next best alternative is worse than their current standard.

Reciprocity or equal exchange. A relational, market-based standard of justice, in which an exchange is held to be fair if freely entered into.

The just price. This is a social standard of legitimacy, in which collective norms of fairness inform what is regarded as an appropriate price for labour or food.

Scott's central argument is that peasants in South East Asia were risk averse: 'subsistence-oriented peasants typically prefer to avoid economic disaster rather than take risks to maximize their average income', and as such 'the problem of exploitation and rebellion is thus not just a problem of calories and income but is a question of peasant conceptions of social justice, of rights and obligations, of reciprocity' (1977: vii). This subsistence ethic was based around the question of 'What is left?' after taxes and rent, rather than 'How much is taken?' Thus:

> Exploitation is thus not a seamless web; each extra basket of rice the land-lord or state takes does not make for an identical quantum of pain. The taxes that smallholders pay may finally reach a point where they must resist or give up the land. The contraction of gleaning rights and food loans may finally oblige a family to go hungry or leave the village. It is for this reason that claims on a cultivator's resources that vary with his capac-ity to pay are experienced as less exploitative than claims that are pressed without regard to his consumption needs.
>
> (Scott, 1977: 178)

The point here is not that Scott's analysis of peasant morality is nec-essarily correct, and certainly not that it is true in all places where rural populations experience hunger and the threat of starvation. Indeed, his argument has been criticized from a number of theo-retical and empirical perspectives (Davis, 2006: 39; Mitchell, 1990; Popkin, 1979). The most important point to take from this discussion is that there are different theories of justice, and different standards and values by which populations pass judgement on particular social arrangements. Thinking philosophically can help make sense of these competing ways of articulating justice claims, and may even help actualize them in some cases.

It can also be helpful to think about this in terms of different forms of legitimacy. Here we can broadly contrast two approaches to the study of legitimacy (Clark, 2007). One is a form of norma-tive theorizing, which starts by deriving criteria for 'legitimate gov-ernance' from first principles or political philosophy (like Rawls), and then assesses actually existing interventions or forms of govern-ance to see how they measure up. The second is a more empirical approach which draws upon the Weberian tradition of asking, in particular circumstances, how certain power relations and forms of authority come to be seen as legitimate, i.e., broadly accepted. Of course, these two aspects of legitimacy – the external and internal or transcendental and phenomenological – are often tightly inter-wined in practice, and the Rawlsian notion of reflective equilibrium reflects the balance between them (see Chapter 1). The standards of legitimacy in a particular community will often be informed by broader philosophical and normative conceptions of what is 'right', and philosophers are also shaped by the communities and traditions within which they exist. But the main point to note for our discussion here is that the growth of movements for food sovereignty signal an assertion that the globalization of fast, cheap, industrially produced food is unjust and illegitimate. This is not on the basis of the fair distribution of resources, or a transgression of individual rights to choose what we consume, but rather on the basis of a violation of a communal moral economy which can be quite difficult for liberal theorists of global justice to incorporate within their framework. Thus, Jenny Edkins (2000: 129), drawing on poststructuralist and postcolonial thinkers, looks for 'a way of maintaining a more avowedly political stance in relation to suffering and disaster, one that acknowledges the need for a continual process of involvement and decisioning and does not try to set up principles or regulate practices according to abstract general rules, and one that does not succumb to modernity's hunger for certainty'.

BUEN VIVIR AND DEGROWTH

Climate change and environmental degradation represent some of the most pressing challenges for global justice in the twenty-first century, as discussed in Chapter 3. One of the particularly significant dimensions of this challenge, beyond simply the implications they pose for the just distribution of goods and bads, is the question they raise over the purpose of development, or economic growth, itself. Economic growth brings industrialization, urbanization, mechanized agriculture, open cast mining, the 'harvesting' of old growth forests, and ever longer and more stressful working days and weeks for the majority of the global population. In 1930 British economist John Maynard Keynes predicted that thanks to machinery and efficiency gains, the average citizen would only work 15 hours per week by 2030. Yet average working hours have increased over the past 50 years: we now work longer (if we are 'lucky' enough to have a job) than we ever have before (Fioramonti, 2013: 79–80). To take just one more observation: a report released in January 2016 predicted that by 2050 there will be more tonnes of plastic in our oceans than tonnes of fish (Wearden, 2016). What sort of world are we creating?

There have always been movements and activists and thinkers who have questioned the premises and values of conventional narratives of development, such as those discussed in earlier chapters. Caney (2005) and Dobson (2003) have articulated influential ways of broaching these issues, whilst staying largely within the liberal paradigm. However, alternative modes of thinking have emerged in recent years which are particularly relevant to debates about global justice, and later in the chapter we will consider how institutions of global governance have articulated alternative visions. First, we consider the emergence of a coalition of leftist governments in Latin America who have promoted the rights of Mother Earth and the concept of *buen vivir*, or living well, in contrast to the doctrine of growth at all costs.

The UN Copenhagen climate conference ended in crisis in December 2009. Tasked with agreeing a multilateral follow-up to the Kyoto Protocol, the negotiations were riven with divisions and acrimony. As it became clear there would be no consensual legal text resulting from the conference, a coalition of powerful countries – the United States, Brazil, India, China and South Africa – met privately and drafted an 'Accord' which was then presented to the rest of the conference. 'In final Plenary at 2am Saturday, seven countries opposed the Accord as undemocratically created, and too weak to save the world: Tuvalu, Nicaragua, Bolivia, Cuba, Venezuela, Sudan, and later Pakistan' (Dimitrov, 2010: 20). The conference collapsed into chaos, and hundreds of negotiators surrounded the intransigent parties. Delegates from Bolivia and Venezuela were physically pressed against the wall of the podium. In the end the conference merely 'took note' of the Copenhagen Accord. Disgusted with the process and the outcome, a number of Latin American states walked away (Bond, 2014; Stevenson, 2014).

The alternative bloc within the climate negotiations were led by the Bolivarian Alliance for the Peoples of Our America (ALBA). This is a coalition initially created by Cuba and Venezuela but which expanded to include Antigua and Barbuda, Bolivia, Dominica,

Ecuador, Grenada, Nicaragua, Saint Kitts and Nevis, Saint Lucia, Saint Vincent and the Grenadines, and Suriname. Signalling their belief in the need for a new direction in climate governance, and led by Bolivian President Evo Morales, these governments organized the World People's Conference on Climate Change and the Rights of Mother Earth in April 2010 at Cochabamba in Bolivia (Bond, 2014; Stevenson, 2014: 10–11). It was attended by around 35,000 people from at least 140 countries, and produced a Universal Declaration of the Rights of Mother Earth (see https://pwccc.wordpress.com/programa/). This is one of the clearest statements of an alternative standard of justice. It begins with the assertion that the peoples and nations of Earth 'are all part of Mother Earth, an indivisible, living community of interrelated and interdependent beings with a common destiny', and that 'every human being is responsible for respecting and living in harmony with Mother Earth'. The implications of asserting rights for Mother Earth will be explored further in the next section, but here it is useful to consider the concept of buen vivir in a little more detail.

The Spanish phrase buen vivir is usually translated as 'good living' or 'well living', and is known as sumak kawsay in the 'cosmovision' of the Quechua peoples, or suma qamaña in Aymara. It was incorporated into the new Ecuadorian constitution of 2008, which proclaims an aim of building 'a new form of public coexistence, in diversity and in harmony with nature, to achieve the good way of living', as well as the Bolivian constitution of 2009 (Balch, 2013). Promoted by decolonial intellectuals like Eduardo Gudynas (2011), and drawing on the work of a previous generation of postcolonial thinkers like Arturo Escobar (1995), it promotes an alternative ethic of social (rather than individual) well-being, radical democracy, and ecocentrism. The differences between the interpretations of buen vivir in the Ecuadorian and Bolivian constitutions are explored in some detail by Gudynas (2011), who shows how in the former it is framed as a set of rights existing alongside other familiar liberal rights, whereas in Bolivia it is presented more as a principle animating the values, ends and objectives of the State. In both versions, however, as well as the many other variations of the concept within Latin American indigenous political thought, Gudynas (2011: 446) sees a fundamental rejection of key elements of Western, Enlightenment, liberal thought, including: 'the division between nature and society, a colonial distinction between modern and non-modern indigenous peoples, the myth of progress as a unidirectional linear path, and a strong confidence on Cartesian science'.

In the alternative moral worldview of buen vivir, development is seen as a 'zombie category' (Gudynas, 2011), rather than an inherent good or natural feature of progressive politics. Here the concept links to the wider influence of 'post-development' theorists, who drew upon poststructuralist and postcolonial critiques of modernity in the 1990s to show how 'the dream of development . . . progressively turned into a nightmare' (Escobar, 1995: 4; see also Sachs, 1999). For Escobar, development is not a universal aspiration, rather it should be understood as a particular political project – or discourse – promoted after World War II by the United States and its allies. This is development as modernization and Westernization, a linear process in which poorer countries are urged to replicate the economic trajectory of the United States or United Kingdom (or, for the more social democratic-inclined, to aim for Denmark or Sweden). Development, for Escobar (1995: 202), was equivalent to 'the resignification of nature as environment; the reinscription of the Earth into capital via the gaze of science; the reinterpretation of poverty as effect of destroyed environments; and the new lease on management and planning as arbiters between people and nature'. Authors like Wolfgang Sachs (1999: x) were haunted by 'one nagging suspicion: that the Western development model is fundamentally at odds with both the quest for justice among the world's people and the aspiration to reconcile humanity and nature'.

The radical vision and philosophy of buen vivir have not always translated into different ways of doing politics, however. As Naomi Klein (2014: 181) points out, leftist regimes in Latin America – in Venezuela, Ecuador and Bolivia – have sought to tackle poverty and inequality through massive new industrial projects, especially concerning the extraction of oil, gas and minerals, rather than through new forms of development in harmony with nature. The difficulty of putting buen vivir into practice in the context of the globalized economy can be seen in the case of the Yasuní-ITT project in Ecuador. Moreover, others have also pointed out new forms of injustice and silencing in the manner in which the ALBA governments have articulated the concept of buen vivir, such as the marginalization of ecofeminist discourses (Stevenson, 2014: 14).

THE YASUNÍ-ITT PROJECT

In 2007 Ecuadorian president Rafael Correa proposed an initiative which would allow him to continue to tackle poverty and inequality in his country, as well as protecting nature and safeguarding the global commons. The Yasuní National Park is an ecologically diverse section of Amazonian rainforest on the eastern edge of Ecuador, and home to two tribes of isolated indigenous peoples. However, it also contains approximately 846 million barrels of crude oil, akin to 20 percent of the country's proven oil reserves. Correa's initiative was simple and attractive: there would be a permanent ban on oil production inside the Ishpingo-Tambococha-Tiputini oil field in exchange for 50 percent of the value of the reserves, or $3.6 billion over 13 years, to be raised from public and private contributions from the international community. How much did the global community value the preservation of pristine rainforest? How committed were sympathetic governments to keeping the oil in the soil?

The Yasuní-ITT Trust Fund was officially launched on 3 August 2010, and contributions were sought from around the world. Declarations of support were received from many sources, including from Ban Ki-moon, Secretary-General of the UN, and the scheme was to be administered by the UNDP. Germany offered $50 million over three years, and there were reports that unnamed corporations had offered Ecuador 'very large' sums to be linked to Yasuní. But by 2012 only $200 million had been pledged, and even less actually deposited. The initiative was abandoned in August 2013. 'The world has failed us', said Correa, and it appeared that the oil beneath the Yasuní park would be drilled and extracted (Krauss, 2013; Martinez-Alier *et al.*, 2013).

The second example of a prominent critique of the premises and values of conventional narratives of development comes from a more surprising direction: international institutions and governments in the developed world. In 2008 Nicolas Sarkozy, President of France, brought together Joseph Stiglitz, Amartya Sen, and Jean-Paul Fitoussi to write a report on the measurement of social and economic progress, motivated by a concern that relying on GDP as a proxy was unsatisfactory. The unifying theme of the report's conclusions was that 'the time is ripe for our measurement system to shift emphasis from measuring economic production to measuring people's well-being' (Stiglitz *et al.*, 2009: 12). The report emphasized that the distribution of income and wealth are as important as levels of aggregate increase (as measured by GDP), and that the sustainability of our economic systems into the future should be considered alongside their ability to meet current needs. These statements may not seem controversial, but they represent an alternative line of economic thinking from the focus on growth and trickle-down economics which had characterized neoliberal orthodoxy for many years (Death, 2010). It was also significant that these comments came from an authoritative, government-appointed report. They made points which could be interpreted as questioning the entire rationale of economic growth. For example: 'consuming the same bundle of goods and services but working for 1,500 hours a year instead of 2000 hours a year implies an increase in one's standard of living' (Stiglitz *et al.*, 2009: 14). The implications of such a statement can be quite profound. In the 1960s and 1970s ecosocialist thinkers like André Gorz (1980: 68–9) envisioned a utopia where the working week would be vastly reduced, declaring that 'the only way to live better is to produce less, to consume less, to work less, to live differently'. Theorists like Hermann Daly, Ivan Illich, Ernest Schumacher and Murray Bookchin all contributed to alternative conceptions of the good life which emphasized simplicity, sufficiency, and well-being above growth, technology and progress (Barry, 2012; Whitehead, 2014), going well beyond the terms of liberal cosmopolitans like Caney in terms of the implications of thinking ecologically.

The dividing line between mainstream thinking and radical alternative perspectives can be quite hard to draw here. At one level we all recognize that economic growth is not the most important measure of development, and that well-being and the good life involves a much wider range of social, cultural and political factors. Well-regarded mainstream economists and politicians frequently make these points. In 1974 Richard A. Easterlin pointed out what became known as the Easterlin paradox: once certain levels of income are reached, further growth does not produce further growth in happiness. Rather it produces 'ever-growing wants' (in Fioramonti, 2013: 67). US GDP per capita has more than doubled from World War II until the early 1990s, yet over this period no studies have shown any empirical evidence of any improvement in perceived happiness (Fioramonti, 2013: 67). Perhaps most famously, US politician Robert Kennedy gave a speech on this subject in March 1968 (3 months before he was assassinated):

> Too much and for too long, we seemed to have surrendered personal excellence and community values in the mere accumulation of material things. . . . Gross national product counts air pollution and cigarette advertising, and ambulances to clear our highways of carnage. It counts special locks for doors and the jails for the people who break them. It counts the destruction of the redwood and the loss of our natural wonder in chaotic sprawl. It counts napalm and counts nuclear warheads and armored cars for the police to fight the riots in our cities. . . . Yet the gross national product does not allow for the health of our children, the quality of their education or the joy of their play. It does not include the beauty of our poetry or the strength of our marriages, the intelligence of our public debate or the integrity of our officials. It measures neither wit nor our courage, neither our wisdom nor our learning, neither our compassion nor our devotion to our country, it measures everything, in short, except that which makes life worthwhile.
>
> (Kennedy, 1968)

These sentiments – profound and inspiring as they sound here – have been widely reflected in the ways we now measure and promote development. Amartya Sen's capability approach was a crucial influence behind the development of the UNDP's Human Development Index which measures literacy and health and other features of well-being. New indexes have been created, such as the New Economic Foundation's Happy Planet Index, which shows the extent to which countries deliver long, happy, sustainable lives for the people that live in them: Costa Rica, Vietnam and Colombia came top of this international ranking in 2012. The OECD has produced a tool called the 'Your Better Life index' which allows users to rank countries according to the well-being criteria which matter to them: if educational indicators are prioritized then Australia comes top of this ranking. The Kingdom of Bhutan has become famous for measuring Gross National Happiness, or sufficiency across a range of indicators, rather than more conventional economic growth (Fioramonti, 2013: 93–6).

From one perspective these proliferating interpretations of development are simply evidence that there are many different visions of the good life and many different substantive conceptions of global justice. In the hands of some thinkers, however, they are a fundamental critique of liberal traditions of modernization and progress. GDP is not one neutral tool among many alternatives, for Fioramonti (2013: 153–4), rather it 'is a way of organising society' in which 'the world is still run by cowboys, plains appear endless, and the gold fever fuels human greed'. For those working in the emerging field of 'de-growth', continual economic growth is simply not possible in a finite world; nor is it desirable given the extent of poverty, violence inequality and environmental degradation produced by centuries of modern 'development'. Giorgos Kallis (2011: 874) defines de-growth as 'a socially sustainable reduction of society's throughput (or metabolism)', where 'throughput refers to the materials and energy a society extracts, processes, transports and distributes, to consume and return back to the environment as waste'. Specific proposals for de-growing the economy include a 21-hour working week, salary caps and basic income grants, new public squares and open spaces, and collective voluntary work in community gardens (Kallis, 2011: 876; Martinez Alier, 2009). But this vision of de-growth entails profound political and economic consequences, since contemporary capitalism (a version of which is accepted by all mainstream global justice philosophers) relies on continual growth. Without growth, 'debts cannot be paid, credit runs out and unemployment sky-rockets' (Kallis, 2011: 875). Profits and accumulation cannot coexist with a just transition to a sustainable economy, from this perspective. In the view of Kallis (2011) and Martinez Alier (2009), the insights of Robert Kennedy or the Sarkozy report lead us inexorably to the realization that the current version of global capitalism is incompatible with genuine well-being. The philosophers of buen vivir in Latin America would agree.

ECOCENTRIC JUSTICE

The third alternative conception of global justice we will consider in this chapter concerns the status of non-human nature. Are humans the only possible subjects of justice? Or, bluntly, 'do trees have rights?' (Stone, 2010). As discussed in Chapter 2, Martha Nussbaum has given extended thought to how the rights of non-human animals might be incorporated within a liberal framework. The abstract debates of philosophers have been given additional recent impetus by the alternative conception of justice articulated by the ALBA nations in the Declaration of the Rights of Mother Earth (see http://www.rightsofmotherearth.com/). This declaration affirmed 'that to guarantee human rights it is necessary to recognize and defend the rights of Mother Earth and all beings in her and that there are existing cultures, practices and laws that do so'. It proceeds to argue that Mother Earth is a living being, 'a unique, indivisible, self-regulating community of interrelated beings that sustains, contains and reproduces all beings', and the 'inherent rights of Mother Earth are inalienable in that they arise from the same source as existence'. As such, 'Mother Earth and all beings are entitled to all the inherent rights recognized in this Declaration without distinction of any kind, such as may be made between organic and inorganic beings, species, origin, use to human beings, or any other status'. These rights, the declaration asserts, 'are specific to their species or kind and appropriate for their role and function within the communities within which they exist', and conflict between rights 'must be resolved in a way that maintains the integrity, balance and health of Mother Earth'.

These rights, the declaration goes on to argue, include:

(a) the right to life and to exist;
(b) the right to be respected;
(c) the right to regenerate its bio-capacity and to continue its vital cycles and processes free from human disruptions;
(d) the right to maintain its identity and integrity as a distinct, self-regulating and interrelated being;

(e) the right to water as a source of life;

(f) the right to clean air;

(g) the right to integral health;

(h) the right to be free from contamination, pollution and toxic or radioactive waste;

(i) the right to not have its genetic structure modified or disrupted in a manner that threatens it integrity or vital and healthy functioning;

(j) the right to full and prompt restoration the violation of the rights recognized in this Declaration caused by human activities;

 (1) Each being has the right to a place and to play its role in Mother Earth for her harmonious functioning.

 (2) Every being has the right to wellbeing and to live free from torture or cruel treatment by human beings.

The declaration goes on to assert the obligations humans have toward Mother Earth, which centre around respect and living in harmony. These assertions are deeply controversial, and indeed they sound odd to many people, especially in western, scientific, humanist cultures in which 'rights' are something specifically and quintessentially human. However, this language has been acknowledged and recognized by the UN in international agreements. The 2012 Rio conference on sustainable development produced a final text which was agreed by the international community, which stated that:

> We recognize that planet Earth and its ecosystems are our home and that 'Mother Earth' is a common expression in a number of countries and regions, and we note that some countries recognize the rights of nature in the context of the promotion of sustainable development. We are convinced that in order to achieve a just balance among the economic, social and environmental needs of present and future generations, it is necessary to promote harmony with nature.
>
> (UN, 2012)

At this point our discussion connects back more directly with established literatures in political theory and philosophy. Questions concerning the rights, or standing, of non-human entities have been a recurrent oncern for many branches of philosophical literatures, although these only rarely interconnect with the global justice debates. There are a number of potential avenues into these discussions. Peter Singer (1975) is one of the most well-known philosophers to make the case that the principle of equality constitutes a sound moral basis for relations with other species, and whilst animal rights differ from human rights a utilitarian outlook still requires us to minimize non-human suffering. He was influential in launching the Great Ape Project (see box; Cavalieri and Singer, 1994). Arne Naess (1983: 343) advocated a philosophy known as 'deep ecology' which valued an appreciation of the world's complex web of natural relationships, and 'biospherical egalitarianism – in principle', including 'a deep-seated respect, or even veneration, for ways and forms of life'. Andrew Dobson (1999, 2003) has considered how the rights of nature might be integrated into, or conflict fundamentally with, liberal theories of justice. A tradition of philosophy known as ecocentrism – putting the ecological community at the centre of value systems, rather than humans as in anthropocentrism – derives much of inspiration from Aldo Leopold who regarded the 'biotic community' as the primary referent of his 'land ethic' (McShane, 2014). In his classic phrase, 'a thing is right when it tends to preserve the integrity, stability and beauty of the biotic community. It is wrong when it tends otherwise' (Leopold, 1949: 189).

THE GREAT APE PROJECT

The Great Ape Project is a campaign which has been running since 1993 to defend the rights of chimpanzees, bonobos, gorillas and orangutans, 'our closest relatives in the natural world' (see http://www.projetogap.org.br/en/). It is an international organization of primatologists, anthropologists, ethicists, and others, including philosophers like Peter Singer, who propose granting three basic rights to these species.

1   The right to life. 'The lives of all great primates must be protected. The individuals can not be killed, with exception for extremely specific situations, such as self-defense.'

(Continued)

(Continued)

2 Individual freedom. 'Great primates can not be deprived, in an arbitrary way, from their freedom. They have the right to live in their habitat. Great primates who live in captivity have the right to live with dignity, in large rooms, to have contact with others of their species to form families and must be protected from commercial exploitation.'

3 Prohibition of torture. 'Intentional imposition of intense pain, physically or psychologically, to a great primate, with no reason or to other's benefits, is considered a kind of torture and is an offense from which they must be protected.'

The basis for these rights includes research which suggests that great apes possess rationality and self-consciousness, and the ability to be aware of themselves as distinct entities with a past and future. Evidence includes documented conversations (in sign languages) with individual great apes, as well as behaviour which appears to show compassion, mourning, grief, empathy, imagination, and a sense of humour (Cavalieri and Singer, 1994). The movement campaigns against the use of great apes in medical and commercial testing, as well as against other cases of cruelty, but the philosophical implications of the concept are extensive (see also Rowlands, 2012). Our capacity to establish a connection with these animals, and imagine ourselves in their position, has stimulated a wide range of artistic and philosophical reflections, such as the novel *Great Apes* by Will Self (1997) in which chimps are the dominant species and keep animalistic humans in captivity, or the 1968 film *Planet of the Apes* (itself originally a book, and spawning a franchise of remakes, spin-offs and sequels). If it is so easy to imagine extending a 'community of equality' to apes, then surely we must consider on what criteria we would deny equality to other species: whales, dolphins, crows, dogs, cats, pigs . . .

A comprehensive engagement with the wide range of literature on animal rights and ecocentric philosophy is impossible here. But there are two strands of the literature which have particular pertinence for our discussion of global justice in this book. The firs strand, poststructuralist work on hybridity and posthumanism, poses some of the biggest challenges to contemporary global justice theory by problematizing core concepts of subjectivity and rationality.

One of the central points of contention between liberal theorists and poststructuralist theorists concerns the nature of human subjectivity, or what makes us different from other entities in nature. Liberalism is predicated on an assertion of a universal humanity, based on rationality, which places us above the beasts. As Descartes said, *cogito ergo sum*; I think, therefore I am. Critical theorists have contested this from a number of perspectives (Edkins, 1999: ch. 2; Hobden, 2014). Marxists reject the notion that we can freely think what we choose, instead arguing that our position in the social structure and the nature of that structure in terms of the predominant mode of production dictate (more or less) what our ideas will be. Freudians suggest that the mind is not the willing tool of rationality Enlightenment theorists had implied, but instead is a terrain of unconscious desires, sublimated drives, and poorly understood fears. Feminists highlight the importance of social and cultural roles structuring what we can think, and widely accepted ideas about proper (gendered) social roles inform the ideal of the rational thinking individual (who, for centuries, was assumed to be male). Judith Butler (1990) argues that identity is performative, meaning that there is no real, pre-existing subject which then enters into contracts or relations with others, rather *who we are* is a function of the social relations and roles we perform. Foucault's (2000) concept of knowledge/power rejects the possibility of a 'truth' free from power relations, and theorists of language and linguistics like Saussure and Derrida showed how the grammatical and discursive rules of language condition what it is possible for us to think, articulate, and be (Edkins, 1999).

Inspired by these theorists and traditions, among others, philosophers like Bruno Latour (1993) and Donna Haraway (1989) have reconsidered the relationship between humans and non-humans. If humans are products of our social class, our unconscious, our gender roles, and powerful discourses of truth and language, then maybe are no more 'free' or rational than other entities? What might politics look like if considered from this perspective? And what would justice mean under such assumptions? There are no clear or easy answers to this, beyond the repeated demand that we might need a 'profound rethinking' of the way in which international political theory incorporates 'the natural world' into its study (Cudworth and Hobden, 2011: 1). But these thinkers have made a number of provocative, interesting and productive suggestions. Latour suggests we call human 'earthlings' to emphasize our rootedness to the planet, and proposed a 'parliament of things' in which it would not be assumed that humans would be sole speakers (Cudworth and Hobden, 2011: 2; Hobden, 2014: 182; Rudy and White, 2014: 123–5). Latour (1993) deployed concepts like networks, assemblages and hybridity to move away from assuming that human agency was the prime and central driver of politics; rather we are enmeshed in networks of technology, ecologies, organic chemistry and other objects. Haraway deployed the metaphor of the cyborg to question the boundaries between the human and the animal, between organism and machine, and between the physical and the non-physical (Hobden, 2014: 180). She deployed a cyborg manifesto as a feminist intervention, emerging from work on non-human primates, as well as using the concept to think through our relationship with dogs and other 'companion species' who co-evolved alongside us and thus complicate the assumption of solely human agency (Haraway, 1989; see also Hobden, 2014: 180–1; Rudy and White, 2014: 126). Haraway's term 'natureculture' implies the impossibility of separating the human from the non-human, echoing Latour's famous claim that 'we have never been modern' with the equally provocative assertion that 'we have never been human'.

If only one thing is clear, hopefully this discussion has shown that we are now a long way away from the world of Rawls, Pogge and Beitz with whom this book started. The implications of claims that non-humans might be subjects of global justice quickly take us into worlds of social and cultural theory that assume very different starting points to those of most participants in mainstream global justice debates. Theorists like Foucault, Derrida, Latour, and Haraway have had profound effects on diverse fields in the social sciences and humanities, but their implications for the global justice debates are neither straightforward nor easy. This being said, it is pertinent that philosophers in the Anglo-American tradition have also began to investigate the case for destabilizing the traditiona relationship between human and non-human, in particular in Sue Donaldson and Will Kymlicka's *Zoopolis* (2011) and also the work of Mark Rowlands (2009, 2012) – a philosopher famous in part for chronicling his life with a wolf – who extends Rawls' original position to include animal species (2002). At the very least, therefore, this section has further opened up the global justice conversation by showing how alternative perspectives on justice raise new issues and problematize core assumptions within mainstream approaches. This can be seen both in the quite specific proposals for the Rights of Mother Earth, or the Great Ape Project, as well as in the all-out attacks by poststructuralist theorists on how we think about subjectivity and rationality.

An interesting and stimulating conversation, however, requires more than just an endless proliferation of issues, critiques and viewpoints. It also requires re-establishing points of connection and common understanding, even if not always agreement. In this spirit, the final part of this chapter considers one more theorist, Robyn Eckersley, whose work is informed both by mainstream debates within political theory as well as by the prospect of a more radical, ecocentric politics.

GREEN STATES AND GLOBAL JUSTICE

Eckersley became most well known for her book *Environmentalism and Political Theory: Toward an Eco-centric Approach* (1992), which set out to relate various strands of environmental theory to the major traditions of political theory, and to argue in normative terms for the cogency and relevance of a 'Green' (emancipatory, progressive) political theory which could also take the status and rights of nature seriously. This project was advanced with the publication of *The Green State* in 2004. Her arguments here are worth considering in some detail, as this book could be seen as an attempt to think about what duties and rights are necessary to make environmental justice possible in contemporary global politics.

Whilst many environmentalists have either given up on formal, state-based politics, or regard the state as one of the causes of environmental harm, Eckersley believes it is possible to rescue a vision of a greener, more democratic state. In order to imagine a state which is capable of advancing both human emancipation and environmental protection, she suggests we need to consider three major stumbling blocks. The first of these concerns the anarchic international system. In a competitive world riven by conflict, how can states cooperate to achieve a just world order? This is the central problem of global justice theory, but Eckersley emphasizes the environmental ramifications of international conflict: transboundary pollution, competitive exploitation of shared resources (such as fish stocks), and global collective action problems (such as climate change). Her answer is that the basic content of state interests are changing as a result of the rise of environmental security considerations, the growing web of international law on environmental issues, and evolving norms of what it means to be a responsible (clean, green) state.

The second obstacle she considers is the relationship between states and capitalism. Marxists have emphasized the role of the state as either the instrument of the ruling classes, or as structurally dependent on continual growth and environmental exploitation. Eckersley responds that processes of reflexive ecological modernization − technological efficiency, civic participation in governance, corporate social responsibility, and so on − are capable of transforming ecologically damaging and unequal state structures into more sustainable and just ones.

The third obstacle is the limits of liberal democracy itself, including both the suggestion that states are too rigid and bureaucratic to respond to new ecological challenges, and the charge that liberalism is too individualistic and defends elites by separating the public from the private sphere. Eckersley's response is that the green state would be post-liberal, and she demands 'the politicization of the private good as well as the re-politicization of the public good' (2004: 96).

Eckersley's green state is therefore, she claims, a very different entity to the liberal, capitalist, competition state. It is a state which would promote ecological democracy, in which 'the opportunity to participate or *otherwise be represented in* the making of risk-generating decisions should literally be extended to *all* those potentially affected regardless of social class, geographic location, nationality, generation, or species' (2004: 112). This proposal is not too far from Latour's vision of a parliament of things, and Eckersley (2004: 112−38) considers in some depth the problems of how to represent those who cannot represent themselves, and how deliberative democracy differs in emphasis from a Habermasian reliance on rational debate (see also Dryzek, 2006).

This green state would have to exist, she concedes, within an international society in which not all states would be as committed to ecological democracy. But she thinks that the spread and expansion of international law, and softer norms of environmental protection, mean that green states would spread by emulation: other states would start to copy successful green states. Such states would be transnational, in that they would have developed their identity and practices of sovereignty beyond a narrow focus on national self-interest. Thus she concludes that 'a proliferation of transnationally oriented green states, which are likely to extend and deepen environmental multilateralism, is also likely to provide a surer path to a greener world than the development of a more overarching cosmopolitan global democratic law' (Eckersley, 2004: 202). In contrast to a more Rawlsian emphasis on a duty to assist, Eckersley defends the principle of green non-intervention, arguing that if sovereignty was properly reconceived along green lines then a strong non-intervention principle would act as a 'green shield' for poorer and weaker states against transnational harm and exploitation (see also Eckersley, 2006: 136–7).

Eckersley is an interesting thinker with which to end this chapter on alternative conceptions of justice. Her theory of the green state is strikingly radical in places, and she rejects liberal theory in unequivocal terms. 'Liberalism's atomistic ontology of the self', she argues, 'its quest for mastery of the external world through the application of instrumental reason, and its corresponding denial of any non-instrumental dependency on the social and biological world have ultimately imperilled rather than enhanced human autonomy for many and environmental integrity for all' (Eckersley, 2004: 242). But others have questioned whether her account is really so far away from a radicalized, democratized, thoroughly 'greened' liberal theory of justice. Meadowcroft (2006) asks whether 'the liberal "dogmas" she repudiates are in fact dogmas *about liberalism* as much as dogmas to which liberals adhere', and suggests that her vision may be less antithetical to versions of liberal theory, as well as aspects of state politics under capitalism, than she implies (in response, see Eckersley, 2006).

Moreover, in her focus on the state – as a public institution with the means of enforcing responsibilities and protecting rights – Eckersley remains more closely engaged with central debates in political theory than some of the other thinkers and movements considered in this chapter. She argues that 'there are still few social institutions that can match the same degree of capacity and potential legitimacy that states have to redirect societies and economies along more ecological sustainable lines' (Eckersley, 2004: 7). It is hard to imagine Latour or Haraway, to take only two examples, framing their political philosophy in quite this way. Finally, though Eckersley is under no illusions about how far we are away from a more ecologically just world, or how difficult it will be to move toward the vision of an ideal green state that she sets out. Like the transition from a feudal to a liberal democratic state, or the long battle for a welfare or more social democratic state, any transition to a green state 'is unlikely to occur without a protracted struggle' (Eckersley, 2004: 2). As such, activists and movements for global justice – whether ecological, indigenous, feminist, racial, or other – are an essential and core component of the politics of justice.

ALTERNATIVES TO JUSTICE?

This chapter extended the conversation about global justice even more broadly than simply engaging with activists, movements and campaigns from various quarters of the world. In this chapter we considered alternative conceptions of justice, and the various points of connection to as well as tensions with mainstream or liberal traditions of political theory. These included the very possibility of universal theories and values, and how to engage with very different ontologies and epistemologies in a diverse world. The problem of difference has been at the heart of this chapter: what does it mean for discussions about global justice to recognize quite radical forms of difference, and can we ever adjudicate between them in deciding what is right? As noted above, there are (at least) two main ways to think about legitimacy, the external and the internal. From an external perspective, we can bring our normative criteria and use that to decide whether a campaign, cause or policy is just. From an internal perspective, we would ask rather whether people seem to accept or reject the institution, policy or position.

In the end, perhaps, all we can say is that politics involves both imensions of legitimacy. Politics is about both power and justice. imply assessing what people are willing to accept in a given moment an lead to a conservative defence of the status quo, the realist man- ·a that might is right. A blind faith in one's own moral superiority nd capacity to judge others as right or wrong leads to the opposite ısk: an inability to consider a different point of view, or recognize radically different system of values and legitimacy (Geuss, 2015). ıs expressed by Edward Hallett Carr in 1939 (2001: 12), 'all healthy uman action, and therefore all healthy thought, must establish a alance between utopia and reality, between free will and determin- m'. A fuller conception of politics is not reducible to the art of the ossible, it is also about who we think we are and what we think is .ght or just.

CONCLUSION

This final chapter briefly casts an eye over the debates and thinke: covered in the course of the book and identifies a number of ke questions which we think remain essential points of common intere for all those committed to the better conceptualization and realiza tion of global justice. In this sense, like all good philosophy, this boo ends with more questions rather than answers. The book ends wit questions in another sense too. Assuming that many of those readin this will be students of global justice, we provide a number of sugge: tions of how the concepts, debates and thinkers covered here migl be drawn upon when coming up with research projects of their own

WHERE HAVE WE BEEN?

We started this book by observing not only the many differer interpretations and understandings of global justice but also the ine: capable fact that global justice seems a very long way away. Eve our own societies are characterized by huge (and often increasing inequalities of wealth and opportunity, but on a global scale, it striking how far one's chances of going to university or to priso: living past 80 or dying before the age of 5 and owning a lapto or living on less than $1.25 per day are structured by the rando:

hance of where one is born and who our parents are. Sadly, we live in a violent world, in which vulnerable people, species and environments are exploited all around us. Our world does not work very well for the majority of the people who live in it.

Yet we have also seen throughout this book that there are a great many rigorous and inspirational thinkers who have devoted their lives to the study of justice and injustice, and whole fields of academic study have arisen around debates structured in terms of communitarians versus cosmopolitans, or globalists versus statists. Even beyond the field of 'global justice theory' narrowly defined, an interest in questions of power and justice to some degree unites all of those working in the disciplines of politics and international relations, as well as many in geography, history, sociology, anthropology, law, philosophy and so on.

KEY THINKERS DISCUSSED IN THIS BOOK

JOHN RAWLS: American philosopher who has shaped the field of global justice in the post-war period. Famous for concepts like the veil of ignorance, the difference principle, reflective equilibrium, and the duty of assistance. Key works: *A Theory of Justice*; *Political Liberalism*; *The Law of Peoples*.

DAVID MILLER: English political theorist known for his defence of nationalism, but who significantly acknowledged that we might still have duties of justice to distant others. Key works: *Social Justice*; *National Responsibility and Global Justice*.

PETER SINGER: Australian moral philosopher known for his utilitarian approach to issues like hunger, foreign aid and animal rights. Key works: *Animal Liberation*; *Practical Ethics*; *The Life You Can Save*.

CHARLES BEITZ: American political theorist who set out the case against traditional approaches to international relations and provided one the first and most compelling cosmopolitan interpretations of Rawls' theory of justice. Key work: *Political Theory and International Relations*.

(Continued)

(Continued)

THOMAS POGGE: German philosopher, supervised by Rawls, but who also criticized him from a cosmopolitan perspective and went on to make significant interventions into global public policy debates on issues like poverty, democracy and human rights. Key works: *Realizing Rawls*; *World Poverty and Human Rights*.

AMARTYA SEN: Indian economist and philosopher, famous for his study of the causes of famine, his notion of development as freedom and the capabilities approach. Key works: *Development as Freedom*; *The Idea of Justice*.

MARTHA NUSSBAUM: American philosopher who has extended the liberal tradition into new areas including feminist theory, disability studies and environmental ethics. Key works: *Women and Human Development*; *The Frontiers of Justice*.

NANCY FRASER: American critical theorist who has emphasized three dimensions of justice – distribution, recognition and representation – drawing on a variety of traditions. Key works: *Unruly Practices*; *Redistribution or Recognition?* (with Axel Honneth).

IRIS MARION YOUNG: American political theorist who sought to broaden the scope of philosophical work on the causes and manifestations of injustice, and argued that activist protest must be taken seriously and not collapsed into processes of deliberative democracy. Key work: *Justice and the Politics of Difference*.

ALISON JAGGAR: American philosopher and influential feminist theorist. Key works: *Feminist Politics and Human Nature*; *Gender and Global Justice*.

BRUNO LATOUR: French philosopher and sociologist of science who has presented a poststructuralist critique of modernity and rejected the idea of a clear division between nature and society. Key work: *We Have Never Been Modern*.

DONNA HARAWAY: American feminist and postmodernist whose work fused studies of science, identity, animality and critical theory. Key works: *A Cyborg Manifesto*; *Situated Knowledges*.

ROBYN ECKERSLEY: Australian political theorist known for her work on ecocentric political philosophy and the 'greening' of political institutions. Key works: *Environmentalism and Political Theory*; *The Green State*.

In addition to the self-identified or professional theorists and philosophers we have discussed, we have also covered a great many social movements which have struggled, lobbied and protested for their own version of global justice. A major aim of this book has been to bring the discussion of political theory into closer contact with the dilemmas, priorities and contributions of those 'on the barricades' for social and political justice. The division between philosopher and activist is not hard and fast: many philosophers like Fraser, Pogge and Singer have lobbied tirelessly and marched on the streets for causes they believe in; and many members of social movements and grassroots campaigns produce original knowledge and conceptual theorizations, as well as systematic defences of their moral positions. But conceived as ideal types, or social roles, the task of the philosopher and the activist can be thought of as complementary, existing in productive tension. No study of global justice, we believe, is complete without serious consideration of the urgent issues and campaigns of the day.

KEY MOVEMENTS DISCUSSED IN THIS BOOK

#RHODESMUSTFALL: South African student movement for justice and transformation in universities, mobilized around a campaign to remove a statue of the racist, colonialist Cecil Rhodes from the University of Cape Town campus.

(Continued)

(Continued)

#BLACKLIVESMATTER: Racial justice and civil rights movement originating in the USA in response to police killings of unarmed black men, now taken forward by groups such as Million Hoodies.

OCCUPY: A worldwide movement which began in Europe and North America against inequality and democratic disempowerment, under the slogan 'We are the 99%'. They took over streets and squares in a challenge to neoliberal capitalism.

WORLD SOCIAL FORUM: Gatherings of movements against globalization and neoliberalism which began in 2001 and at their peak attracted hundreds of thousands of activists to talk and build solidarity, usually in the Global South.

JUBILEE 2000: International coalition calling for the cancellation of third world debt by the year 2000.

KALAHARI BUSHMEN (BASARWA): Movement for the right to maintain an indigenous lifestyle and culture in the Kalahari Desert, Botswana.

BDS ISRAEL: The Boycott, Divest, Sanctions movement against the Israeli occupation of the Palestinian territories seeks to uphold international law and pressure Israel and her allies through a commercial, artistic and educational boycott.

FOSSIL FUEL DIVESTMENT: A movement to 'leave the coal in the hole, the oil in the soil, and the gas under the grass', i.e. for climate justice, principally by urging institutional investors to sell (divest) their stocks in fossil fuel companies.

FOOD SOVEREIGNTY: Coalition of peasant and agricultural producer movements worldwide, from France to Brazil, calling for the rights of local communities to control what they grow and what they eat.

BUEN VIVIR AND DEGROWTH: Movements and philosophies of well-being which contest the idea that economic growth is the root to global justice. Particularly strong in Latin America where several countries have recognized the rights of Mother Earth in their constitutions.

GREAT APE PROJECT: Campaign started by Peter Singer to recognize the rights of chimpanzees, bonobos, gorillas and orangutans to life, freedom and dignity.

It is not possible to recap all of the debates, concepts and issues we have discussed in this book. Instead, we hope that these two brief lists of key thinkers and key movements will help you recall the subjects in the previous chapters. Neither is it particularly easy, in an introductory text like this, to bring everything together in a neat conclusion which encapsulates the 'state of the discipline'. This is particularly difficult in such a deeply contested field as global justice, where methodologies, epistemologies and ontologies are so varied and have so much at stake. Instead, therefore, we end by briefly reflecting on some of the key questions we think remain essential points of common interest for all those committed to the better conceptualization and realization of global justice.

WHERE ARE WE GOING?

This book started with questions such as 'who is owed what?' and 'what duties to each other do people have?' These questions remain essential components in a world of vastly differing levels of wealth, different personal and social capabilities, and different vulnerabilities. In a world divided by states into particular communities, yet which is increasingly interconnected and interdependent, the question of how we relate to distant others is just as important as the duties we have to those closest to us.

The specific challenge of 'global justice', however, is 'why it is so far away?' This entails asking 'what are the causes of injustice?', and this is a question which has both more empirically and more normatively orientated lines of answer. For some, the lack of an international government or sovereign fundamentally compromises the potential of a more just world order. The realist insistence that in a situation of international anarchy, only self-interest is wise or principled is a maxim that all the thinkers and activists discussed in this book would reject and contest. Remembering the prime importance of insisting that a better world is possible is something which can bring global justice philosophers together, even when the debates become highly divisive.

What role should states play in the quest for global justice? Are they the primary agents of justice, or merely instrumentally useful institutions which could and should be bypassed if they violate individual rights? Would 'greener' states lead to a more environmentally sustainable international system, or would this become a pretext for some states to dictate to weaker communities how they should live their lives? Despite the rise of corporate power and the fragmentation of national identities in some places, states remain one of the few political institutions with the capacity and legitimacy to promote and enforce justice. What role they can and should play, and in what conditions, are vital questions for political theorists and philosophers.

What role should social movements play in the quest for global justice? In one sense this question could be seen as nonsensical or self-evident: if global justice is to have any political weight and significance it will have to be pushed and promoted and struggled for by activists and campaigners. It has always been thus. But how should movements best deliberate upon and decide what visions of justice they want to promote? How should they recruit members, choose tactics, and struggle most effectively against powerful adversaries? Will education win-out, or in some contexts is civil disobedience and even perhaps violence needed?

There are many other questions we could reiterate here. How universal are notions of human rights, civil liberties, political freedoms? Are issues of gender and environment foundational or secondary questions of justice? What is the best balance between dimensions of distribution, recognition and representation? Methodologically, are abstract thought-experiments more or less useful than practice- or context-dependent explorations of justice? But in order to unpack these questions, and more, there is only one answer. As James Baldwin said: 'read, read, read, never stop reading. And when you can't read any more . . . write!'

With this in mind, perhaps the best place to end this book is with some suggestions for how to use this book to inform and design your own research projects on global justice. These guidelines are intended to be of use to projects at the high school level, to undergraduate dissertations or self-directed research essays, and even postgraduate theses. The three main questions highlighted here are: what, why, and how?

What? Start with a research question. This can be broad, like those above, or narrower, such as 'what would a just energy policy look like in South Africa?' If it is broad you will need to find a way to narrow it down, so think about using a particular theorist to help answer it, or exploring it in the context of a particular movement or country. If you have a narrow and well-focussed question, remember that the best projects manage to make the connection to the big questions in the field: questions like 'what are the causes of injustice?' You also need to think about what sort of question you are asking: is it a 'should' question (more normative in focus), or a 'how' or 'why' question (more empirical in focus)? If you are interested in a particular theorist or tradition, think about what sorts of questions tend to be asked by other people working in this area. Can you adapt or modify their questions, and build upon them?

Why? By this point you may already have a clear idea of the answer to the 'why?' question. But keep asking yourself this. So what? Why is this topic important: to you, to academics working in this area, to activists and policy-makers, and to the world? There are no right or wrong answers here, but you need to come up with a clear and convincing answer of some kind, and be prepared to defend it. Typical answers might be that there is an important theoretical debate or disagreement which you are seeking to help resolve or advance; that a new issue or empirical topic has emerged which needs new research to cast light on it; or that there is a problem or puzzle which others have struggled with and you could present very differently by taking a different set of concepts or theories. Ultimately, when working on global justice, don't be afraid to say that you are working on this because it is one of the most important and urgent issues in global politics. Injustice is too important *not* to do research on!

How? Thirdly, you need to think about how you are going to answer your question. Which theorists will you use, and which parts of their work? Who do they draw upon, or argue with, and do you need to read them too? Given how quickly your reading list can spiral out of control, how will you limit the scope of what is relevant for your purposes? How will you know when you have read enough? Running out of time is not the best answer (although it may be a truthful answer for many of us!). Instead use the literature review to explain why certain authors are key, and if you have left out other obvious authors then explain why. Just as you need to limit the authors you engage with, so you need to identify certain key concepts or debates. You cannot write a good essay, or dissertation, or thesis on 'justice', 'democracy', 'freedom', 'human nature', and 'feminism' all together. You must pick your central concepts and debates and focus on two or three them. The research which changes the world often starts from a deceptively simple position – such as someone cutting a cake knowing they will be last to choose a slice – and then unpacks and unfolds the consequences of this in a structured and logical way.

Much more could be said about how to do good research on global justice. Your next step could be to get a pile of books together and spend an afternoon in the library. Or go and talk to your teachers, lecturers, supervisors and colleagues about your ideas. Both are excellent ideas. Whatever you do, the next stage in the struggle for global justice is up to you, and whether you are a philosopher or an activist (or hopefully, both!), remember to draw whatever inspiration you can from those who have gone before.

> I have walked that long road to freedom. I have tried not to falter; I have made missteps along the way. But I have discovered the secret that after climbing a great hill, one only finds that there are many more hills to climb. I have taken a moment here to rest, to steal a view of the glorious vista that surrounds me, to look back on the distance I have come. But I can rest only for a moment, for with freedom comes responsibilities, and I dare not linger, for my long walk is not yet ended.
>
> (Mandela, 1995: 751)

BIBLIOGRAPHY

Adorno, Theodor W. and Max Horkheimer (1997 [1944]) *Dialectic of Enlightenment*, London: Verso Books.

Almond, Gabriel and James S. Coleman (eds) (1960) *The Politics of the Developing Areas*, Princeton, NJ: Princeton University Press.

Almond, Gabriel and Sidney Verba (1963) *The Civic Culture: Political Attitudes and Democracy in Five Nations*, Princeton, NJ: Princeton University Press.

Anderson, Mark (2015) 'UK passes bill to honour pledge of 0.7% foreign aid target', *The Guardian* (UK), 9 March. Available at www.theguardian.com/global-development/2015/mar/09/uk-passes-bill-law-aid-target-percentage-income (accessed 2 June 2016).

Ansar, Atif, Ben Caldecott and James Tilbury (2013) *Stranded Assets and the Fossil Fuel Divestment Campaign: What Does Divestment Mean for the Valuation of Fossil Fuel Assets?* Oxford: Smith School of Enterprise and the Environment.

Armstrong, Chris (2012) *Global Distributive Justice: An Introduction*, Cambridge: Cambridge University Press.

Arnold, Thomas Clay (2001) 'Rethinking moral economy', *American Political Science Review*, 95, 1, pp. 85–96.

Audard, Catherine (2007) *John Rawls (Philosophy Now)*, Montreal and Kingston: McGill-Queen's University Press.

Bain, William (2003) *Between Anarchy and Society: Trusteeship and the Obligations of Power*, Oxford: Oxford University Press.

Bakan, Abigail B. and Yasmeen Abu-Laban (2009) 'Palestinian resistance and international solidarity: The BDS campaign', *Race and Class*, 51, 1, pp. 29–54.

Balch, Oliver (2013) 'Buen vivir: The social philosophy inspiring movement in South America', *The Guardian* (UK), 4 February. Available at www. theguardian.com/sustainable-business/blog/buen-vivir-philosophy-south america-eduardo-gudynas (accessed 2 June 2016).

Banai, Ayelet, Miriam Ronzoni and Christian Schemmel (2011) 'Global social justice: The possibility of social justice beyond states in a world of overlapping practices', in Ayelet Banai, Miriam Ronzoni and Christian Schemmel (eds) *Social Justice, Global Dynamics: Theoretical and Empirical Perspectives*, London Routledge, pp. 46–60.

Barghouti, Omar (2011) *Boycott Divestment Sanctions: The Global Struggle for Palestinian Rights*, Chicago: Haymarket.

Barry, Brian (1973) *The Liberal Theory of Justice: A Critical Examination of the Principal Doctrines of a Theory of Justice by John Rawls*, Oxford: Clarendon Press.

Barry, John (2012) *The Politics of Actually Existing Unsustainability: Human Flourishing in a Climate-Changed, Carbon-Constrained World*, Oxford: Oxford University Press.

BBC (2014) 'Scarlett Johansson quits Oxfam role over SodaStream row', *BBC* (UK), 30 January. Available at www.bbc.co.uk/news/world-us canada-25958176 (accessed 2 June 2016).

Beitz, Charles (1983) 'Cosmopolitan ideas and national sovereignty', *Journal of Philosophy*, 80, pp. 591–600.

Beitz, Charles (1999 [1979]) *Political Theory and International Relations*, Princeton NJ: Princeton University Press.

Beitz, Charles (2000) 'Rawls's law of peoples', *Ethics*, 110, 4, pp. 669–96.

Bohman, James (2007) *Democracy across Borders: From Dêmos to Dêmoi*, Cambridge MA: MIT Press.

Bond, Patrick (2014) 'Justice', in Carl Death (ed.) *Critical Environmental Politics* London: Routledge, pp. 133–45.

Brock, Gillian (2009) *Global Justice: A Cosmopolitan Account*, Oxford: Oxford University Press.

Brock, Gillian, ed. (2013) *Cosmopolitanism Versus Non-Cosmopolitanism: Critiques Defenses, Reconceptualizations*, Oxford: Oxford University Press.

Brock, Gillian (2015) 'Global justice', in Edward N. Zalta (ed.) *The Stanford Encyclopedia of Philosophy* (Spring 2015 Edition). Available at http://plato.stanford edu/archives/spr2015/entries/justice-global/ (accessed 8 November 2016).

Brown, Chris (1992) *International Relations Theory: New Normative Approaches* New York: Columbia University Press.

Brown, Chris (2002a) *Sovereignty, Rights and Justice: International Political Theory Today*, Cambridge: Polity.

Brown, Chris (2002b) 'The construction of a "realistic utopia": John Rawls and international political theory', *Review of International Studies*, 28, pp. 5–21.

Buchanan, Allen (2000) 'Rawls's law of peoples: Rule for a vanished Westphalian world', *Ethics*, 110, 4, pp. 697–721.

Burns, Tony and Simon Thompson (eds) (2013) *Global Justice and the Politics of Recognition*, Basingstoke: Palgrave Macmillan.

Butler, Judith (1990) *Gender Trouble: Feminism and the Subversion of Identity*, London: Routledge.

Butt, Daniel (2009) *Rectifying International Injustice: Principles of Compensation and Restitution between Nations*, Oxford: Oxford University Press.

Calhoun, Craig J. (2002) 'Imagining solidarity: Cosmopolitanism, constitutional patriotism, and the public sphere', *Public Culture*, 14, 1, pp. 147–71.

Campbell, Lyle (2012) *Endangered Language Catalogue*. Available at: http://ling.hawaii.edu/research-current/projects/elcat/ (accessed 31 May 2016).

Caney, Simon (2002) 'Survey article: Cosmopolitanism and the law of peoples', *The Journal of Political Philosophy*, 10, 1, pp. 95–123.

Caney, Simon (2005a) 'Cosmopolitan justice, responsibility and global climate change', *Leiden Journal of International Law*, 18, 4, pp. 747–75.

Caney, Simon (2005b) *Justice beyond Borders: A Global Political Theory*, Oxford: Oxford University Press.

Caney, Simon (2014) 'Two kinds of climate justice', *Journal of Political Philosophy*, 22, 3, pp. 125–49.

Carr, Edward H. (2001) *The Twenty Years' Crisis 1919–1939: An Introduction to the Study of International Relations*, Basingstoke: Palgrave Macmillan.

Cavalieri, Paola and Peter Singer (eds) (1994) *The Great Ape Project: Equality beyond Humanity*, London: St Martin's Press.

Césaire, Aimé (1972) *Discourse on Colonialism*, translated by J. Pinkham, New York: Monthly Review Press.

Chakrabarty, Dipesh (2000) *Provincializing Europe: Postcolonial Thought and Historical Difference*, Princeton, NJ: Princeton University Press.

Chandler, David (2006) *Empire in Denial: The Politics of State-Building*, London: Pluto Press.

Chang, Ha-Joon (2002) *Kicking Away the Ladder: Development Strategy in Historical Perspective: Policies and Institutions for Economic Development in Historical Perspective*, London: Anthem Press.

Chaturvedi, Sanjay and Timothy Doyle (2015) *Climate Terror: A Critical Geopolitics of Climate Change*, London: Palgrave Macmillan.

Chesterman, Simon, Michael Ignatieff and Ramesh Thakur (eds) (2005) *Making States Work: State Failure and the Crisis of Governance*, Tokyo: United Nations University Press.

Chinigò, Davide (2016) 'Re-peasantization and land: Reclamation movements in Malawi', *African Affairs*, 115, 458, pp. 97–118.

Clapp, Jennifer (2012) *Food*, Cambridge: Polity.

Clark, Ian (2007) *International Legitimacy and World Society*, Oxford: Oxford University Press.

Clarke, Kamari (2009) *Fictions of Justice: The International Criminal Court and the Challenge of Legal Pluralism in Sub-Saharan Africa*, Cambridge: Cambridge University Press.

Cohen, Gerard (2001) *If You're an Egalitarian, How Come You're So Rich?* Cambridge: Harvard University Press.

Collier, Paul (2007) *Bottom Billion: Why the Poorest Countries Are Failing and What Can Be Done about It*, Oxford: Oxford University Press.

Collier, Paul (2008) 'The politics of hunger: How greed and illusion fan the food crisis', *Foreign Affairs*, 87, 6, pp. 67–79.

Collste, Göran (2015) *Global Rectificatory Justice (Global Ethics)*, New York: Palgrave Macmillan.

Crick, Bernard (1967) 'Philosophy, theory and thought', *Political Studies*, 15, pp. 49–55.

Cudworth, Erika and Stephen Hobden (2011) *Posthuman International Relations: Complexity, Ecologism and Global Politics*, London: Zed.

Culp, Julian (2014) *Global Justice and Development*, Basingstoke: Palgrave Macmillan.

Davis, Mike (2001) *Late Victorian Holocausts: El Niño Famines and the Making of the Third World*, London: Verso.

Davis, Mike (2006) *Planet of Slums*, London: Verso.

Death, Carl (2010) *Governing Sustainable Development: Partnerships, Protests and Power*, London: Routledge.

Death, Carl (ed.) (2014) *Critical Environmental Politics*, London: Routledge.

Death, Carl and Clive Gabay (2015) 'Doing biopolitics differently? Radical potential in the post-2015 MDG and SDG debates', *Globalizations*, 12, 4, pp. 597–612.

de Bres, Helena (2013) 'Disaggregating global justice', *Social Theory and Practice*, 39, 3, pp. 422–48.

Della Porta, Donatella, Massimiliano Andretta, Lorenzo Mosca and Herbert Reiter (2006) *Globalization from Below: Transnational Activists and Protest Networks*, Minneapolis: University of Minnesota Press.

Denney, Lisa (2011) 'Reducing poverty with teargas and batons: The security development nexus in Sierra Leone', *African Affairs*, 110, 439, pp. 275–94.

Devereux, Stephen (2009) 'Why does famine persist in Africa?', *Food Security*, 1, 1, pp. 25–35.

Dimitrov, Radoslav S. (2010) 'Inside Copenhagen: The state of climate governance', *Global Environmental Politics*, 10, 2, pp. 18–24.

Dobson, Andrew (ed.) (1999) *Fairness and Futurity: Essays on Environmental Sustainability and Social Justice*, Oxford: Oxford University Press.

Dobson, Andrew (2003) *Citizenship and the Environment*, Oxford: Oxford University Press.

Dobson, Andrew (2006) 'Thick cosmopolitanism', *Political Studies*, 54, 1, pp. 165–84.

Dobson, Andrew (2007) *Green Political Thought*, fourth edition, London: Routledge.

Doherty, Brian and Timothy Doyle (2014) *Environmentalism, Resistance and Solidarity: The Politics of Friends of the Earth International*, Basingstoke: Palgrave Macmillan.

Donaldson, Sue and Will Kymlicka (2011) *Zoopolis – A Political Theory of Animal Rights*, Oxford: Oxford University Press.

Dryzek, John S. (2006) *Deliberative Global Politics: Discourse and Democracy in a Divided World*, Cambridge: Polity.

Duffield, Mark (2007) *Development, Security and Unending War: Governing the World of Peoples*, Cambridge: Polity.

Easterly, William (2006) *The White Man's Burden: Why the West's Efforts to Aid the Rest Have Done So Much Ill and So Little Good*, Oxford: Oxford University Press.

Eckersley, Robyn (1992) *Environmentalism and Political Theory: Toward an Ecocentric Approach*, New York: SUNY Press.

Eckersley, Robyn (2004) *The Green State: Rethinking Democracy and Sovereignty*, Cambridge, MA: MIT Press.

Eckersley, Robyn (2006) 'The state as gatekeeper: A reply', *Politics and Ethics Review*, 2, 2, pp. 127–38.

Edkins, Jenny (1999) *Poststructuralism and International Relations: Bringing the Political Back In*, London: Lynne Rienner.

Edkins, Jenny (2000) *Whose Hunger? Concepts of Famine, Practices of Aid*, Minneapolis: University of Minnesota Press.

Enloe, Cynthia (2014) *Bananas, Beaches and Bases: Making Feminist Sense of International Politics*, Berkeley: University of California Press.

Erskine, Toni (2002) '"Citizen of nowhere" or "the point where circles intersect"? Impartialist and embedded cosmopolitanisms', *Review of International Studies*, 28, 3, pp. 457–78.

Erskine, Toni (2008) *Embedded Cosmopolitanism: Duties to Strangers and Enemies in a World of 'Dislocated Communities'*, Oxford: Oxford University Press.

Eschle, Catherine (2001) *Global Democracy, Social Movements, and Feminism*, Boulder, CO; Westview.

Escobar, Arturo (1995) *Encountering Development: The Making and Unmaking of the Third World*, Princeton, NJ: Princeton University Press.

Fanon, Frantz (2004) *The Wretched of the Earth*, translated by R. Philcox, New York: Grove.

Fioramonti, Lorenzo (2013) *Gross Domestic Problem: The Politics behind the World's Most Powerful Number*, London: Zed.

Flikschuh, Katrin, Rainer Forst, Darrel Moellendorf, Valentin Beck and Julian Culp (2013) 'On the role of the political theorist regarding global injustice Interview of Katrin Flikschuh, Rainer Forst and Darrel Moellendorf', *Global Justice: Theory, Practice, Rhetoric*, 6. pp. 40–53.

Forst, Rainer (2005) 'Justice, morality and power in the global context,' in Andreas Follesdal and Thomas Pogge (eds) *Real World Justice*, Dordrecht Springer, pp. 27–37.

Forst, Rainer (2007) 'First things first: Redistribution, recognition and justification', *European Journal of Political Theory*, 6, 3, pp. 291–304.

Forst, Rainer (2012) *The Right to Justification*, New York: Columbia University Press.

Foucault, Michel (2000) 'The subject and power', in *Power: Essential Works of Foucault 1954–1984*, Volume 3, New York: The New Press, pp. 326–48.

Fraser, Nancy (2008) *Scales of Justice: Reimagining Political Space in a Globalizing World*, Cambridge: Polity Press.

Fraser, Nancy and Alex Honneth (2003) *Redistribution or Recognition? A Political-Philosophical*, Exchange, London: Verso.

Freedom House (2015) 'Afghanistan'. Available at https://freedomhouse.org/report/freedom-world/2015/afghanistan (accessed 2 June 2016).

Fukuyama, Francis (2004) *State Building: Governance and World Order in the Twenty-First Century*, Ithaca, NY: Cornell University Press.

Gardiner, Stephen (2011) *A Perfect Moral Storm: The Ethical Tragedy of Climate Change*, Oxford: Oxford University Press.

Geuss, Raymond (2005) *Outside Ethics*, Princeton, NJ: Princeton University Press.

Geuss, Raymond (2015) 'Realism and the relativity of judgement', *International Relations*, 29, 1, pp. 3–22.

Gill, Stephen (2005) 'Toward a postmodern prince? The battle in Seattle as a moment in the new politics of globalisation', in Louise Amoore (ed.) *The Global Resistance Reader*, London: Routledge, pp. 150–7.

Gorz, André (1980) *Ecology as Politics*, translated by Patsy Vigderman and Jonathan Cloud, Boston: South End Press.

Grady-Benson, Jessica and Brinda Sarathy (2016) 'Fossil fuel divestment in US higher education: Student-led organising for climate justice', *Local Environment: The International Journal of Justice and Sustainability*, 21, 6, pp. 661–81.

Gudynas, Eduardo (2011) 'Buen Vivir: Today's tomorrow', *Development*, 54, 4, pp. 441–7.

Habermas, Jürgen (1989) *The Theory of Communicative Action – Volume 2*, Cambridge: Polity Press.

Habermas, Jürgen (1992 [1962]) *The Structural Transformation of the Public Sphere*, Cambridge: Polity Press.

Habermas, Jürgen (1997) *Between Facts and Norms: Contribution to a Discourse Theory of Law and Democracy*, Cambridge: Polity Press.

Haraway, Donna (1989) *Primate Visions: Gender, Race, and Nature in the World of Modern Science*, London: Routledge.

Hassoun, Nicole (2014) *Globalization and Global Justice: Shrinking Distance, Expanding Obligations*, Cambridge: Cambridge University Press.

Hegel, Georg W.F. (1991) *Elements of the Philosophy of Right*, ed. Allen Wood, Cambridge: Cambridge University Press.

Hirschkind, Charles and Saba Mahmood (2002) 'Feminism, the Taliban, and politics of counter-insurgency', *Anthropological Quarterly*, 75, 2, pp. 339–54.

Hobbes, Thomas (1982 [1651]) *Leviathan*, London: Penguin Classics.

Hobden, Stephen (2014) 'Posthumanism', in Carl Death (ed.) *Critical Environmental Politics*, London: Routledge, pp. 175–83.

Hobson, John M. (2012) *The Eurocentric Conception of World Politics: Western International Theory, 1760–2010*, Cambridge: Cambridge University Press.

Hodgson, Dorothy L. (2009) 'Becoming indigenous in Africa', *African Studies Review*, 52, 3, pp. 1–32.

Hoffman, Paul (2016) 'African walkout from ICC runs contrary to obligations', *Business Day* (South Africa), 4 January. Available at www.bdlive.co.za/opinion/2016/01/04/african-walkout-from-icc-runs-contrary-to-obligations (accessed 2 June 2016).

Holloway, John (2005) *Change the World Without Taking Power: The Meaning of Revolution Today*, London: Pluto Press.

hooks, bell (1994) *Teaching to Transgress: Education as the Practice of Freedom*, New York: Routledge.

Inayatullah, Naeem and David L. Blaney (2004) *International Relations and the Problem of Difference*, London: Routledge.

Jackson, Patrick T. (2015) 'Fear of relativism', *International Studies Perspectives*, 16, pp. 13–22.

Jackson, Robert H. (2005) *Classical and Modern Thought on International Relations: From Anarchy to Cosmopolis*, New York: Palgrave Macmillan.

Jaggar, M. Alison (2014a) 'Introduction: Gender and global justice: rethinking some basic assumptions of western political philosophy', in Alison M. Jaggar (ed.) *Gender and Global Justice*, Cambridge: Polity Press, pp. 1–17.

Jaggar, M. Alison (2014b) 'Transnational cycles of gendered vulnerability: A prologue to a theory of global gender justice', in Alison M. Jaggar (ed.) *Gender and Global Justice*, Cambridge: Polity, pp.18–39.

James, Aaron (2005) 'Constructing justice for existing practice: Rawls and the status quo', *Philosophy & Public Affairs*, 33, 3, pp. 281–316.

James, Aaron (2012) *Fairness in Practice: A Social Contract for a Global Economy*, New York: Oxford University Press.

Jamieson, Dale (2010) *Climate Ethics*, Oxford: Oxford University Press.

Jamieson, Dale (2014) *Reason in a Dark Time: Why the Struggle to Stop Climate Change Failed – and What It Means for Our Future*, Oxford: Oxford University Press.

Jones, John R. (1966) *Prydeindod*, Llyfrau'r Dryw: Llandybie.

Kallis, Giorgos (2011) 'In defence of degrowth', *Ecological Economics*, 70, pp. 873–80.

Kant, Immanuel (1983 [1792]) *Perpetual Peace and Other Essays*, London: Hackett Classics.

Kant, Immanuel (1996) 'On the common saying: That may be correct in theory, but it is of no use in practice', in Mary Gregor (ed.) *Practical Philosophy*, Cambridge: Cambridge University Texts, pp. 273–310.

Keck, Margaret E. and Kathryn Sikkink (1998) *Activists beyond Borders: Advocacy Networks in International Politics*, Ithaca, NY: Cornell University Press.

Kennedy, Robert F. (1968) 'Remarks at the University of Kansas', March 18. Available at www.jfklibrary.org/Research/Research-Aids/Ready-Reference/RFK-Speeches/Remarks-of-Robert-F-Kennedy-at-the-University-of-Kansas-March-18-1968.aspx (accessed 2 June 2016).

Klein, Naomi (2005) 'Culture jamming: Ads under attack', in Louise Amoore (ed.) *The Global Resistance Reader*, London: Routledge, pp. 437–44.

Klein, Naomi (2014) *This Changes Everything: Capitalism vs. the Climate*, London: Allen Lane.

Krauss, Clifford (2013) 'Plan to ban oil drilling in Amazon in dropped' *New York Times* (USA), 17 August. Available at www.nytimes.com/2013/08/17/business/energy-environment/ecuador-drops-plan-to-ban-drilling-in-jungle.html?_r=0 (accessed 2 June 2016).

Kukathas, Chandran and Philip Pettit (1990) *A Theory of Justice and Its Critics*, Cambridge: Polity Press.

Kumar, Rahul and Kok-Chor Tan (2006) 'Special issue: Reparations', *Journal of Social Philosophy*, 37, 3, pp. iv–v, 323–482.

Kuper, Andrew (2000) 'Rawlsian global justice: Beyond the law of peoples to a cosmopolitan law of persons', *Political Theory*, 28, 5, pp. 640–74.

Lamony, Stephen A. (2013) 'Is the international criminal court really picking on Africa?', *African Arguments* blog (UK), 16 April. Available at http://africaarguments.org/2013/04/16/is-the-international-criminal-court-really-picking-on-africa-by-stephen-a-lamony/ (accessed 2 June 2016).

Landes, David (1998) *The Wealth and Poverty of Nations*, New York: W.W. Norton.

Latour, Bruno (1993) *We Have Never Been Modern*, Cambridge, MA: Harvard University Press.

Lee, Richard P. (2013) 'The politics of international agri-food policy: Discourses of trade-oriented food security and food sovereignty', *Environmental Politics*, 22, 2, pp. 216–34.

Leopold, Aldo (1949) *A Sand County Almanac: With Essays on Conservation*, Oxford: Oxford University Press.

Ling, L. H. M. (2014) *Imagining World Politics: Sihar and Shenya, A Fable for Our Times*, London: Routledge.

Linklater, Andrew (1998) *The Transformation of Political Community: Ethical Foundations of the Post-Westphalian Era*, Columbia: University of South Carolina Press.

Locke, John (1980) *The Second Treatise of Government*, London: Hackett.

Longhurst, Rose (2015) 'A woman's place is in the audience: The joy of all-male panels', *The Guardian* (UK), 28 October. Available at www.theguardian.com/global-development-professionals-network/2015/oct/28/a-womans-place-is-in-the-audience-the-joy-of-all-male-panels (accessed 2 June 2016).

Loomba, Ania (1998) *Colonialism/Postcolonialism*, London: Routledge.

Lu, Catherine (2011) 'Colonialism as structural injustice: Historical responsibility and contemporary redress', *The Journal of Political Philosophy*, 19, 3, pp. 261–81.

McKibben, Bill (2012) 'Global warming's terrifying new math', *Rolling Stone*, 19 July.

McMahon, Sean F. (2014) 'The Boycott, divestment, sanctions campaign: Contradictions and challenges', *Race and Class*, 55, 4, pp. 65–81.

McMichael, Philip (2008) 'Peasants make their own history, but not just as they please . . .', *Journal of Agrarian Change*, 8, 2–3, pp. 205–28.

McShane, Katie (2014) 'Ecocentrism', in Carl Death (ed.) *Critical Environmental Politics*, London: Routledge, pp. 83–90.

Maffettone, Sebastiano and Aakash Singh Rathore (eds) (2012) *Global Justice: Critical Perspectives*, New Delhi: Routledge.

Mamdani, Mahmood (2001) *When Victims Become Killers: Colonialism, Nativism and the Genocide in Rwanda*, Oxford; James Currey.

Mandela, Nelson (1995) *Long Walk to Freedom*, London: Abacus.

Mandle, Jon (2006) *Global Justice: An Introduction*, Cambridge: Polity Press.

Marchand, Marianne H. (2005) 'Some theoretical "musings" about gender and resistance', in Louise Amoore (ed.) *The Global Resistance Reader*, London: Routledge, pp. 215–25.

Martinez-Alier, Joan (2009) 'Socially sustainable economic de-growth', *Development and Change*, 40, 6, pp. 1099–1119.

Martinez-Alier, Joan, Nnimmo Bassey and Patrick Bond (2013) 'Yasuni ITT is dead: Blame President Correa', *EJOLT* blog, 17 August. Available at: www.ejolt.org/2013/08/yasuni-itt-is-dead-blame-president-correa/ (accessed 2 June 2016).

Marx, Karl (1867/1990) *Capital: A Critique of Political Economy*, Volume 1, London: Penguin.

Marx, Karl (2000) *Selected Writings, Second Edition*, ed. David McLellan, Oxford: Oxford University Press.

Meadowcroft, James (2006) 'Greening the state', *Politics and Ethics Review*, 2, 2 pp. 109–18.

Mill, John S. (1991 [1862]) *Considerations on Representative Government (Great Books in Philosophy)*, Buffalo, NY: Prometheus Books.

Miller, David (2000) *Citizenship and National Identity*, Cambridge: Polity Press.

Miller, David (2007) *National Responsibility and Global Justice*, Oxford: Oxford University Press.

Miller, Richard (2010) *Globalizing Justice: The Ethics of Poverty and Power* Oxford: Oxford University Press.

Mitchell, Timothy (1990) 'Everyday metaphors of power', *Theory and Society* 19, pp. 545–77.

Molomo, Mpho G. (2008) 'Sustainable development, ecotourism, national minorities and land in Botswana', in Kojo Sebastian Amanor and Sam Moyo (eds) *Land and Sustainable Development in Africa*, London: Zed pp. 159–83.

Monbiot, George (2005) 'Stronger than ever: Far from fizzling out, the global justice movement is growing in numbers and maturity', in Louise Amoore (ed.) *The Global Resistance Reader*, London: Routledge, pp. 361–2.

Morgenthau, Hans (1946) *Scientific Man Versus Power Politics*, Chicago, IL University of Chicago Press.

Morgenthau, Hans (1948) *Politics among Nations: The Struggle for Power and Peace* New York, NY: Alfred A. Knopf.

Mouffe, Chantal (2005) *On the Political*, London: Routledge.

Moyo, Dambisa (2009) *Dead Aid: Why Aid Is not Working and How There I Another Way for Africa*, London: Allen Lane.

Mulhall, Stephen and Adam Swift (1996) *Liberals and Communitarians: An Introduction*, second edition, Chichester: Wiley-Blackwell.

Munck, Ronaldo (2013) 'The Precariat: A view from the South', *Third World Quarterly*, 34, 5, pp. 747–62.

Musschenga, Albert W. (1998) 'Intrinsic value as a reason for the preservation of minority cultures', *Ethical Theory and Moral Practice*, 1, 2, pp. 201–25.

Naess, Arne (2005 [1983]) 'The shallow and the deep, long-range ecology movement: A summary', in John S. Dryzek and David Schlosberg (eds) *Debating the Earth: The Environmental Politics Reader*, Oxford: Oxford University Press pp. 343–7.

Nagel, Thomas (2005) 'The problem of global justice', *Philosophy and Public Affairs*, 33, pp. 113–47.

Nussbaum, Martha (2001) *Women and Human Development*, Cambridge Cambridge University Press.

Nussbaum, Martha (2002) 'Women and the law of peoples', *Politics, Philosophy and Economics*, 1, 3, pp. 283–306.

Nussbaum, Martha (2006) *Frontiers of Justice: Disability, Nationality and Species Membership*, Cambridge, MA: The Bellknap Press of Harvard University Press.

Odysseos, Louiza (2011) 'Governing dissent in the central Kalahari game reserve: "Development", governmentality, and subjectification amongst Botswana's Bushmen', *Globalizations*, 8, 4, pp. 439–55.

Okin, Susan M. (1989) *Justice, Gender, and the Family*, New York: Basic Books.

Orford, Anne (2009) 'What can we do to stop people harming others?', in Jenny Edkins and Maja Zehfuss (eds) *Global Politics: A New Introduction*, London: Routledge, pp. 427–53.

Owen, Robert (1991 [1815]) *A New View of Society and Other Writings* (Penguin Classics), London and New York: Penguin Books.

Oxfam (2016) '62 people own same as half world', press release 18 January. Available at www.oxfam.org.uk/media-centre/press-releases/2016/01/62-people-own-same-as-half-world-says-oxfam-inequality-report-davos-world-economic-forum?intcmp=HPWWLWP_grid_davospr (accessed 2 June 2016).

Pattison, James (2010) *Humanitarian Intervention and the Responsibility to Protect: Who Should Intervene?* Oxford: Oxford University Press.

Pears, Elizabeth (2014) 'Should we be compensated for slavery', *The Voice* (UK), 1 February. Available at www.voice-online.co.uk/article/should-we-be-compensated-slavery (accessed 2 June 2016).

Petersen, V. Spike and Anne Sisson Runyan (2005) 'The politics of resistance: Women as nonstate, antistate, and transstate actors', in Louise Amoore (ed.) *The Global Resistance Reader*, London: Routledge, pp. 226–43.

Pettit, Philip (2010) 'A republican law of peoples', *European Journal of Political Theory*, 9, 1, pp. 70–94.

Phillips, D. Z. (1993) 'Pam Achub Iaith?', *Efrydiau Athronyddol 56*, Cardiff: Gwasg Prifysgol Cymru, pp. 1–12.

Pizzi, Michael (2015) 'South Africa threatens to withdraw from ICC, alleging anti-African bias', *al Jazeera*, 12 October. Available at http://america.aljazeera.com/articles/2015/10/12/south-africa-threatens-to-withdraw-from-icc-alleging-anti-african-bias.html (accessed 2 June 2016).

Pleyers, Geoffrey (2004) 'The social forums as an ideal model of convergence', *International Journal of the Social Sciences*, 182, pp. 508–17.

Pogge, Thomas (1989) *Realizing Rawls*, Ithaca, NY: Cornell University Press.

Pogge, Thomas (1998) 'The bounds of nationalism', in J. Couture, K. Neilsen and M. Seymour (eds) *Rethinking Nationalism*, Calgary: University of Calgary Press, pp. 463–504.

Pogge, Thomas (2001) 'Critical study: Rawls on international justice', *The Philosophical Quarterly*, 51, 203, pp. 246–53.

Pogge, Thomas (2007) *John Rawls: His Life and Theory of Justice*, Oxford: Oxford University Press.

Pogge, Thomas (2008 [2002]) *World Poverty and Human Rights: Cosmopolitan Responsibilities and Reforms*, second edition, Cambridge: Polity Press.

Pogge, Thomas (2011) 'Allowing the poor to share the Earth', *Journal of Moral Philosophy*, 8, 3, pp. 335–52.

Popkin, Samuel L. (1979) *The Rational Peasant: The Political Economy of Rural Society in Vietnam*, Berkeley: University of California Press.

Prebisch, Raúl (1950) *The Economic Development of Latin America and Its Principal Problems*, New York: United Nations.

Prebisch Raúl (1959) 'Commercial policy in the underdeveloped countries', *American Economic Review*, 49, pp. 251–73.

Pufendorf, Samuel (1994) 'The political writings of Samuel Pufendorf', in Craig L. Carr (ed.), Oxford: Oxford University Press.

Quill, Lawrence (2005) *Liberty after Liberalism: Civic Republicanism in a Global Age*, London: Palgrave Macmillan.

Rathore, Aakash Singh (2012) 'The romance of global justice: Sen's deparochialization and the quandary of Dalit Marxism', in Sebastiano Maffettone and Aakash Singh Rathore (eds) *Global Justice: Critical Perspectives*, London: Routledge, pp. 163–175.

Rawls, John (1993) 'The law of peoples', in Stephen Shute and Susan Hurley (eds) *On Human Rights: The Oxford Amnesty Lectures*, New York: Basic Books, pp. 41–82.

Rawls, John (1999) *The Law of Peoples*, Cambridge, MA: Harvard University Press.

Rawls, John (2001a) *Justice as Fairness*, Cambridge, MA: The Belknap Press of Harvard University Press.

Rawls, John (2001b) *Collected Papers*, new edition, Cambridge, MA: Harvard University Press.

Rawls, John (2005 [1993]) *Political Liberalism*, expanded edition, New York: Columbia University Press.

Rawls, John (2005 [1971]) *A Theory of Justice*, reissue edition, Cambridge, MA: Harvard University Press.

Reidy, David (2007) 'A just global economy: In defense of Rawls', *The Journal of Ethics*, 11, pp. 193–223.

Reyes, Oscar (2015) 'Seven flies in the ointment of the Paris climate deal euphoria', *Global Justice* blog (UK), 15 December. Available at www.globaljustice.org.uk/blog/2015/dec/15/seven-flies-ointment-paris-climate-deal-euphoria (accessed 2 June 2016).

Risse, Mathias (2012) *On Global Justice*, Princeton, NJ: Princeton University Press.

Rodrik, Dani (ed.) (2003) *In Search of Prosperity: Analytical Narratives of Economic Growth*, Princeton, NJ: Princeton University Press.

Ross, Michael L. (1999) 'The political economy of the resources curse', *World Politics*, 51, 2, pp. 297–322.

Rousseau, Jean-Jacques (2011) *On the Social Contract*, London: Hackett.

Routledge, Paul and Andrew Cumbers (2009) *Global Justice Networks: Geographies of Transnational Solidarity*, Manchester: Manchester University Press.

Rowlands, Mark (2002) *Animals Like Us*, London: Verso.

Rowlands, Mark (2009) *The Philosopher and the Wolf: Lessons on Life, Death and Happiness from the Wild*, London: Granta.

Rowlands, Mark (2012) *Can Animals Be Moral?* Oxford: Oxford University Press.

Rudy, Alan P. and Damian White (2014) 'Hybridity', in Carl Death (ed.) *Critical Environmental Politics*, London: Routledge, pp. 121–32.

Sachs, Jeffrey (2005) *The End of Poverty: Economic Possibilities for Our Time*, London: Penguin.

Sachs, Jeffrey, Roseline Remans, Sean Smukler, Leigh Winowiecki, Sandy J. Andelman, Kenneth G. Cassman, David Castle, *et al.* (2010) 'Monitoring the world's agriculture', *Nature*, 466, 29, pp. 558–60.

Sachs, Wolfgang (1999) *Planet Dialectics: Explorations in Environment and Development*, London: Zed Books.

Saugestad, Sidsel (2001) *The Inconvenient Indigenous: Remote Area Development in Botswana, Donor Assistance, and the First People of the Kalahari*, Uppsala: Nordic Africa Institute.

Schlosberg, David (1999) *Environmental Justice and the New Pluralism*, Oxford: Oxford University Press.

Schlosberg, David (2004) 'Reconceiving environmental justice: Global movements and political theories', *Environmental Politics*, 13, 3, pp. 517–40.

Scoones, Ian, Joseph Chaumba, Blasio Mavedzenge and William Wolmer (2012) 'The new politics of Zimbabwe's Lowveld: Struggles over land at the margins', *African Affairs*, 111, 145, pp. 527–50.

Scott, James C. (1977) *The Moral Economy of the Peasant: Rebellion and Subsistence in Southeast Asia*, New Haven, CT: Yale University Press.

Self, Will (1997), *Great Apes*, London: Bloomsbury.

Selwyn, Ben (2014) *The Global Development Crisis*, Cambridge: Polity.

Sen, Amartya (1980) 'Equality of what?' in S. McMurrin (ed.) *The Tanner Lectures on Human Values*, Volume 1, Salt Lake City: University of Utah Press, pp. 195–220.

Sen, Amartya (1983) *Poverty and Famines: An Essay on Entitlement and Deprivation*, Oxford: Oxford University Press.

Sen, Amartya (1999) *Development as Freedom*, Oxford: Oxford University Press.

Sen, Amartya (2009) *The Idea of Justice*, London: Allen Lane.

Shilliam, Robbie (2011) 'Non-western thought and international relations', in Robbie Shilliam (ed.) *International Relations and Non-Western Thought: Imperialism, Colonialism and Investigations of Global Modernity*, London: Routledge, pp. 1–11.

Singer, Peter (1972) 'Famine, affluence and morality', *Philosophy and Public Affairs*, 1, 1, pp. 229–43.

Singer, Peter (1975) *Animal Liberation: A New Ethics for Our Treatment of Animals*, New York: HarperCollins.

Slaughter, Steven (2005) *Liberty beyond Neo-liberalism: A Republican Critique of Liberal Governance in a Globalising Age*, Basingstoke: Palgrave Press.

Smith, Jackie (2004) 'The world social forum and the challenges of global democracy', *Global Networks*, 4, 4, pp. 413–21.

Spivak, Gayatri C. (1988) 'Can the subaltern speak?', in Cary Nelson and Lawrence Grossberg (eds) *Marxism and the Interpretation of Culture*, Urbana IL: University of Illinois Press, pp. 271–313.

Starr, Amory (2005) *Global Revolt: A Guide to the Movements against Globalization*, London: Zed Books.

Stevenson, Hayley (2014) 'Representing green radicalism: The limits of state-based representation in global climate governance', *Review of International Studies*, 40, 1, pp. 177–201.

Steward, Corrina, Maria Aguiar, Nikhil Aziz, Jonathan Leaning and Daniel Moss (2008) *Towards a Green Food System: How Food Sovereignty Can Save the Environment and Feed the World*, Boston: Grassroots International.

Stiglitz, Joseph, Amartya Sen and Jean-Paul Fitoussi (2009) *Report by the Commission on the Measurement of Economic Performance and Social Progress*. Available at www.insee.fr/fr/publications-et-services/dossiers_web/stiglitz/doc-commission/RAPPORT_anglais.pdf (accessed 1 June 2016).

Stone, Christopher D. (2010) *Should Trees Have Standing? Law, Morality, and the Environment*, Oxford: Oxford University Press.

Tan, Kok-Chor (2000) *Toleration, Diversity and Global Justice*, University Park: Penn State University Press.

Tan, Kok-Chor (2004) *Justice Without Borders: Cosmopolitanism, Nationalism and Patriotism*, Cambridge: Cambridge University Press.

Tan, Kok-Chor (2012) *Justice, Institutions and Luck: The Site, Ground, and Scope of Equality*, Oxford: Oxford University Press.

Tarrow, Sidney (1998) *Power in Movement: Social Movements and Contentious Politics*, second edition, Cambridge: Cambridge University Press.

Taylor, Charles (1992) *Sources of the Self: The Making of the Modern Identity*, Cambridge, MA: Harvard University Press.

Thompson, E. P. (1964) *The Making of the English Working Class*, New York: Pantheon Books.

Thompson, E. P. (1971) 'The moral economy of the English crowd in the eighteenth century', *Past & Present*, 50, pp. 76–136.

Tutu, Desmond (2014) 'We need an apartheid-style boycott to save the planet', *The Guardian* (UK), 10 April.

UN (2000) *Millennium Declaration*, 8 September. Available at www.un.org/millennium/declaration/ares552e.htm (accessed 2 June 2016).

UN (2012) '*The Future We Want, Outcome Document*, 22 June. Available at https://sustainabledevelopment.un.org/futurewewant.html (accessed 2 June 2016).

UNFCCC (2015) *Paris Agreement*, 12 December. Available at http://unfccc.int/resource/docs/2015/cop21/eng/l09r01.pdf (accessed 2 June 2016).

Valentini, Laura (2011) *Justice in a Globalized World: A Normative Framework*, Oxford: Oxford University Press.

Van Parijs, Philippe (2011) *Linguistic Justice for Europe and for the World*, Oxford: Oxford University Press.

Wallerstein, Immanuel (1974) *The Modern World-System I: Capitalist Agriculture and the Origins of the European World-Economy in the Sixteenth Century*, New York: Academic Press.

Wallerstein, Immanuel (1983) *Historical Capitalism*, London: Verso.

Waltz, Kenneth N. (2001 [1959]) *Man, the State, and War*, New York: Columbia University Press.

Waltz, Kenneth N. (1979) *Theory of International Politics*, New York: McGraw Hill.

wa Thiong'o, Ngũgĩ (1986) *Decolonising the Mind: The Politics of Language in African Literature*, London: Heinemann Educational.

Wearden, Graeme (2016) 'More plastic than fish in the sea by 2050, says Ellen MacArthur', *The Guardian* (UK), 19 January. Available at www.theguardian.com/business/2016/jan/19/more-plastic-than-fish-in-the-sea-by-2050-warns-ellen-macarthur (accessed 2 June 2016).

Wenar, Leif (2008) 'Property rights and the resource curse', *Philosophy and Public Affairs*, 36, 1, pp. 2–32.

Wenar, Leif (2013) 'Fighting the resource curse', *Global Policy*, 4, 3, pp. 298–304.

Whitehead, Alfred N. (1979) *Process and Reality: Corrected Edition*, New York: The Free Press.

Whitehead, Mark (2014) 'Sustainability', in Carl Death (ed.) *Critical Environmental Politics*, London: Routledge, pp. 257–66.

Williams, Huw L. (2011) *On Rawls, Development and Global Justice: The Freedom of Peoples*, Basingstoke: Palgrave MacMillan.

Williams, Huw L. (2014) 'Wacky races: Miller, Pogge and Rawls, and conceptions of development in the global justice debate', *Journal of International Political Theory*, 10, 2, pp. 206–28.

Williamson, John (1989) 'What Washington means by policy reform', in John Williamson (ed.) *Latin American Readjustment: How Much Has Happened*, Washington: Institute for International Economics.

Williamson, John (2004) 'The strange history of the Washington consensus', *Journal of Post Keynesian Economics*, 27, 2, pp. 195–206.

Wilson, Japhy (2014) *Jeffrey Sachs: The strange case of Dr Shock and Mr Aid*, London: Verso.

Wittgenstein, Ludwig (2009) *Philosophical Investigations*, fourth edition, translated by G.E.M. Anscombe, Chichester: Wiley Blackwell.

Wollner, Gabriel (2013) 'The third wave of theorizing global justice: A review essay', *Global Justice: Theory, Practice, Rhetoric*, 6, pp. 21–39.

Young, Iris M. (2001) 'Activist challenges to deliberative democracy', *Political Theory*, 29, 5, pp. 670–90.

Young, Iris M. (2006) 'Responsibility and global justice: A social connection model', *Social Philosophy and Policy*, 23, 1, pp 102–30.

Ypi, Lea (2012) *Global Justice and Avant-Garde Political Agency*, Oxford: Oxford University Press.

INDEX

Taylor & Francis eBooks

Helping you to choose the right eBooks for your Library

Add Routledge titles to your library's digital collection today. Taylor and Francis ebooks contains over 50,000 titles in the Humanities, Social Sciences, Behavioural Sciences, Built Environment and Law.

Choose from a range of subject packages or create your own!

Benefits for you

» Free MARC records
» COUNTER-compliant usage statistics
» Flexible purchase and pricing options
» All titles DRM-free.

REQUEST YOUR FREE INSTITUTIONAL TRIAL TODAY

Free Trials Available
We offer free trials to qualifying academic, corporate and government customers.

Benefits for your user

» Off-site, anytime access via Athens or referring URL
» Print or copy pages or chapters
» Full content search
» Bookmark, highlight and annotate text
» Access to thousands of pages of quality research at the click of a button.

eCollections – Choose from over 30 subject eCollections, including:

Archaeology	Language Learning
Architecture	Law
Asian Studies	Literature
Business & Management	Media & Communication
Classical Studies	Middle East Studies
Construction	Music
Creative & Media Arts	Philosophy
Criminology & Criminal Justice	Planning
Economics	Politics
Education	Psychology & Mental Health
Energy	Religion
Engineering	Security
English Language & Linguistics	Social Work
Environment & Sustainability	Sociology
Geography	Sport
Health Studies	Theatre & Performance
History	Tourism, Hospitality & Events

For more information, pricing enquiries or to order a free trial, please contact your local sales team:
www.tandfebooks.com/page/sales

Routledge
Taylor & Francis Group

The home of
Routledge books

www.tandfebooks.com